AN ARMSFULL OF BIRDS

A Personal Field Guide to Love, Loss, and Commitment

CARA BENSON

Health Communications, Inc.
Mt. Pleasant, South Carolina

www.hcibooks.com

Library of Congress Cataloging-in-Publication Data
is available through the Library of Congress

ISBN-13: 978-07573- 2555-7 (Paperback)
ISBN-10: 07573-2555-6 (Paperback)
ISBN-13: 978-07573- 2556-4 (ePub)
ISBN-10: 07573- 2556-4 (ePub)

Publisher: Health Communications, Inc.
1240 Winnowing Way, Suite 100
Mt. Pleasant, SC 29466

Cover, interior design, and formatting by Larissa Hise Henoch

Praise for AN ARMSFULL OF BIRDS

"I opened it up to read the first few pages and then spent five hours reading the rest. Beautifully done. Poignant, human, authentic."

—**Jenny Lawson,** The Bloggess and #1 *New York Times* bestselling author of *How to Be Okay When Nothing Is Okay*

"This is a book about many profound things, but one of them is healing, and in particular the healing possibilities of the physical world around us. Of course, as Benson recognizes, healing needs to—and can—go both ways. A valuable book!"

—**Bill McKibben,** author of *Here Comes the Sun*

"Cara Benson feels everything so deeply and tells her stories so honestly. Part recovery story, part eco-travelogue, part grief memoir, *An Armsfull of Birds* is a nuanced, thoughtful book about what it means to live fully, even when that means surviving your most beloved people. A memoir that will break your heart and put it back together again."

—**Amy Shearn,** award-winning author of *Animal Instinct* and *Unseen City*

"As a poet, a lover, a close observer of nature, and a warts-and-all fighter, Cara Benson delivers an elegant and gimlet-eyed tale of disaster, recovery, and vulnerability."

—**Neal Allen,** co-author of *Good Writing: 36 Ways to Improve Your Sentences*

"A powerful memoir of addiction and recovery, love and loss, and embracing life. *An Armsful of Birds* is written with grace, poetry, and wit. It's also a page turner. Full of insight about mental health issues and many other things, the story is compelling and moving. Raw at times, at times heartbreaking, there is also joy and love. A beautiful book."

—**Jennifer Michael Hecht,** author of *Stay: A History of Suicide and the Philosophies Against It*

"This is a memoir as it should be: ruggedly brutal, unflinchingly honest, and emotionally intense. It is a journey both tumultuous and cathartic, an embrace of hard realities and whispers of hope. Read this book and you will be changed. Guaranteed!"

—**Anthony D. Fredericks,** best-selling author of *The Healing Wisdom of the Forest: Timeless Lessons of Renewal, Tranquility, and Joy*

"In the wake of her partner's suicide, Cara Benson performs a compelling close examination of their relationship, their individual and joined dynamics, and the nature of love and loss. In gorgeous, arresting prose, she seamlessly weaves in elements of their passions and commitments—birds, hiking, animal love, environmental stewardship, and sobriety. *An Armsfull of Birds: A Personal Field Guide to Love, Loss, and Commitment* is required reading for anyone who has ever been confronted by the gaping questions surrounding a loved one's passing, or really anyone who has loved and lost."

—**Sari Botton,** author of *And You May Find Yourself . . . Confessions of a Late-Blooming Gen-X Weirdo,* and the editor-in-chief of *Oldster Magazine*

"Gorgeously written, with every page full of heart, Cara Benson's story perfectly captures what it is to be human in an often unforgiving world. Through the brutal years of addiction, the hard work of recovery, and profound love and loss, I couldn't put this book down. If you're looking for inspiration or comfort, it is here."

—**Lisa Smith,** author of the award-winning memoir *Girl Walks Out of a Bar*

"Like any true field guide, Cara Benson's *An Armsfull of Birds* is about wanting to know—how to care for the natural world and its myriad creatures, how to live an engaged and ethical life, and, at heart, how to survive (and learn from) indelible loss. 'Loss,' Benson writes, 'has everything to do with loving.' This keenly observed, honest, and emotionally resonant memoir opens a way for us all."

—**Steve Edwards,** author of *Rare Good: Essays on Art, Autism, and Astonishment*

"*An Armsfull of Birds* is a powerful book about a woman coming into herself by stepping more fully into the world around her. It's an important story about connections—romantic, familial, and platonic—and the difficult process of caring for ourselves and others. This book could only have been written by someone with a poet's heart, and Benson's is full."

—**Tove Danovich,** author of *Under the Henfluence*

for Jon

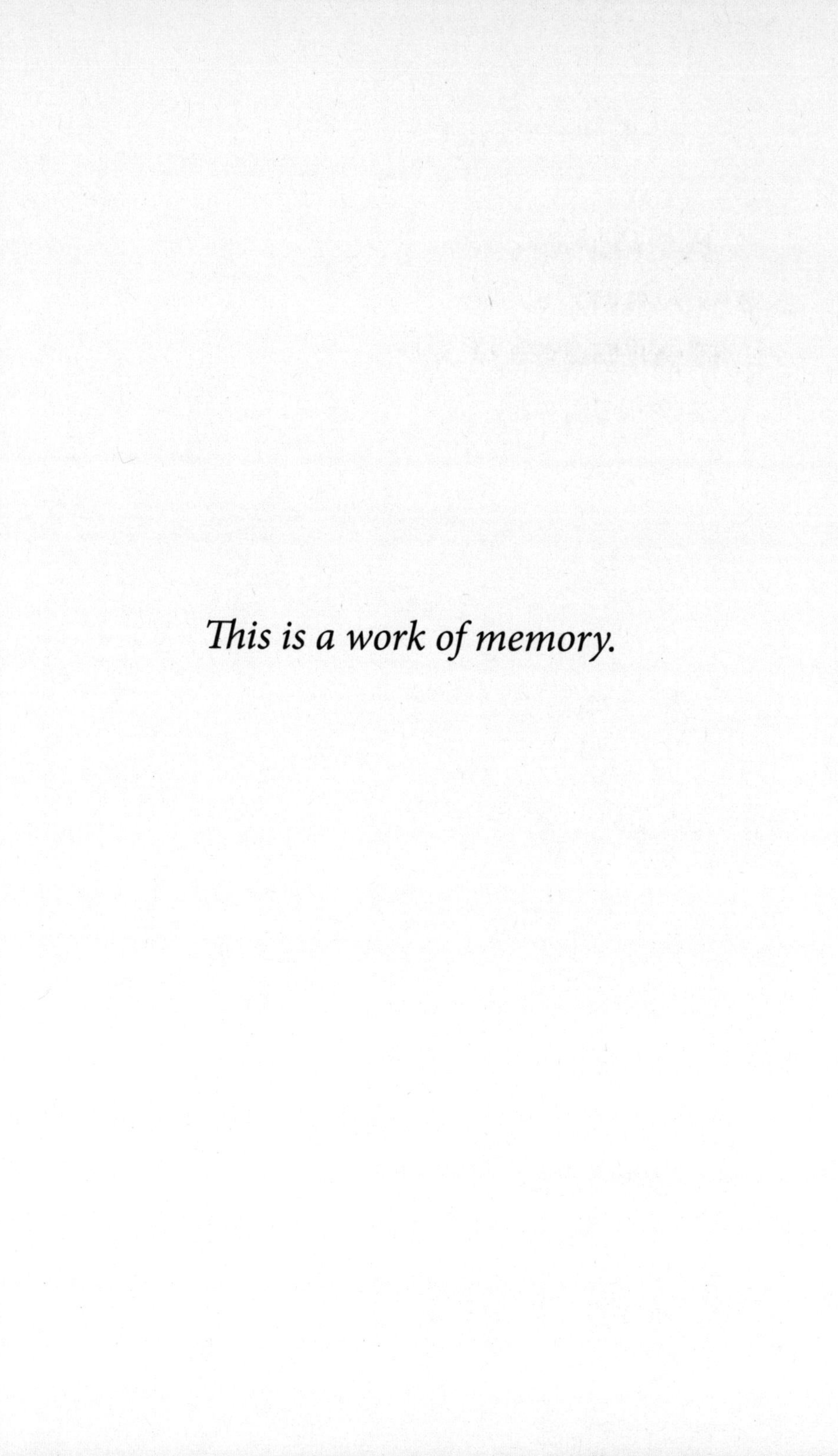

This is a work of memory.

CONTENTS

PROLOGUE

After, a beginning

We're up ridiculously early to be moving at the halting pace that is required for the morning's activity. Hushed conversations, but mostly no talking. A pip or chur or bssssht, and in near unison everyone stops, all heads turning, pulling up binoculars to scour the leafy canopy for a flash of color. The true birders have their ears cocked, a look on their faces of scanning the environment against their internal sound banks for an id, when a broad grin breaks out if they've landed the particular species. This often reminds me of the old game show *Name That Tune* or of Deadheads catching the briefest of strains of the beginning of a new jam and then sending cheers up into the crowd, the song identified! The pleasure in recognizing "St. Stephen" or "Terrapin Station," whatever song was coming into being.

In our case, the blackburnian warbler. Or a particular vireo. It is spring in the northeastern U.S., and the migrants are making their way through to summer breeding grounds in the area and farther into Canada—seemingly ever farther north as all of earth's intricate rhythms are under exceptional duress in a radically changing climate.

I'm new to bird walks, to birding generally with any kind of integrity. While hiking in the woods has become a necessary reset for my addled brain chemistry, my hikes are more like hauling ass up whatever's in front of me than stop and gander the flora and fauna strolls. But the layers of presence in the environment through which I move have been deepening of late. Or should I say expanding? I have so much to learn; there is always more, and while I have come to appreciate the intimate relationship I have with terrain *because of* moving through it aggressively—its contours, slopes, roots, and rocks make for footing that requires a particular attunement to the land when I'm truly booking—a staggering event in my life has disrupted everything I know about how to walk in the world. The minute has me in its grip. I am sensitized to the particular and want to miss none of it. In a way, it's a quality of paying attention that drew me to Jon, the man with whom I have most experienced the rewards and existential challenges of being resolutely committed.

Look! Everyone's heads turn. Not our official aim, but a porcupine lumbers through the brush downhill from where the dozen or so of us are gathering. There is no urgency to the spiky creature's gait. They're notoriously unconcerned with possible predators, so well-defended is their flesh, which isn't to say they won't make their way up a tree if pressed (they still seem to do it with a casual confidence). But this I would learn later, their particular traits and behaviors, on yet another walk, another focus for the learning—mammal tracking. Then it was spring ephemerals. An initial foray into mushrooms. Books and talks and more walks on reading the forested landscape to determine how the topography can show where a previous homestead was located or that white pines in the understory signal the return of wild turkeys to the area. Everything in the woods has a story, and I was desperate to know them all.

The porcupine makes its way away from us, and we, too, move down a path, binocs at the ready and eager for encounters with the spring avian visitors. We're shuffling in a hush, save for the swish of rain pants and slickers. It's not only early but wet and cold for all the creeping along, then standing stock-still, unless one counts the shivering. I'm used to staying warm by being in motion, so I'm dressed less for birding than for stripping layers once I get a sweat going. At fifty-one, I might be the youngest of the bunch. Though I'll come to meet new generations, this particular group for my first serious bird walk gives me pause (they all do). What kind of nature nerd have I become? I remind myself that I'm nowhere near the kind of expert that makes this charge truly leviable, which actually feels worse. Then the long line of a winter wren's song threads through the branches and I'm happily back in the fold.

The leader of the walk takes the opportunity to remind us that birding is a lot of listening. It is an art, a moving with intent for connection that takes time. A willingness to walk sometimes for an entire morning with little reward. Putting in what an animal tracker I've studied with calls "hours on the ground." Some days it can feel like a confrontation with emptiness. It is always a reckoning with desire. I have so much desire to be engaged with the nonhuman world! Engaged, I'll say, not mauled. Learning the bigger picture of the wildly interconnected planet doesn't mean I will disregard a grizzly bear's nature. Quite the opposite, in fact. As I've heard it put, we can consider all of animated life socially, which does not always imply sociability. (It's not very friendly to be eaten alive.) But it does entail agency. Not land and its creatures as background, but as players. Comrades. Lovers. Family. Yes, even the deadly ones. This was always within me, this creaturely sense of connection with and respect for my environment, if not fully recognized or cultivated the way that I have come to believe is crucial to survival, my own and most urgently the planet's. I had flashes here and there, but never a dedicated approach to developing the relationship, the way I learned to be connected with Jon.

We break for a snack on the bank of a creek, the day has warmed a little. This is the first real opportunity to chat with any volume and the usual *What brings you here?* questions float into the air. I am unusually taciturn. There is so much I'm keeping to myself this morning. So much I don't say. The circumstances of my excruciating longing. My love story. Of digging deeply into that which is more than a feeling. Of devoting oneself to the welfare of the other despite a grievous lack of guarantees. The commitment that transcends a lifetime. Into geological time. And perhaps into a realm that is inconceivably without chronology. But first, the matter at hand. The story of Jon and me, of two profoundly wounded people learning how to love. And of my waking up from alienation from self and other and planet. *Shhhhhh.* Listen.

CHAPTER 1

AMERICAN GOLDFINCHES

(Jon and I meet)

2006

The river bottoms affording all the timber which is to be seen in the country they are filled with innumerable little birds that resort thither either for shelter or to build their nests. when sun began to shine today these birds appeared to be very gay and sung most enchantingly. . . .

—Meriwether Lewis, journal entry, June 8, 1805

Considering the fact that Jon and I met because we were fucked, or had been, that in one way or another we'd both gone to desperate lengths to kill the parts of ourselves that were damaged—call it the death drive run amok, call it addiction, call it soul sickness, whatever it was we were two of too many people on the planet who get battered by the way the world works and nearly take ourselves out of the game in response—considering all this, it's a miracle we were willing to risk any iota of pain by opening up to each other, but one night at a recovery meeting he did just that, and our journey began.

I'd known Jon through these meetings for about a year. We'd both been "in the rooms" for well over a decade at that point, separately working through our own versions of withdrawal, of disbelief, of trying to get through a minute, then another minute, and then just one more, counting all the excruciating increments of time leading up to days, that finally accumulated into months, building up the years away from all sorts of behaviors we'd been compelled to partake in for all the reasons addicts do. We'd listened to each other's stories in bits and pieces during short and longer shares as a means of saving our own lives. These scenes are familiar from movies. The dingy church basement or scrappy community room adorned with tattered posters of recovery slogans: "Keep Coming Back," "One Day At A Time," and "Think Think Think" often turned upside down. The hands raised, the confessions of horrible behavior, the defensiveness, the denial. Jon and I were no different. We unleashed on and with our fellows our own gritty details of serial one-night stands, crippling debt, dope sniffing, the mornings after, the morning drink, and the accompanying regret and lament and self-recrimination.

But also the recovery. The first night I became aware of Jon it was his voice that got me. His voice, and that he was talking about drinking more water as a matter of taking care of himself. It was irrefutable proof of my complete overhaul as a human being that I found this mundane behavior sexy. But so was his humor. His sensibility.

His way of expressing himself. He felt familiar to me, as if I'd already known him. Not *you remind me of my father, so let's move in together and work out all the ravages of childhood on each other,* though maybe that, too, but a deeper form of recognition. I don't believe in predestination, per se, nor the rom-com trope of soul mates, but perhaps the spiritual-not-religious intellectual's equivalent. He is my people, I thought.

Despite the attraction, we didn't date right away. I'd made the conscious choice to defer the possibility out of respect for the rules of engagement for where we'd met. It wasn't advised to treat this community as a dating pool, though many of us did (myself included), but I was trying to do it differently by then. Also, I had the feeling that he wasn't ready for me yet, though it was far more appropriate for me to admit that I wasn't at all ready for him. I was still growing up, an adult daughter whose mother was in the throes of an excruciating, three-year struggle with ovarian cancer. I was busy holding her hand during hours of slow dripping chemo. I received the calls in the middle of the night to drive her to the ER when the pain was too great. I sat with her at the table while she shakily signed checks, eager to exert some control in her retracting life. I was deep in the challenge of loving her while losing her. And still, Jon caught my attention. I could do nothing at the time but file him away as a yes, I could "go there," but no, I'm not going to at the moment, if ever. Uncharacteristically, I was exhibiting restraint and patience.

And then, after the better part of a year of grieving the death of my mother, I wrote the final poem in a draft of my project as a belated grad student and shared about it at a meeting. Jon was there that night, and he, also uncharacteristically, approached me afterward to talk with me about it. I would come to learn that he'd written stories and poems, too. That he read broadly, inhaled music, adored movies, craved scientific understanding. That he was constitutionally enthralled by the magnificence and terror of—what can I call it?—*existence, the breadth of life?* The intricacies of the ways of the world and universe and ant tunnels and cantilevers and throat singers and black holes and extinct dodo birds and how the way certain languages use the cardinal directions demonstrates a sophisticated relationship with land and sea? All of it. He was taken with all of it.

I was, too, ostensibly, and by trade. I was, after all, a *poet.* And he truly could not have been more admiring of that fact, so much so that he broke through his usual Midwestern reserve to approach me after the meeting to say so.

"I give you so much credit," he said. I was talking with another woman who happened to be a musician. "Both of you. It takes a lot of courage to do what you're doing."

"Uh huh." Ever the charmer, me. I was unswayed and, also, jealous. Unswayed because courage felt like the prize everybody gets for playing. I didn't want to be courageous. I wanted to be a fucking rock star, or whatever the equivalent for my dumb choice of career would be. Jealous because suddenly I didn't want to share this weak compliment, or more to the point, to have his attention also on this other woman.

"No, really," he forged on in what would turn out to be a consequential move for both of our lives. "You should be proud of yourself."

This was clearly for me and me alone. Fortunately the other woman was awkwardly shy and took the opportunity to escape, leaving me to bask in his attention. I was my usual gracious self in response to the compliment.

"You know, poems are completely ineffectual in the capitalist marketplace."

Now it was his turn. "Uh huh."

"No, really."

Thankfully he was undeterred, hungry as he was for conversation about reading and ideas and literature. So much so that he was practically ebullient, or his Midwesterner's version of it, about the writers that got him through high school. Of hiding the Kurt Vonnegut novels he'd been forbidden to read between the pages of textbooks. And of the authors who felt like treasured friends to him now, decades later. Louise Erdrich. Umberto Eco. Sherman Alexie. Dorothy Allison. Virginia Woolf. At least as much I was required to read for a master's degree, and he was doing it all of his own accord. How did I not know this about him?

I remember the moment that night that everything shifted. I can still see him standing in the diffuse, yellow glow of the lighting outside the building where the meeting had taken place, everyone in the usual clusters of twos and threes chatting, until they weren't, and the two of us were still talking without realizing the others had left. It was so easy, our sentences building excitedly one upon the other. He was so damn charming! Quick to laugh, an attentive listener, and when he spoke his responses were clearly considered, not prefabricated. And he was handsome, too, though he would never have thought any of that about himself. The background around us blurred, and he clicked into focus. His fluffy ginger brown hair and trim beard. His shiny cheeks and sparkling blue eyes. That wide smile. I was entranced. Of course the entire exchange was helped along by the flood of bodily chemicals and neurons firing, and *could* it be that we'd been Viking royalty together in another life?

And then, the next consequential turn, he offered: "If you ever want to share a poem of yours with me, I'd love to read it."

You never have to ask a poet this twice.

Of course I would send him something! We would exchange e-mail addresses. I wasn't entirely sure if this was appropriate, but I had a pen in my car behind the building, so I led him down the alley, out of the light in front, toward the dark back lot. I remember him saying something like, "Where are you taking me?" He was joking, and not. We were both scared.

And so our courtship began, though he later said that I was dating him well before he was dating me. He might not have been able to continue if he'd thought there was the potential for romance between us. I did my best to talk him into it without literally talking him into it. We began by e-mail. I sent him a poem, as agreed, then second-guessed that particular one as well as every single word in the e-mail itself while waiting for him to respond. A day or two later he e-mailed back with such careful attention. I don't remember exactly what he wrote, but it was complimentary without being saccharine. I expected a slight to come, but one never did.

As our correspondence grew, I spent an enormous amount of energy refraining from sending too many e-mails, not always successfully. There was the night I came home from the gym, super jazzed to find something from him in my inbox after mope-jogging that I hadn't heard from him in a few days. I had the movie *The Sting* playing in the background and began sending lines of dialogue in a version of play-by-play in successive e-mails. "Everything's jakey." [send] [but was it, jakey?] "Nah, I'd only blow it." [send] [shit! he'll think I'm a fuckup] "You know me. I'm the same as you. It's two in the morning and I don't know nobody." [send] [too close to the truth] "You follow?" [send] [was I threatening him now?] Eventually I stopped, but not before I sent eight e-mails to his one. I cringed thinking about him seeing them lined up in his account the next morning. "Well, it was nice while it lasted," I tried to comfort myself, certain I'd blown it. But then there was an e-mail back from him before the end of the next (very long) day.

I did a ton of hiking. It was a strategy I developed in sobriety to manage my malleable mental health. I poured the overwhelming excesses of energy that coursed through me into churning up mountains instead of exploding in situ. I was a goat. A lion. I felt feral. The day the phone call came when he finally said it would be nice to have a conversation in real time and would I like to get together tonight to do so (jesus, Jon, just ask me out already), I nearly vomited into the phone. Somehow I managed to respond, "Why yes, Jon, that sounds lovely," then immediately threw my always-ready backpack into the car to drive 75 miles per hour in a 40 zone to a favorite hill for a panting, sweaty, exuberant pulsing push all the way up 1,900 feet in 1.8 miles and back down, then home for a shower in under three hours because I couldn't hold my *holy shit I've been waiting for this, for you, for us, for all of my life* excitement in. The goal was to exorcise myself of myself, and mostly it worked.

I drove to where we'd agreed to meet for dinner while breathing in, then out, then in take this exit, then out there's the turn, then in cough cough sputter, then out, Cara, you can do this, as all my people had assured me I could do. Jon was already in a parking spot on the phone with a friend for the encouragement he also needed when I pulled into the lot. I didn't know this. I had no idea when I was readying to present myself by swigging on a travel bottle of mouthwash that he was two spaces over and could see me swish, tip my head back to gurgle to the heavens, then open my car door to spit.

Here it must be said that I am not, and never have been, any good at spitting. It takes multiple tries and usually I don't clear my own body. There's often spittle. Then wiping with the back of my hand. He saw it all. He was actually waving to me to get my attention, telling his friend on the phone that I'd arrived, that what he was so nervous about was set to begin. He put his hand down, afraid that I'd be embarrassed, and faced forward in his car. It helped to ease his tension he later said.

But I didn't know any of that when I got out of my car, also nervous, clutching a paper I'd written about teaching poetry in prison, the class I was leading weekly for my degree. I was certain there was confirmation within this text that we had the most important things in common and was convinced he would agree if he read it. We met out front of the restaurant we'd planned to eat at, but it was closed. In the delicate flush of early romance it felt like this could derail everything! Handily, there was an Italian restaurant open just a few doors down that had a booth available for us. We settled in across from each other.

He put his phone aside and said, "Okay, entertain me." He was joking. It was a thing one of his sons from his defunct marriage did, also as a joke.

"I'm nervous," I said, and then, in an ill-advised move, ordered beans and greens, a dish notorious for its liberal use of garlic. Did I also get pasta? I had no clue what I was doing. I handed him the paper. He looked uncertain. It was one thing to consider a poem, but twenty pages of academic writing?

"Just read it," I said, but didn't insist on him reading it right then and there, though likely I wanted him to. In the paper I'd posited the idea that words in a poem could be considered as strings on a sitar vibrating off each other, in a version of what musicians call sympathetic resonance. An alluring notion to be sure and one that could certainly apply to more than writing, but all the more so because he'd happened to mention in our early e-mail correspondence how much he appreciated that some strings exist solely for the purpose of vibrating in response to others. He'd had no idea that I, too, adored this concept. Not only did I adore it, I'd already written it into a philosophy of teaching. Then I spit out my car door.

He said he would read it, the paper, then asked me why I was nervous. I shifted around in the booth, beaming like a silly sunflower, and told him it was because I liked him. Those exact words. I felt like the kindergartner who asked Mark Elliott to be my valentine by passing him a piece of colored construction paper with "I lik U" scrawled in magic marker over sloppy hand-drawn hearts. Then it was Jon's turn to wriggle and blush. We were schoolkids, really, in adult bodies. Most people are in early romance, but addicts are always extra. They say people coming into recovery are the emotional age of their first acting out behaviors in their addictions, so we were decidedly psychologically in early adolescence. I even had a few freshly sprouted pimples.

We agreed to go for coffee after the meal. I stashed the many leftovers on the back seat of my car. The original plan had been to meet for dinner, then go to one of our meetings, a bookend that might keep the situation from getting away from us. Or if it was going horribly awry, we both had an out. But we chose to continue. We took the risk of parting, then joining together at another venue, of breaking the face-to-face spell in our own cars, back to our individual selves, then to reconnect and claim the choice to sit together all over again, that same night. This felt notable. An attraction that could withstand the challenges of closed restaurants and following each other through traffic lights, even if I was anxious the whole drive over, nervously checking my rearview mirror to see if he was still behind me.

After coffee, we stood out front of the shop, awkwardly of course, but smiling. A few feet apart. I remember looking at his shoes, right there on the ground. Loafers. Jeans. His beaming face. Would he kiss me? Should we? He kept a respectful distance, but clearly he was happy to be standing with me. As I was with him. We would part, this was nice. Did we say we'd do it again? I don't remember how we left it, except that probably it included my reiterated request that he read the paper.

I got back to my car a few spots away and opened the door to a rush of the odor of leftovers. I called out to him across the lot, "My car smells like garlic!" I don't know why I did. I also don't know why that tickled him, but he would bring it up for years to come. This was our first date that he still did not think was a date. We both held secrets that night that we were excited for the time when we would reveal them. The moment when he got home and hit upon sympathetic resonance in my paper. The time after a month of dating that he told me he'd pulled into the parking lot before I arrived, and I immediately knew that he'd seen me spit. The delight of original response. Of experiencing something more than our own echoes off the cave wall. We were vibrating.

CHAPTER 2

ROCK DOVE, FERAL–AKA COMMON PIGEON

(I flee New York City)

1993

The squabs stay in the nest for between 24 and 30 days when they leave, fully feathered and the same size as their parents. This is why you might think you have never seen a baby pigeon, because by the time they leave the nest they are almost indistinguishable from adults. Young birds are fed by their parents for a further 2 weeks after leaving the nest.

—"Things you need to know about PIGEONS!" *A Shot of Wildlife* (YouTube)

My relationships with men had nearly killed me. With women, too. With bosses and colleagues. Friends, boyfriends, friends of boyfriends, and boyfriends of friends. Bartenders and dope dealers. Pretty much all bodies of matter and spirit I crossed paths with, even the earth herself. But most especially I was at war with myself, and I came damn close to losing.

It really was as dramatic as that. A true face-to-face with death as an event. Addicts and alcoholics commonly act contrary to their instinct for survival, and this can unfold by a million cuts or in hefty fell swoops. My downward trajectory was both, in a way, all of it expedited, hard, ragged. I went from film student, comedy club publicist, burgeoning environmental activist, and writer and performer of some promise to being unemployed and unemployable in a few short years, scraping along a macadam bottom in New York City, walking into fists as large as baseball mitts and throwing myself against plateglass windows while pissing and vomiting anywhere and everywhere. It wasn't pretty. (It often isn't.)

I crept through sooty, rat-filled subway tunnels with other trespassers of the night. I gave blowjobs to strangers in littered doorways for bags of dope to snort. I sold all of my possessions to buy cigarettes, booze, and drugs to smoke. When I ran out of my own things to sell, I learned to dig through Upper East Side garbage cans for the stuff rich people discarded that could be wiped off and laid out on the sidewalks of the Lower East to fetch a price. I told myself I was doing the world a service, keeping all of these items out of a landfill. Finally I found a man who felt about me the same way that I did, which is to say that he both loved and abhorred me, mostly the latter. It was his fists that forced me to choose in a flash. *Live or die, Cara. Live or die.*

I'm not sure I was specifically choosing life, but I found in that moment I didn't want to die. I crawled across the floor of my once enviable, now demolished East Village apartment, head ringing, throat hoarse from screaming through the dirty sock Tony had gagged me with, bleeding from my vagina, and shakily put my fingers into the holes of the phone to draw the dial around from 9, then 1, then 1. My emergency was this: The man who says he loves me is coming back to kill me.

New York City cops in the early 1990s likely had scant training in dealing with battered women, with battered anyone, and perhaps they still don't, but for sure the two that showed up that night in response to my call had no clue how to help this beaten, bloodied, and bruised woman other than to begrudgingly drive her away from the scene of the crime.

"This isn't a taxi service," I remember one of them saying from the front seat while I was shivering with fear and nausea behind the bulletproof divider. I was confused. I couldn't remember any of my friend's addresses. I had the clothes on my body and somehow had had the presence of mind to grab my passport. I didn't know where to tell them to take me, just please hurry the fuck up because that man will kill me, especially if he sees me with police.

Everything was dark. The night. The apartment where Tony had shut the circuit breaker. The jagged humor of the police. My body was clenched in terror, my nails trying to get purchase in the hard vinyl while I scanned the faces of passersby for my perpetrator. *There!* I saw him through the crowd on the sidewalk on his way back, just as he had said. I slid down in the seat, afraid he'd see me, which surely he did because in an instant he disappeared back into the crowd. I said nothing to the cops about spotting him.

"East 9th Street. Can you drop me on East 9th?" They'd been unwilling to drive farther than their precinct boundaries to get me to a safer spot in the West Village. East 9th was where Scotty lived, a fellow writer and performer. He, like many of my friends at that time, had refused to continue performing with me or even to hang out at all if I couldn't show up sober, which I was less and less able to do, and then not at all. But I couldn't think of where else to go.

"There's his building."

I was terrified to get out of the car. In my mind the man who beat me had magical powers, could have been lurking in a doorway or behind garbage cans, having somehow tracked the vehicle from two blocks away where he'd seen me being driven off. It wasn't rational, but it was real. I didn't want the police to leave until I knew Scotty was home and would let me in. It is entirely possible that they waited, but they absolutely did not walk with me up to the door. At the top of the steps I buzzed his apartment. Was it midnight? 1 AM? Whatever the time, I was ashamed. Desperate. In need of rescue in the night, a burden.

He buzzed me in without question. I scuffed the many steps of the walk-up in a daze. The scratchy bricks of the stairwell. The echoing of my footfalls. I was both wincing in pain and bewilderingly numb. As I grabbed the banister to help me up the flights, I could see the cuts on my wrists where I'd been tied with extension cords so tight my fingers tingled for weeks afterward. When I got to his floor, Scotty was on the landing in front of his door. He gave me a hug as if he'd been waiting for this moment for months, which he and nearly everyone else in my life had been. He brought me into his place.

Whatever one expects of a downtown performance artist's apartment, Scotty's fit the bill. The walls were painted black. There were loose buttons scattered about, baroque picture frames sans pictures, and uncomfortable furniture. We sat on the floor across from each other. He handed me a button to focus on while I recounted enough of the gory details for him to say, "Wow. I'll never fantasize about getting raped ever again."

When I said nothing, he continued, "I want you to remember that button."

I looked at it in the palm of my hand.

"I want you to have something else to remember this night by. So that it isn't only tragedy. There's this button. Remember it."

God love him, but even the sanest of my friends at the time was truly fucking nuts.

In the bathroom I stuffed toilet paper between my legs and splashed water as gently as I could on my swollen face. When I got back into the room Scotty said we needed to "hatch a plan." There was talk of pressing charges. Of how to find the man who knew how to vanish underground at the hint of capture. I wasn't so sure I could deal with the police again. Nor that they would do their due diligence in helping to keep me safe. Tony could be anywhere. Going back to my apartment, where Tony would surely return, wasn't an option. Even if I could stay with Scotty, which wasn't a given, to be walking and working the same streets Tony frequented was too risky.

"I guess I need to leave town," I finally conceded.

"Yes you do, honey. At least until things cool down."

It was decided that I'd try my mother. It was not an easy call to make. How could I deliver the news that the daughter she'd carried in her body had been on the verge of being beaten to death and had the black eyes, torn vagina, and chipped tooth to prove it? I took a deep breath. Scotty handed me the phone.

"Mom?"

Immediately she knew what had happened, or some version of it she had been imagining.

"I can't go home. He'll . . ."

"I know. I'm here."

She remained remarkably calm as she had been counseled by Domestic Violence Services to do. She'd known for months I was in particular danger and had reached out to them to see if they had a plan for how she could save her daughter. She'd been trained for this moment.

"Can you get to the train station safely?"

I could hear her husband in the background. Had I woken them up? No. They had friends over. It was earlier than I thought, even as it felt so very late.

I didn't have any money. I was afraid to leave the apartment. I was certain Tony was waiting on the street to finish what he'd started. My panic escalated.

Scotty spoke up. He would get me into a cab, but we would wait until daybreak. It was agreed I would go to my father's on Long Island first; the train fare was cheaper, and Scotty only had so much. It would be good enough for the next move, and that was all I could handle. Each next step.

At dawn, we went down the stairs I'd climbed hours ago. I was pale, sweating. Wordlessly, Scotty went out to the street to hail a cab while I waited inside. I stayed as far back from the door as I could. Finally he waved, and I moved cautiously forward, then bolted down the steps to the curb. We hugged, and I ducked into the back seat.

"Please hurry," I said to the cabdriver.

"What time is your train?"

"Just get me out of here as fast as you can."

He punched the gas. I was thrown back against the seat and let out a scream. The first of many times in my life that the startle response victims of violence live with would kick in, but in that moment all I knew was that I was leaving home and had no idea when I'd be back.

After a few nights on the couch circuit going from my father's house to my sister Donna's apartment and back to my dad's again, I got on another train. This time I was heading to my mother's in upstate New York. Now I had a small overnight bag that various family members and friends had helped me to assemble and I was a few days away from the terror of the last beating. Somehow I figured out how to get my hands on a bottle of scotch to carry in my bag. Ridiculously, I ensured it was a fine single malt. Though I'd had my fair share of vodka that tasted slightly worse than rubbing alcohol, things had been rough. I felt I deserved a bit of the good stuff.

On the train I watched as the scenery flew by, the marshy shoreline on one side, the wide expanse of the Hudson River on the other. I was headed farther afield to see if distance could solve the spectacular mess I'd made of my life. It's what I later learned people in recovery call making a geographical cure for what ails us internally, but it was true that anything I might have hoped for my life wouldn't be possible if I couldn't stay alive. And so I left my beloved Manhattan in an ignominious retreat to my mother's house in a forested area outside Saratoga Springs in the foothills of the Adirondack Mountains.

I wasn't happy about it. Though it was killing me, gritty sidewalks, active street corners, and an embarrassment of bars were my milieu, the society I'd become accustomed to operating in. The stillness and isolation of my mother's place disturbed me, but what choice did I have? Besides, I told myself, I wouldn't be there long. I just needed a little breathing room to shake Tony.

My mother picked me up at the station. Seeing the look of both relief and heartbreak on her face was tough. So was the ride to her house, where it started setting in more deeply just how remote her place was. To many people my mother's home was like a vacation rental in the woods. It was situated well back from a sparsely populated road. A former Boy Scout camp turned sizable nature preserve bordered the forest behind her yard. There were no neighbors' houses visible from hers, save for one, but then only in winter when the leaves of the thick forest were down. To the city girl I'd become, this was the definition of the boonies. Which is to say that the place was unnervingly quiet and a whole other level of dark when the sun went down.

That night I struggled to sleep. I lay in bed, my ears ringing, and reeking of the cigarette smoke that permeated all of my clothing and hair. I stuffed my head under the pillow. I needed noise. I needed action. I needed to get away from myself. I was both unbearably tender and absolutely savage. Good god, get me access to any kind of hub where there was trouble to be had like dope or a car to drive way too fast so I could hang out the window screaming. I could feel my heart beating in my chest. My breathing was shallow. My dreams when I finally slept were filled with growling dogs and knife blades glinting in moonlight. I woke, sweating and cold. I swigged on my bottle. Clearly I needed a plan, and fast. I was not going to last possibly even another night way the fuck out here.

It wasn't safe to go back to NYC, but maybe I could try another city? Swig. I thought Los Angeles. Slurp. Maybe New Orleans. Chug. The more I drank, the more I was convinced I was onto something. I'd show them. Once I got myself established as a writer in the industry (leaning toward LA), everyone would get off my back. I just needed a fresh start. This kind of bullshit is so predictable it's cliché. I'm sure on some level I knew I was full of it, but alcoholic thinking can be damn convincing.

Not to everyone, however. The next morning my mother presented a very different idea of what my next move should be. She wanted to take me to see the good people at the local Domestic Violence Services office in the so-called city center. I don't remember if she had to talk me into it or if I momentarily wanted it myself, but for some reason I agreed to go. I also don't remember the conversation with the counselor once we got there, none of it, but I can still picture the Polaroids she took of my battered body, the bruising, the cuts, the rip across my belly. It was documentation in case I did decide to press charges. More importantly, when I made the attempts that were surely coming to convince myself things really weren't that bad, here was the irrefutable proof. The problem with this strategy for keeping me safe from myself was that it depended on me wanting that, which wasn't at all a given.

"How would you feel about staying here for a while?" my mother asked. We were driving back through town.

I looked out the window. What I saw was the definition of quaint. Baskets bursting with colorful flowers were hanging from street posts, and pedestrians ambled casually on the sidewalks. A few elaborately designed historical buildings in marble, granite, and brick anchored one of the larger intersections. The rest of the main street was lined with boutique storefronts, ice cream and gelato spots, and a plethora of upscale restaurants. But where there were restaurants, there would be bars.

"What do you mean?" I knew what she meant, but when in doubt, push back.

"I mean, how about I help you get an apartment, and you can take some time to get back on your feet."

I knew I had to do something. I couldn't keep on with the couch circuit indefinitely. Still, I wasn't keen on living in such a small town. But then no one, absolutely not one person in my life would have supported me taking off into the sunset on my own. I had zero resources. No car. The status of my driver's license was questionable at best after a brief but notable teenage driving career. And then there was that gaping hole on my résumé.

"When you say here, you mean downtown, right?"

I was twenty-five, still slightly concussed, my mother was offering to set me up in an apartment, and all I really wanted to know was whether I could walk to the bars from wherever I'd be living. Also, I'd prefer it if the lease was monthly as it wouldn't be too long before I'd be ready to move on. She said she would see what she could find. She seemed relieved. I wanted out of the car.

I asked her to drop me in town. No time like the present to take a look around and see if there was work to be had. How much would a cab back cost? And could I have a few extra bucks in case I wanted to grab some lunch? We both knew I wasn't getting food or looking for work and that likely I'd figure out how to get a ride back to her house from someone I'd become fast friends with between rounds. She must have been picking her battles because she pulled over at a street corner and handed me some money.

"Will you be back for dinner?"

"Of course I will."

Of course I wouldn't.

"Please be careful, okay?"

I wanted to laugh. What did she think could happen in a town as fucking cute as this?

CHAPTER 3

WILD TURKEYS

(We engage in courtship)

2005

Fun Fact! Turkey droppings tell a bird's sex and age.
Male droppings are j-shaped; female droppings are spiral-shaped.
The larger the diameter, the older the bird.
—U.S. Fish & Wildlife Service

After that first date that Jon did not think was a date, we went on another one. And then another. It finally became clear to him, to both of us, that though we were adolescents nearing midlife, full of heart-wrecks and drive-bys and the stunted emotional growth that addicts come into recovery with, we also had been on the path long enough to have stabilized (mostly) and to have experienced a certain amount of healing. More than that, though, we were undeniably drawn to each other in what felt like a "good" way, which is to say a different way from what we'd both known, enough to spur us to give the relationship thing with each other a try.

And so we became lovers.

We became lovers in our gazes. Lovers in holding hands. Lovers in our cheeks and smiles and animated gestures. We became lovers in laughing. In recurring jokes. In my spit takes. In his not taking offense. In the cultural currency of the community we shared. In telling each other the doings of our days. We became lovers in perpetual conversation.

We were lovers in our cars, making out after the movies. After a public reading by a favorite author. After dinner at one of the many restaurants in the region where Jon was treated like one of the family—so personable was he to nearly everyone he met. We blushed. We kissed. We nuzzled our faces into each other. We yearned. We were working to balance tremendous and overwhelming all-consuming attraction with such banal tasks as our daily lives commanded. Laundry. Work. Study. Showers. Meetings. Oh my god, can you see me tonight?

We let each other into our living spaces. His a divorced dad apartment that held the overcrowded remnants of having had his now-grown children on Wednesdays and every other weekend. Mine the immaculate three-bedroom house I inherited when my mother died. We were the kind of lovers where my weeping at the loss of her was understood as part of the journey. And also it was something that took up a lot of space between us. *Don't touch me. I'm crying.* Even if he didn't always understand, which he sometimes notably didn't, he eventually learned to wait at the edge of it for my waves of grief to subside.

We oozed. We gooed. We annoyed people. We inspired them. Our friends were delighted. Relieved. Happy we had each finally found someone that could meet the many quirks of our individual personalities. (Maybe me the most, but then thinking that would be one of the quirks.)

"You two are such a good fit!"

"If ever a couple was supposed to be together . . ."

And because between us we'd each been through countless therapy sessions, we processed *everything.* Long talks, facing each other, practicing repeating what the other person is saying to be sure that it was heard, and the ever popular "When you ______, I feel _______" communication tricks. As in "When you interrupted me, I felt angry." Or "When you showed up late, I felt disrespected." Who were these people, calmly stating what could have easily been barked in the heat of the moment or repressed into seething resentment to be sprung on the other in a future argument? I felt like we were aliens in a pod, or cult members, but it did seem to be working, except when my (not so) old ways leaked through and I blurted something moronic. We were lovers who were going to have to withstand a lot of fucking it all up.

Starting with the first time we played tennis. We didn't so much play a game as hit the balls past each other, then chase after them. I was horrified by our incompetence. He didn't seem to care, at all. For him the fun was—what did he say it was? I don't remember, but he laughed a lot, letting one hit of mine after another whiz right past him. What kind of sport was this? He was the one who had the rackets, and this is the kind of play he's got? And good god, those shorts. I was appalled, the sweet spell of romance broken. I knew it would come, but so soon?

"I guess the honeymoon's over," I said at lunch afterward.

The confused and slightly hurt look on his face snapped me out of it. I did my best to maneuver past the moment, but the line became another one of those that stuck. “Honeymoon’s over,” he’d say, and I’d slump dramatically to get him to laugh, which he usually did. We were lovers of self-deprecating humor.

We shared our origin stories. Our dating histories, even though much of this we already knew from hearing each other talk about the bad, the ugly, and the downright illegal at recovery meetings. We shared our bodies. We tumbled around on his bed, tucked into a corner of his apartment, his cat Titi walking circles around us, stepping on my hair, until finally Jon would push him down. We fooled around on my bed, the king in the master bedroom I had taken as mine, us writhing and wriggling, my cat Ed sensibly avoiding us. Occasionally me panicking.

“Should we be doing this?” I sat up one night at exactly the wrong moment.

“What?” He was, I think it’s fair to say, stunned.

“We’re only three [or two or five] months in. Are we rushing it?”

He cleared his throat, gathering himself from the ecstatic, now interrupted. “Um, I don’t think so?”

“It’s good that we’re asking, though, right? You know, checking in with ourselves?”

This wasn’t the often told story of a woman putting the breaks on the sexual while the man wants nothing more than to pursue penetration. This was something far more comprehensive—and terrifying. We were lovers at the precipice of intimacy.

Up until this point, relationships meant a total loss of self, an enmeshment that produced what an earlier boyfriend of mine had once called “that saltine feeling.” The one where you don’t need anything or anyone but your lover, a tiny apartment lit by a bare bulb hanging down on a wire, and a box of crackers to live on. At thirty-nine I had far more experience pursuing this version, not to mention the violence that had almost erased me entirely, and I was eager for something greater. This did not mean I knew how to do it. Some days the best I could do to maintain a sense of myself with Jon was to throw some spiky speed bumps into our process of getting close. I'm not sure what it says about him that he hung in there with me, but then Jon had his sneaky ways of keeping me at bay, too. Of course dopamine got us over more than a few of these humps, as it is designed to do, but being under its influence had led to such disastrous consequences in both our histories that it's astonishing we kept at it. We were lovers in mutual risk.

We risked heartbreak and misfiring neurotransmitters. We risked depression. Mood disorders. Making all the same mistakes we'd already made. We became willing to walk away from each other if that's what it took to live with integrity. In fact, at one point he did just that. We both did. He cut it off when one weekend early on I pushed the limit of how much was too much too soon by talking him into a trip to New York City with me. He needed space. He needed not to go forward. He needed not to be dating. And I . . . I let him go. I needed someone who would stick it out. Who could say no to me but not leave me. This became our weekend of moping, at the end of which he changed his mind. He called. He'd made a mistake. He got some bad advice. Would I be willing to keep trying? Yes, Jon. Yes. We were lovers in leveling up.

When did we first say the word? We spoke around it. We prolonged it. We were holding out for the good stuff. The right time. The big payoff. None of that is really true. We were speechless and breathless and overflowing with too much to say. Our love of language stitched our stories together. We picked up each other's catchphrases. We used with ease our pets' various nicknames. Certain expressions became flash points and shorthand, the way lovers develop their own vocabularies.

One of the things I'd said early on that he latched onto in my *I'm not convincing you to date me, but here's why we should keep trying* efforts was that while there are some things that one must heal on one's own, equally as important, there are some wounds that can only be healed in relationship. It was something a therapist once said to bust me out of a rut. It sounded good, so I tried it on us, and it worked, so much so that he would bring that up eons after I'd said it, at the point in our relationship when I wondered why he'd taken me seriously. Like the poem I wrote for him that included these lines:

fly from my chest

an armsfull of birds

when I see you

I wasn't aware at the time how much he loved birds, how they fascinated him. Their behaviors. Their colors. Their unique personalities. Their place in the ecosystem. He could stare out a window for hours watching them flutter around a feeder and delighted in spotting hawks on a roadside perch. Much of this I would come to learn about him over time, but not everything. (Some things we keep to ourselves.) It's an unpredictable process, the act of discovery. This exercise in becoming known.

We read aloud to each other, me my writing to him, and in turn I listened to him read out of some of his most treasured books. One time he became so hysterical trying to get through a few pages of Bill Bryson's *Thunderbolt Kid* that he was shuddering and crying because he was laughing so hard. We were lying together in his bed when he picked up the book and sent us both into waves of orgiastic laughter.

We were lovers walking to the supermarket near his apartment, the first time we would shop for and cook a meal together, broaching the domestic in the tiny kitchen of his scrappy one bedroom. We were lovers with our plates on our laps, sitting on his futon, watching *Some Like It Hot* or the kind of movie he'd describe as *shit blows up real good.* We were lovers while the DVDs played in the background, the empty plates now on the floor, our hands and crevices and mouths and flesh eager for the luscious friction of willing bodies rubbing against each other.

We were lovers in talking politics. In takedowns of consumer culture. In lamenting exploitation. Environmental degradation. The profit motive. We were lovers with compatible worldviews, with differing strategies, with tempering and invigorating influences on the other. I was the obvious activist, protesting organizing agitating, to his preferred stance of sly commentator. I knocked on doors, spoke through bullhorns at rallies, rode the bus to DC. He had a business card made that read "Capitalist Tool." We were lovers in arguing which was the more effective strategy. In loving the argument itself.

He became willing to hike with me! I went to progressive rock concerts with him! We were expanding each other's orbits of experience and knowledge. Surely this was the greater love. One afternoon while dutifully writing a paper for grad school I listened to his copy of *Music for Airports* on repeat as he ventured to a favored mountain of mine to give my kind of walking uphill a try. I was already a Brian Eno fan, but nowhere near to the extent that he was. Jon, however, was not really an active outdoors guy, even if he did have a far more sophisticated understanding of the workings of the natural world than I did for all my time in the woods. He much preferred going to matinees. And while he'd had periods of physical fitness playing high school football and working construction, he wasn't in one of those when I met him. But he was currently in a routine of going to the gym, so I fostered the conviction that I'd lure him into the backcountry with me sooner or later. We were lovers in talking ourselves into all sorts of things.

For this first attempt, Jon insisted on going without me. I was cranky about it, stuck home at a computer while he was out meeting a hill that I'd hiked so many times it felt like a friend, but thrilled he was going and begrudgingly grateful he was still willing to say no to me. It was a glorious fall day. The light streamed through the windows where I wrote. The soothing repetition of the music worked on me and especially that it had come from him. I stared out at the trees flaming into glorious color and wondered how he was faring on the trail. Was he hating it? Second-guessing the whole relationship? Was I? I began to get concerned, I hadn't heard anything for longer than I expected. Finally he called, filled with stories! He'd made it to the summit and had met nearly everyone on the way, a far more gregarious person than he believed himself to be. His incredible attention to people and the slope and events up and down gave rise to an exciting afternoon to report on. I lapped up every word. In turn he asked me about my paper, and I told him how the music had helped me to persevere. We were lovers of alchemy.

Jon described our relationship as unfolding. I said we were sniffing each other's butts. At last we said the words. *I love you.* We teased it out of each other simultaneously, entwined on my mother's couch in the living room of the house that was clearly too big for me alone. We were filled with the swelling emotion of growing romance. We called this love, the way everyone does, and it was. And this is always only the beginning.

CHAPTER 4

CRESTED CARACARA

(My Hail Mary last gasp drinking)

1994

The word "caracara" comes from a South American indigenous word that refers to their guttural, rattling calls that apparently sound like running a stick along a fence. Look for them foraging on a carcass . . . and near dumps. . . .

—San Antonio River Authority Blog & News

"Is everything all right?"

I was passed out on the grass when a freshly showered woman with two young kids in tow addressed me.

I roused myself, fluttered my eyes open, and squinted up toward her. "What?"

"Oh, goodness," she said. "You're our waitress from last night."

That got my attention. I propped myself up on one elbow, putting the other arm up to block the sun. "I am." I had no idea if that was true.

"Your shift was late?" she hoped.

"That's it. A late shift."

"At first I thought you were, I don't know, drunk?" Her kids were clustered behind her legs, peeking out at me.

"Ha, ha! Ha. I'm fine. Just wanted to get some sunshine before my shift tonight."

It was indeed a sunny day. A downright Chamber of Commerce postcard day in one of Saratoga's many elaborately manicured parks. Rolling lawns, marble fountain sculptures, Victorian gazebos, couples on blankets, groups playing frisbee, and families setting up for picnics filled the idyllic setting. Then there was me, cheek stuck to grass, my body sprawled, limbs akimbo in a raggedy tank top, bra showing, baggy black pants, and sweating last night's booze and makeup I hadn't washed off, despite staggering home for a few hours of drooling sleep before inexplicably stumbling early the next morning (noon) down to flop out in the town park. Only to be interrupted by this inquisitive do-gooder.

"Well, it's a beautiful day for it," she hedged.

"Yes! *So* much," I overcompensated. "It's so . . ."

It took me way too long to find a next word. Her kids started fidgeting.

"Beautiful," I finally repeated.

"Well, good luck," she said.

Earlier in my drinking career I might have been offended. What made her think I needed luck? It's a good bet I would have snapped at her. Ranted about the luck *she'd* need living the banal and pedestrian life of suburban small-town soccer mom in waiting, polluting the planet with more humans to gobble up resources, and so on. Acerbic swill I'd be fabricating as I went, fast, furious, ill-informed, insulting, pushing words out of my mouth like vomit. That I didn't have it in me to be obnoxiously offensive as my best defense could have been a sign of some kind. A tell that I was nearing the end of trying to convince myself of my rightness by making everyone else wrong about my drinking. Instead, I sheepishly thanked her. On some level I must have known I needed it, maybe lots of it—luck.

It's curious that I was as embarrassed as I was. I'd done far more egregious acting out since acquiescing to my mother and moving into a small piece of an apartment, that's what I called it, getting a cat and a polyester uniformed waitressing job that seemed impossible to get fired from, and continuing to perform my pain in plain view of Saratogians on a daily basis. Just up the hill from the very spot where I was plastered to the lawn was a bench that I'd taken to on weekday afternoons, sucking on a bottle in a bag and chain-smoking Marlboro Reds, crushing the finished filters in a pool around my feet. My coat was too big, a clunky army-colored cloak with huge pockets for storing supplies. My tan Timberline boots were tattooed, Tony had branded them with black marker, and I was ever-undershowered. These sessions often devolved into cry-singing, gurgly hacking, slobbering. I wasn't even trying to hide it.

Nights I'd become fast known in the bars. My predilection for single malt (when I had some dosh) and then whatever swill someone would buy me when I didn't often aroused comment, the way everyone shouts, *Norm!* each time he enters the bar on *Cheers*, only far less cheery. Which isn't entirely true as certain types of drunks do like other drunks. Or rather, we need one another. If everyone around me is drinking the way I drink, then clearly that's the thing to do. De rigueur, if you will. Which is to say I readily acquired compatriots. Fellow "regulars." We didn't so much as drink together, but in proximity.

Of course I developed a crush. Was it a crush? More like a hammer I took to using on myself. I might have relocated, but I certainly hadn't changed. The object was a bartender who had a quasi-girlfriend, but in the mores of the circuit, that didn't much matter. I suppose he encouraged my flirting with him because when I had money I was a good tipper and was always a lively addition to the roster, even when I turned ugly, which surprisingly wasn't as often as one would think. I could convince myself that he did have a semblance of attraction to me, possibly credibly, and the will-we-won't-we took on a significance far greater than the paltry amount of time we interacted would have warranted. I spun these stories out, savoring every last gesture, parsing the attention, reading way too much into all of it. I spent more time on replay in my mind, the original alternate reality, than I did in my actual life, all the while using booze and other substances if they were to be had as lubricants for the distortions.

I loved regaling others with the ins and outs of these elaborate tales. In a way, I lived for it. Anything in my life could be endured if I was able to bring others along for the ride. "I have stories, ladies!" I'd promise the other house cleaners I worked with at the first job I got before the waitressing gig. "Just wait until break, and I'll spill everything." I think it got us all through room after room of tedium. Cleaning a hotel wasn't my first choice for work. At the time it was my only choice. Though my high highfalutin career days and nearly completed bachelor's degree might have made me eligible for a salaried position rather than hourly shift worker, I was far too removed from that period of my life to present myself for that kind of job. Besides, as I kept reminding everyone (okay, my mother), there was no way this two-bit town had anything even half interesting enough to receive all that I had to offer. Both notions of self I believed to be true. I was worthless. I was a superstar. I became a maid.

This is not to disparage maids. The job is incredibly taxing, I soon found out. And it all started at the shock of dawn, which was an hour I'd only seen on the way to passing out, not prepared for after a night of rest, a shower, and whatever else it is that morning people do in the morning. It's a wonder I lasted as long as I did. In fact, I almost lost the job early on when I slept through my alarm after a night of drinking. I had no phone at my apartment, so the inn called my mother's house, the only number I had to list when I went for the interview. My mother drove the twenty minutes into town to yell through my window to wake me up. I'd not heard her at the door, and I scrambled into my uniform and she drove me to my shift in silence. What did I possibly say to appease everyone? I don't remember, and maybe there really wasn't anything to say, or it was that the inn was in such dire need of the labor that I was good enough to keep on.

Plus, the other maids covered for me. As I did for them when I could or it was needed, which were both less often than the other way around. But I was earning my spot as the entertainer, the storyteller of our little tribe, so they seemed to want me around. I'd stagger in, eyes watery and bloodshot, still tottery, often smelling of booze even after brushing my teeth and splashing water on my face, and they'd know they were in for details of my antics from the night before that I'd parcel out over the course of the morning and into our lunch. While shoving the heavy carts onto the service elevator they'd pry for details.

"Did you see Mark last night?"

"How many free drinks did you get?"

None of it was of any real consequence, but I made good use of volume modulation, timing, and my gift for zinging one-liners in all directions. There was always an embarrassing moment to recall, and they loved those the most. I don't remember most of them now, but I'm sure I fell down. Said exactly the wrong thing at precisely the right time. My boobs would have popped out of my bra. I'd have been crass. Grabbed my crotch. Slurred and swayed while lecturing about the ways we were destroying the earth. I do remember drunkenly wandering supermarket aisles late at night, stuffing my face with powdered donuts and sneaking behind the empty deli counter to make long distance calls on the store phone. At checkout, I had sugar all over my face and down my shirt while a tiny packet of gum rolled down the conveyor belt as my sole purchase.

And then there was the time I stood in front of a jam band playing in a local venue, holding my arms up before them as conductor because I didn't like the guitar player but was enjoying the horns. I kept trying to get him to tone it down and to bring the trombone and trumpet up. In my mind they were responding to my Bernstein-esque gesturing, that they were following my truly inspired take on their playing, so I kept it up. Who the hell knows what the band members thought. At minimum, the guitar player probably wasn't pleased. For me, it was just another night of cringeworthy behavior added to all the others. I'm not sure I shared that one with my coworkers.

I was getting tired. So very fucking tired. There's a saying: "sick and tired of being sick and tired," which likely means something's about to change. Part of me knew I was nearing the end, without knowing what could possibly come next or even exactly what would be ending. I couldn't see how to live any differently. I vowed in the mornings! So typical. I'm *not* drinking tonight. Then my shift would end, and I simply could not face going back to my apartment to sit with myself, so then there I was again, at the bar, trying to squeeze out of the bottle, the people, and the pretending enough juice to jolt me into getting through another day.

I made one last run on NYC. Aching for the honeymoon phase with Tony, I was willing to take the risky gamble that I could catch it just right and get out before his switch flipped. I hid my return bus ticket in the lining of my bag. Under no circumstances was he to know where I'd moved, that much I was committed to, but please, baby, love me for as long as you can. I don't remember how I found him, except that I knew his haunts both above- and underground. This time he was staying down in the subway tunnels in an alcove tucked into the wall off the Broadway line. He'd tapped into the electricity and had a light going, some blankets, a little radio. The rule was no food down there (rats) and make sure no one's looking when slipping past the end of the platform to descend to the tracks and slide along the wall to the side room. I did all this. I lay with him in the dirty dark, in a place where no one would have ever found me if he'd beaten me to death, which I knew for certain he had it in him to do.

I'd planned ahead for a lost weekend. By then I was working both jobs, cleaning hotel rooms by morning and waitressing in the evening, lord knows why, and I'd called out for a few days. But there's no telling what will happen once a drunk picks up her first drink, and I doubled down on the bet by staying one more day, and then another, calling no one to tell them anything, where I was, when I'd be home.

I was riding the wave between Tony and me that was swelling precipitously by the minute. I knew I was risking everything, my life and even, or especially, my cat's. I'd left a big bowl of dry food out for Ed, but surely it was empty or close to it. The bomb was ticking.

At first our time was delicious, celebratory even. I came into town ready to blow the cash I should have been saving for rent, so we immediately stocked up on quart bottles and pints. Cigarettes and some smoke. Did we get food? We must have eaten. Tony was on his best behavior. Abusers can be perfectly charming. Sexy. Sweet. Solicitous. Attentive. Everything I craved. We walked the streets, hanging all over each other, bumping into whoever and whatever we wanted, while he serenaded me with a scratchy Satchmo version of "Is You Is or Is You Ain't My Baby." We sacrificed precious dollars for a bag of peanuts to feed soaked gray squirrels from a park bench. We sat in the cold drizzle under a canopy of city trees, tossing nuts in their shells out to the critters who, one by one, then two by three, scampered in closer for nosh.

One day floated into the next. Dark and light were inconsequential. Nights elapsed on sidewalks and in urban parks, and days were spent down in the tunnels. All feeling of the consequences of time was distorted, except that deep inside me I knew it was finite. I thought of my cat, Ed. If I couldn't get out to save my own life, I knew I had to get back to save his.

So when I insisted we spend some of the last of the money for a strip of pictures of the two of us in a photo booth, Tony must have sensed the shift in me. "You're never coming back, are you." It was a statement, not a question.

"I am!" I insisted. "I just want something to hold onto until the next time."

This was dangerous territory, of course it all was, but batterers are most likely to do irreparable damage when the object of the abuse is thought to be leaving.

"Sure you are."

The menace in his voice told me it was a matter of a day, at most. My plan was to take the bus the next morning. Down in the alcove we sucked on a pint, pausing our conversation when trains thundered past. They came in waves, increasing during peak times, accompanied by platform announcements, screeching brakes, passenger conversations, all sounds that reverberated in our hideaway. *Bing bong stand clear of the closing doors please.* We had boomeranged back into having a good time. We were laughing, alive with the energy of invention, imagining the lives of people whizzing by. And then that switch flipped. I was lying on the blankets with my legs stretched out and feet propped against a girder, having a rare moment of feeling confident in myself, riffing on whatever song we were listening to or spinning some story out of the air, when he ripped into me.

"You fat fuck. You think you're so fucking clever. You're just trash."

I quickly sat up, pulling my feet into myself, and looked at the ground. Of course I was a piece of shit. Of course I deserved whatever was coming. Of course I'd take it all and come back for more.

Only this time, I was done. If I could get out of there alive, I would not come back. I didn't know why, or even how I knew, but this time was different. I kept myself as compliant as possible that night and somehow extricated myself for the bus the next morning, sweating, looking over my shoulder to see if he'd followed me to the terminal. I took one last look around and climbed onto the bus. I slid into a seat, slumping down as low as possible, and headed back to Saratoga to face what I'd abandoned.

Miraculously, my beautiful Ed was alive and happy to see me. I sobbed walking in the door to his purring welcome. My mother, while again incredibly grateful I'd made it home alive, was decidedly not purring when I finally called her, and I lost the hotel job entirely. Waitressing at Friendly's? I was right. Almost impossible to get fired from. I still had shifts if I wanted them.

As it turned out, that gig would be part of my salvation.

CHAPTER 5

BOHEMIAN WAXWINGS

(Jon agrees to go backpacking)

2006

The Bohemian Waxwing is a fascinating bird of the boreal regions. Its unique biology, unpredictable migratory behaviors, and striking plumage make it a must-study species for ornithologists. . . . Observing these flocks in motion is a memorable experience.

—BirdzNow

As far as I was concerned, the time had come. We'd done all the sleepovers. Been to the art museums. The depressing or impossibly inspiring documentaries, the independent flicks, the occasional super dumb Hollywood shit. Free jazz that wasn't free and Henry Rollins talking nonstop at an impossible clip for an hour. Jam bands. Dinners out and breakfasts in. We were having sex on the regular without me interrupting in a panic, or not always, often talking about it all with novel and tender forthrightness afterward, sometimes before. Occasionally, the delicate dance of during. My cat, Ed, who'd become primary in my life, didn't pee on Jon's disrobed clothes or tear at his forehead when we got intimate (things he'd done to other men I'd dated). I met Jon's adult children, who mostly approved as well. People in the rooms were particularly encouraging, and even my recovery sponsor was cautiously optimistic. Jon's, too. We kept on with our own activities. Going to the gym. Him to the office to design buildings, me to the books I was writing about for grad school. And we eagerly shared it all, or much of it. We combined our workout times. Talked about poems and joist beams. We'd survived the "honeymoon's over" debacle, though we never did play tennis together again. We even went back to the mountain he'd insisted on hiking without me to see how, or I suppose if, we could survive climbing to the top together. Not only did we make it, but he said he'd be willing to do it again. With me. This I took as a sign that our relationship was ready to go to the next level. It was time for us to go backpacking.

"See how we'll be walking with the contour lines? It's mostly on the flat," I said as innocently as possible. We were leaning over a topographical map of a section of the Adirondacks spread out on my kitchen table. This in the very house I'd thought unnervingly isolated when I first fled the city, now hoping I could convince my newfound love to go even farther into the woods with me for an overnight.

"I can read a map, Cara."

"Of course you can." I stepped back slightly. I didn't want to blow it by coming on too strong.

He studied the map in silence while I watched his eyes dart back and forth over the proposed route. The man sure knew how to take his time processing information, especially when it came to anything that pushed him out of his comfort zone, which seemingly was everything I wanted to do.

"There's a waterfall, you said?"

This was looking good.

"Yep. Right in front of the lean-to." I pointed to the spot.

"There's a water crossing."

He did know how to read a map.

"Yes, but it should be doable."

"Should be?"

"Well, it depends on the water level, but they wouldn't put the lean-to on the other side if you couldn't get to it, right?"

"I thought you'd been there." Not panic, exactly, but rising discomfort in his voice.

"I have. And yeah, the crossing can be a little tricky, but I'm here to tell you about it."

He looked back to the map. I needed to act.

"You are going to love camping next to the sound of flowing water. There's nothing like it. And lying out under the stars? It's magical."

It was true that I'd been there before and had been transformed by the experience. It was a site I'd been guided to for my first backpacking venture in the Adirondacks, so I told him it was the "absolutely perfect" choice for his. He both believed and doubted me, but finally he agreed to go. As trip prep, he reread Bill Bryson's *A Walk in the Woods,* alternating between heaving laughter and putting the book down to interrogate me about how this might go down. Will there be bears? Is it easy to get lost? Just how much will we need to carry? While I had experience in the backcountry and even on some big mountains at that point, I still lacked quite a bit of gear, and it could be said that my judgment had its limitations, but I had enthusiasm enough for the both of us.

We picked a date and set about borrowing gear. I got my hands on a friend's camp stove. Jon was able to get a loaner of an old-school exterior frame backpack. I bought a half dozen citronella candles in tins, a ridiculous weight to carry, but the lean-to we were aiming for was an open three-sided structure, and mosquitoes in the Adirondacks are a force come summer. Trip reports are often filled with words like *miserable, a wall of bugs* and *there isn't enough DEET in the world.* My goal was for him to want to go again, so I was willing to heave the extra pounds in if it would make the experience more palatable. I purchased portable French press mugs for morning coffee and a pouch of precooked Chana Masala for dinner, Indian food being one of his preferred cuisines. Neither one of us had sleeping bags yet, but we'd have blankets, sleeping pads, and body heat. I couldn't wait to get out there with him. This would be the start of so many adventures for us—I was sure of it.

And it was! So perfectly a Cara and Jon start, which is to say that half a mile on the way in to the lean-to the rain came. The kind of incessant pelting rain that soaks through even the best of waterproof gear, which neither one of us had. God love him, Jon kept right on behind me. He complained some, asked how far it was a few times. Then we heard a noisy bunch heading toward us that turned out to be a group of Eastern European men on a bachelor party adventure. They were drenched but undiminished in spirit. One of them was wearing a superhero costume complete with cape and chest icon. He excitedly exclaimed as we passed each other on the trail: "I'm getting maaarrr-eeeeeeeee-ed!" This boosted our resolve and became another catchphrase added to our repertoire.

But that didn't stop the rain from coming, which only made the crossing of the brook that Jon had noticed harder to navigate. We could see the lean-to across the rushing water, and its dry interior was a great motivator. Besides, we were already soaked. What did it matter if our feet walked in the water so long as we didn't get sucked down the falls. We slipped and slid our way over and dove into the lean-to out of the weather. After a few minutes of a futile attempt at shaking ourselves off, I convinced him to try a bushwhack with me, an off-trail attempt at two of the mountains that stretched up for miles behind our site. The rain hadn't let up at all, so I'm not quite sure what I was thinking, but I took a compass bearing, and we trekked into the wet, farther and farther from marked trails and the lean-to, away from any sign of human activity. We treaded carefully across beaver dams and picked up faint animal runs, but at some point we were full on in the thick of it, getting whacked in the face with spruce limbs and sliding downslope in mud. These weren't new conditions for me to hike in, but dragging Jon, who could still be reluctant to say no to me, eroded my push to climb. After about twenty minutes more of uphill slogging, the storm surged even harder, finally convincing me to save us both from further misery. I suggested, and he instantly agreed, that we turn back. I reversed my compass bearing, and down we went.

Excitingly, I overshot the lean-to. I reasoned that as it was on a brook we couldn't get completely lost. But not being lost was not the same as being where our shelter was. I wasn't sure if the lean-to was due east or due west of where we came out on the water. It was one direction or the other, so I turned east like that was what I'd intended all along. At some point, I officially second-guessed it and told him I thought we might be headed in the wrong direction. We turned back until I second-guessed that at some point, too. For longer than anybody cared to, we walked up and down the brook in a state of quiet panic. Nobody wanted to sleep in the teeming rain. Everybody was concerned they'd made all sorts of mistakes. I felt the pressure to say something, anything, to talk my way out of the mess if I could.

"Don't worry. Our honeymoon will be drier."

Jesus, Cara. Of all words.

Jon wisely said nothing. Perhaps he didn't hear me. It was still raining quite forcibly. At last I committed to a direction, and we returned to the familiar location where our stuff was waiting for us, far closer to where we'd first emerged than I'd given myself credit for. There would be no lying on a boulder looking up at the stars that night, but we did have an intimate time of it in our bedding with the lemongrass bug-repelling candles flickering in a semicircle around us.

In the morning, I opened my eyes to the sun filling the lean-to. It was gentle and warm, an embrace made all the more enjoyable after the consistent battering of the previous day. We weren't comfortable, exactly—sleeping on a wood floor with nothing more than a thin mat to buffer the unforgiving platform isn't plush—but it was pleasant enough that I was unwilling to heed my full bladder or need for coffee that required retrieving the stove and food from where we'd stashed it off in the woods, all of which meant actually moving my stiff body. I rolled over and curled into Jon, who was already awake.

"Bense! Look."

Reluctantly, I pulled my face from nuzzling into his side and followed his sightline. Out in the clearing in front of the lean-to was a blanket of black butterflies, or were they moths? Whichever the species, I knew nothing at the time, there were easily a hundred of them covering the rocky ledges and bushes spreading out in the grace of the sunlight before us. The slow steady winking of their wings was mesmerizing. Jon was particularly enraptured. He seemed to breathe with them. Open. In. Closed. Out. Open. In. Closed. Exhale.

I was moved, sure, but not like he was. I had to pee, and then there was the extra effort required to get the coffee going. I roused myself. He stayed put, watching. At some point he made his way into the water to stand calf-high in a shallow, his gaze trained on the bug striders pulsing across the surface. I had no doubt he would have been engaged for hours, homing in on minute details of the ecosystem in front of him. I walked a cup of coffee out to him, rubbed his shoulder, and made my way back up to the lean-to to start repacking our gear. I had a pretty good feeling he'd try this again with me. As I stuffed blankets and candles into my backpack, I looked over to him stock-still in the water. He must have felt me watching because he looked up, smiling. How lucky, both of us. How happy.

The next trip was decidedly less magical. That one became known between us as the Pharaoh Mountain fiasco, three days that nearly ended our relationship. What I'd wanted most when he asked what he could do for my birthday that year was for him to go on another backpacking adventure with me. By then we'd done more day hikes together, more working out, more negotiating the things that even new-ish couples need to negotiate, and then there was the eventual success of that first overnight in the woods. So birthday girl upped the trip to two nights, quintupled the mileage, added a mountain to climb right in the middle of the loop, which would require hauling our full backpacks up and over, and to top it all off, picked a wilderness area where the trailhead was only accessible via a high clearance four-wheel drive vehicle that neither one of us owned. All of which Jon actually agreed to, and as the consequences of being an addict can have a long reach, especially in finances, he even took the risk to ask his boss for use of a credit card to secure a rented SUV as part of his gift to me.

The big day came. On my end, it got off to a rough start as it was the first birthday after my mother's passing. I'd done enough bereavement counseling to know about the challenges of the year of firsts and thought I had a pretty good plan to honor the rite of passage. A ritual in the making, even. What I did not account for was a prickly run-in with a cranky neighbor over what I called a walk in the woods to the pond where we'd scattered her ashes, but he called trespassing. (For the record, I might have been in the wrong, but he was the asshole.) When Jon arrived to gather me up, I was still upset. He did what he knew to do when I was telling him how raw I was, how hurt and angry, which was the exact opposite of what I needed. He tried to hug me.

"Please don't," I said, stepping back.

"But hugs make you feel better."

"I don't need a hug," I said. "I just need you to listen."

They make T-shirts out of this shit.

He truly was mystified. Who was this creature who didn't want to be hugged when she was crying? And I couldn't understand how he couldn't understand or why he seemed to be taking it so personally. Were we not going to the same recovery meetings where words like *boundaries* and *listen to each other without comment* were thrown around like rice at a wedding? Things escalated quickly. I was mad that he was mad, and so was he. We were compound mad. But daylight was ticking by, so we officially "dropped it," and off we went.

The drive down the washed-out, boulder-studded off-road road to the trailhead should have been a sign. We nearly tipped over multiple times, continuously scraped the undercarriage, backed up, teetered ahead, both of us wincing and him sweating behind the wheel that his boss was legally financially responsible for. Finally we made it to the muddy clearing where a few other vehicles were parked and began the process of getting everything we would need for the next three days and two nights onto our backs. There was some grumbling, a bit of talking to ourselves, to our gear, stuffing, heaving, huffing, and then swinging the full packs up, straps over the shoulders, and belts and chest straps clipped. His first few steps looked a bit iffy, but he steadied. Our target for the first night was an isthmus sticking out into Pharaoh Lake, another site I'd camped at previously and one I knew to be stunning. Rock ledges, tall swaying pines, and a lean-to situated with an open view onto dazzling water that glimmered in the sun, which miraculously was on our side this time. If we could just make it to the site, maybe we could reset the monstrous start to the trip with the beauty of the woods and water smoothing everything over.

Unfortunately, we were not the only ones who were after the allure of this particular location. We trudged nearly four miles to discover a group of young twenty-somethings had already claimed the area. There were at least eight of them buzzing around. They had a tent erected in the lean-to, another tent set up right next to it, gear strewn everywhere, bottles of booze stacked like a minibar, and a radio was drowning out the tender sounds of the forest. Had I been a hiker in my drinking days, this might have been me, or worse, but that didn't make it right. Besides, I wasn't now that person (mostly). I waved upon approach and attempted some casual reminders about backcountry etiquette concerning radios, forgoing a self-appointed citizen ranger position by withholding comments on the inappropriate tent sitings. All was civil. The radio got turned down, if not off, and Jon and I walked out farther along the shoreline to a rocky spot under the pines to discuss what to do. We had no tent. No desire to spend time in earshot of the group, but also not enough daylight left to make it to the next lean-to. At least we had a common enemy. We could keep each other warm in our blankets, cuddled together under the night sky that this time would be twinkling in all the glory of being far from light pollution and without a wisp of a cloud. That settled it. We would stay the night and move on in the morning, as planned.

What we did not plan on was just how rough that night would be. We had an inkling we were in for it when a few of them were fairly randy well before dark. Drinking alcohol rarely decreases volume, and true to form we were kept awake by both their music, which got steadily louder, and someone named Scooter erupting at all hours, despite my talking to them twice and even some in their own group trying to get Scootman to *chill, dude.* Thin blankets on cold rocks suck. Every time someone zipped a tent open or closed, Jon thought it was a bear. We were shivering. Supremely uncomfortable. Tired. And we loathed Scooter. Rise and shine, lovebirds, time to climb the mountain. We pulled it together as quickly as possible, feeling some urgency to get to the next site before it would be similarly overrun, and off we trekked.

The rest of the trip went downhill from there, even as much of it was uphill. There was the excessively baking sun, discovering I'd forgotten my head meds, a fight about Yo-Yo Ma that was not about Yo-Yo Ma, another uncomfortable night even though it was only the two of us in the lean-to, spilling the last of the precious coffee the next morning, then hiking ten-plus miles to get back to the trailhead where we ran into Scooter and crew just in time to share some unpleasantries before coming dangerously close to wrecking the rented SUV on the road back to civilization.

Relieved as we were to be back on paved roads, the mood between us was tense. We pulled into a convenience store off the highway to decompress with snacks and beverages. We sat at a picnic table in the shade of the building and began the lengthy process of deconstructing just what the fuck had happened between us. It wasn't so much the circumstances, though they exacerbated everything. We were deeply shaken by our inability to "get" one another. This was honeymoon's over on steroids.

Somehow, we were oddly convinced that if we spent enough time laboriously explaining to the other what had happened, preferably in chronological order, labeled, categorized, and annotated, we could repair the rift. What began roadside, continued on couches. At restaurants. In bed. Despite these repeated attempts, often hours at a clip, the only thing that became clear was that we both kept showing up to the conversation. We both wanted in. So when we each found ourselves in need of new places to live at the same time, though we were a mere nine months into our relationship, it seemed to me as if "the universe was nudging us to move in together." (Yes, that's a thing I said.)

CHAPTER 6

COMMON STARLINGS

(I crash into sobriety and into the woods)

Mid-1990s

Love them or hate them, there's no doubt the European Starling is a wildly successful bird.

—National Invasive Species Information Center, U.S. Department of Agriculture

Not surprisingly, I dated my way into the rooms. That's not the full picture. I also waitressed my way in. Rather, I waitressed, and the rooms came to me. Every night Friendly's filled with sober alcoholics after their nighttime meetings ended, and they took over the smoking section for the "meeting after the meeting." Lo and behold, I fit right in with them. Not the sober part, but the personalities.

The quips back and forth. The caustic humor. I got to know them by name, and mine they readily knew from my ever so friendly name tag. They called it out and waved enthusiastically when I ran into them in town, which began happening regularly. Christ, they were everywhere. Were there always this many people in the world actively and specifically not drinking?

One day I came across a few of them sitting in the very park where I'd done much of my drinking, and they invited me to join them on their blanket. They were smiling and seemed so happy to include me, this drinker they might attract into the program. Their recovery speak floated in the air, enough that I started using phrases like "surrender to win" and "let go let god" without a clue what that meant or having a belief in anything with a capital G (though once, under the influence of an extraordinary amount of psychedelics, I thought I saw all the molecules of Washington Square Park vibrating). I was still drinking. Still bullshitting. But now here I was hanging out with people who went to meetings and were not drinking, even if it was strange to me that they were spending time with a fuckup like me.

The men who swarmed, I understood better. Even if I'd never heard of the infamous thirteenth step, I recognized the behavior. Typically it's someone who's been in the rooms longer than the other person, and it's often predatory in nature. The newbie is coming in as if they've been in a car crash, and in swoops the elder statesperson to "help" the newcomer with their program.

In my case, the reverse was true. I was using these men to get closer to the rooms without actually dropping the drink or drugs. There were two in particular, but more were hanging around the edges. Maybe it was mutual, the using. Were they getting vicarious pleasure from spending time with someone who was actively partaking? Was I a good candidate for rescuing? The damsel in dysfunction? I got one of them to drive me around when I was drunk. Buy me things. Middle-of-the-night meals when I had a lush's craving for eggs and hash browns at 2 AM to soak up the booze. When I was short on rent I got repeated temporary loans. My mess was obvious. Part of my charm.

I was actively trying to hide my drinking from the other man. Frank was older, inappropriately so, but he was clean and sober and a thoroughbred trainer with strong hands and an intuitive sense with animals, which were very appealing. It was Saratoga Springs, summer home of historic horse racing, so the lure of being privy to backstretch connections, to being *on the scene* was also a draw. I was a taker, flat out. He was the father of one of the girls I used to clean hotel rooms with. She initially regretted introducing us, which was not uncommon for people to feel about me.

Our first date was memorable for the half bottle of beer I let sit with great restraint to prove a point. All I could hear all dinner long was that beer calling to me, but I did it. I abandoned it for the waitress to clear when we left the restaurant. Surely I asked him to drop me home so I could go out drinking afterward. I held out for a few weeks, but before long I showed up insultingly late and thoroughly intoxicated for an evening together and blew my cover as someone who did not, absolutely under no circumstances, have a problem with alcohol or drugs. It was hard to be convincing while slurring the words. Frank wasn't having it. He couldn't be around me if I was going to drink like that. I don't know why that got my attention because plenty of people had cut me out of their lives due to my various and sundry forms of acting out over the years, but this time it rattled me.

And then there was my mom. She'd been watching my self-destruction, driving me around town when I needed a ride while I kept up the act that everything was fine. One day, at a traffic light, she turned to me in the car and asked very plainly, "Do you think you drink too much?" She wasn't accusing. There was no rancor or recrimination in her voice. She simply wanted to know what I thought. I was stumped. Trapped, really. My shucking and jiving and tap dancing weren't going to work anymore. I didn't even have it in me to whip it up to try to convince myself. I offered something like, "Yes, but it's okay?," my lack of conviction reflected in the rising tone.

Then those damn alcoholics again, back in Friendly's night after night. Sobriety was closing in on me. A friend in program once described the closed mind of the alcoholic like a lock. All the tumblers have to be perfectly aligned for the message to get through. Something in me was shifting. I was opening up to the idea that not only did I have to stop drinking, that wasn't new, but that I *could*. It still took another week, maybe more, of waiting on and kicking it with everyone after they piled into the smoking section, then swapping my polyester fudge-coated uniform for civilian duds and heading downtown to drink after my shift. Waitress. Drink. Repeat.

Until one night, instead of going out after my shift I sat down in a booth with a few of the people from the rooms. I didn't tell them what I was trying to do, to not drink, but I'm sure they knew. We talked about everything but alcohol. Or did we talk only about alcohol? Either way, I went home without drinking that night. Same the following night and the one after that, until finally I walked down the musty stairs of one of seventeen churches in Saratoga and entered my first official meeting.

The room itself was cavernous, echoey, and adorned with discomfiting religious posters. It was a church, after all—not a building I'd have been found in typically, save a cousin's wedding here or there. About fifty people filled the rows of chairs that faced a table at the front, where one person sat with a gavel in hand amid framed recovery slogans facing back at the crowd. I recognized him from Friendly's. If *this* guy was in charge of the whole thing, I thought, then how in the hell were these people being helped?

I took a seat in back. A few of the other regulars turned around and nodded to me. I was embarrassed. The guy whacked the gavel on the table, and the meeting began. There was a format and rituals I didn't understand, much like church the few times I'd been to services, without the down on the knees, back on the seat, stand to sing activity. This meeting involved raising of the hands, identifying with first names, and talking a lot of shit. Someone was going on and on about his in-laws and another person talked about resentments. There was a lot of head nodding, vocalized agreement, and a bit of side conversation.

This went on for an hour, then suddenly everyone was up on their feet in unison, holding hands in a circle to say a prayer. I joined, mumbling along without knowing what I was saying. As soon as the meeting broke, the room exploded in conversation and action. People were laughing, stacking chairs, cleaning up the coffee cups, and putting away materials. I stood alone, watching from the back.

The whole event was baffling. But then so was how to fill the hours I would have been drinking, thinking about drinking, or regretting drinking. So if sitting in a church basement listening to some guy complain about his wife's parents would keep me from that "first drink" that everyone was talking about, well then I guess that was what I would do. A few people came over to tell me to keep coming back and that it would get better. I didn't want anyone to stand too close. This was going to be grim.

I dragged myself through the motions of those initial days. I felt like giving up all the time. On the way to somewhere early on—a meeting, waitressing, a grocery store? Was I putting food in my fridge? Getting a pack of cigarettes, most likely—I simply couldn't keep at it. I was done putting one foot in front of the other as everyone was telling me to do, and I sat down on the sidewalk right where I was, buried in dark, baggy clothes in the bright, hot sun, deflated like a float after the parade is over. I was a puddle of self-pity, both exaggerated and justified, even if I was wrong about the reasons why on each count. Was this any better than being hungover on the grass in the town park? I didn't know. I got up anyway. Hoofed it to wherever it was I was going.

Fortunately for such a small town, there were a lot of meetings, almost always in churches, usually in the basement. There was one above a recovery bookstore, but it was first thing in the morning. I did manage to get there a few times. It was down the hill from my apartment so I could stumble to it easily enough, sleepy and filled with doubt. There were lumpy couches, always a coffee pot, usually cookies. Sugar and caffeine and alcoholics often become fast friends once the drink is down. Most meetings at the time had a halftime break at the thirty-minute mark so that we could "smoke 'em if we had 'em"—which I did—and gobble up pecan sandies or Toll House goodies, washed down with various shades of percolator coffee in Styrofoam cups.

The standing around the entrance to meeting rooms, bantering, chewing, smoking, swigging, I understood. It was everything else that was foreign. Recovery wasn't quite in the zeitgeist the way it has become, but even if it was, I would have been out of my skin and mind and nerve endings in a way that made the world bewildering, technicolor, angering. I snapped at customers. I slapped Ed's back once. Hard. I immediately regretted it and chased him across the apartment to apologize, but he was not impressed. The next morning I awoke to find one of the unframed art posters that I'd tacked up on the wall absolutely shredded on the floor. We called it even.

Bursts of temper were followed by sobbing, in between long stretches of numb. Nothingness. Lying face down on my apartment floor, like a prostrate Jesus on the cross, emanating low growling sounds that should have concerned Ed, but didn't (fucking cats). Once I started speaking at meetings, I didn't stop, venting like the guy whose in-laws were a pain in the ass. I even outright barked like a rabid dog and was still encouraged to keep coming back. It was super annoying. I was physically dizzy for at least the first month. I wondered for a while if I was iron deficient, which was a thing I had considered in my life never. Finally I mentioned it to someone else in the rooms who clued me in that I was probably in alcohol withdrawal. Compared to the bone marrow ache of heroin withdrawal I'd gone through earlier in my using, this was mild, so it hadn't even crossed my radar.

I walked everywhere. Long walks, the longer, the better, sometimes counting my steps to give the piranha tank of my head chum to feed on. One of the walks I took regularly was out an extended unpaved road away from town past the polo field, it was Saratoga after all, and I'd walk in all the dust that the occasional, usually speeding truck kicked up, leaving me coughing, spitting, cursing, while horse flies buzzed around my head from all directions. It seemed fitting. The external matching my interior. But for the first time since I began drinking in earnest as a preteen, I was doing it. I was going for days, then weeks, then months without a drink or a drug—except cigarettes, coffee, and cookies of course—but this addict could only do so much at one time.

I also wasn't ready to give up the way I interacted with men. Frank was still in the picture. It was a common suggestion not to get into a relationship in the first year of sobriety, but I argued that I was already in it with him when I got to the rooms. Didn't they also say no major changes early on, too? Which does not mean that I was entirely faithful to him. There was the inappropriate back rub from Lenny, the full-body hugs from Timothy, the motorcycle ride with whatever his name was where I clung to his back while my shirt blew all over the place revealing my spicy black bra. And then there was Steve. Not only was Steve in the rooms, but we also worked together at Friendly's. After our night shifts, he started walking me home. It was only a matter of time before he was inside my apartment in the dark and we were kissing. Okay, it was the very first time, but I stopped it at that, kissing, and then told him I would need to be "rigorously honest" with Frank about it, in the parlance of the program.

"Bbbut, Cara. Doesn't it say except when to do so would injure people? I'm just not sure how it would help."

Steve was not happy about the idea. In fact, he was scared.

"I mean, Frank's big."

"I don't know if I can stay sober if I'm not being honest."

"Are you fucking kidding me? You're out here kissing another guy, and now you're worried about your recovery?"

"Better late than never?"

I spared Steve the naming but did confess to Frank. I wasn't sure that admitting what I'd done would serve anything, except for me to feel like I was changing my behavior, which despite all appearances, I really was trying to do. For his part, Frank was rightly pissed but not enough to end the relationship. I didn't promise him I'd never do it again or that *now* I was going to buck up and be on the straight and narrow. I simply said I'd fucked up. I was sorry. I would understand if he never wanted to see me again. I did say that I was going to try to do better, but that wasn't for him. Or us. I wanted to do it for me. For my recovery. As a fellow addict, he got it—the fucking up. The trying. Perhaps what made a difference was my honesty, after all. Whatever his reasons, he stayed in.

I was changing in other ways, too. My walks were taking me farther from town, out to the edges of the woods, and I began experiencing a curiosity about getting up into the Adirondack Mountains that everyone was talking about. Even back in my New York City days I'd read about these mountains in Anne Labastille's book *Woodswoman.* In it she writes about canoeing into the backcountry and camping out for nights on her own and about building a log cabin out there to live in, far from any infrastructure. I remember being intimidated and terrified in a way that was compelling, so much so that I inexplicably believed that this, or something like it, was something I should do with my life. Me, city girl, dyed black hair, combat boots, chain-smoking, heroin snorting, pavement dependent—*sure, you, right, Cara.* I drowned the thought, and many others, in an ocean of drugs and alcohol.

Now that I was sober and lived closer, the inkling resurfaced. Maybe it was time to try? Or was it that I wanted an out? As in, get me out of day after day after day of the same people saying the same shit at the same fucking meetings. Get me out of myself. Whatever the cause, I had an urge—always with the urges—to get into the woods, so when a sober friend asked if I wanted to go backpacking in the Daks, as they were known, I said yes.

Between the two of us, Liz and I had no clue how wholly unprepared we were for an overnight in the woods. But like good alcoholics, that wasn't going to stop us. I did look at a few library books about hiking the region to get an idea about what we might be in for, but mostly this served to put delusory notions in my head about adding a few mountains to climb to our agenda.

We got a late start (of course we did). When we got to the High Peaks Information Center, a hiker's hub at a convergence of trailheads, some of them leading to the tallest mountains in the state, the staff took one look at us and steered us in the opposite direction of the big hikes. Liz and I conferred. Neither of us had ever climbed a mountain. We had no tent, no stove, no boots. She at least had a backpack and a sleeping bag. I was improvising with a gym bag carried vertically in a way that it was never designed to be used, having to loop my arms through the handles so that the straps pulled taut against my armpits and would likely cut off circulation. I'd stuffed it with a wool blanket, an enormous amount of chocolate, a box of crackers, a jar of peanut butter, and a roll of paper towels. Basically, I'd grabbed a bunch of stuff from my kitchen with no regard for compactibility or weight. Maybe they had a point. I was disappointed, and offended, but they ultimately convinced us we were too late to tackle anything more substantial anyway.

Within minutes on the trail, my arms were tingling with numbness, but I was on my feet and moving. And moving was good, always good. At three miles in, I was fairly lightheaded and had a rash forming in my armpits, but we'd made it to the junction with the brook that needed to be crossed to get to the lean-to. Liz and I stood at the edge of the water. Could this be right? We could see the lean-to on the other side, but we couldn't understand it. Surely there had to be a foot bridge like all the ones we'd been grateful for on the way in. We looked left and right. Walked back to the main trail. Then back again to the brook. Yup, this was it. We would have to hop on rocks, just above a tumble of boulders that created a rushing waterfall. It was going to be dicey going, especially with bags on our backs, but the thought of facing the Information Center staff without having made it to the "easier" site spurred me onward. I leapt out. Liz leapt. We wobbled and hesitated, our arms shooting out in the air for balance, creatively contorting our bodies to avoid falling over and into the water. Both of us had a few near misses, but at last we were across.

We dropped our bags and walked around the site. The lean-to was basically a small three-sided log cabin with a sloping roof toward the back, and there was a fire ring in front of the open end. It was surrounded by tall, leafy trees swaying gently in the wind. The water from the brook was burbling and whooshing down the falls. It was as iconically beautiful as one might imagine, a location many would savor. I, however, was alarmed. Suddenly it struck me that this was to be where we would be stuck, doing absolutely fuck-all, from what I could see, for the rest of the day and all through the night until an escape could be made the next morning. This was not a recipe for enjoyment. It was a setup for psychological claustrophobia.

"Let's get out of here."

Liz looked at me with concern.

"I mean, let's go exploring. See what's farther down the trail."

She must have read the distress in my face because she agreed. We stashed our stuff in the lean-to and hopped back across the brook, easier to do without gear, but still tricky. On the other side we climbed up to the trail. We had no map, but it was a right to go onward and a left to head the three miles back to the parking area. We turned right. It didn't matter to me *in the least* so long as we were in motion.

Very quickly we ran into large swaths of mud masquerading as the trail. It seemed to be getting thicker and wider the farther we went. I tiptoed carefully, squishing as delicately as I could in sneakers that would have been swallowed whole if I'd stepped straight in. There were footprints right through the middle of the trail. Were these people walking directly in it? Yes, they were. In boots, of course, not Keds. After what I wanted to think was a few miles but was probably more like a thousand feet, we turned around.

Back to the brook to leap, hop, muster up courage, then make that one particularly tricky bound over a deep gap in the boulders to get to the lean-to and wait it out til morning, or so I thought. Turned out, there were lots of things to take care of. Our first order of business was to figure out where to hang the food bag so bears wouldn't get it. In my ever so precursory research, I'd seen pictures of cubs on top of mama's shoulders pulling down such contraptions, so apparently you couldn't pick any old spot.

Liz had an idea to hang it out over the brook. There was one branch that seemed like it could work if we could get the rope up and over it. She began to tie the rope around a rock to help loft it up and over the high branch. She got it wrapped round and round, knotted it some kind of way, then stood back to launch it through the air. One, two, three, and up it went sailing. We watched as mid-arc the rock flew out of the rope bundle and plunked into the water ten feet away.

We found different-sized rocks. Tried varying knots. She threw. I threw. The rope got stuck more than once and had to be tugged and shimmied out of a tangle of branches. I have a vague recollection of the plastic supermarket bag of our goodies hanging in the air briefly, but also I know for sure that it didn't last there. And now the dark sky

I'd been worried would never come was upon us, and we couldn't see well enough up into the branches. We finally admitted defeat. But oh my, those *stars*! I couldn't remember ever seeing them so brilliant as they were above us that night.

We grabbed a few granola bars, maybe she had a sandwich, and carefully made our way to a boulder protruding out of the water. We laid back and let the sky cast its magic on us. We talked about desire. What kind of lives we wanted to live. The night was full with possibility and a feeling that all the good stuff we wanted could actually happen. I needed that more than I knew, still achingly raw and ravaged. I'd say we were transported, and we were, but only by being in that very spot as the vehicle. We giggled. My gym bag! Sneakers in the mud! The food bag fiasco!

Ah, yes. The food bag. We still needed to hang it. We hoisted ourselves up from the boulder of miracles and creaked our stiffening bodies back to the pile of gear. Should we just sacrifice it? The plan was to hike out first thing in the morning. If I could make that without coffee, I could definitely do it without food. We did need to do something with it if we didn't want to draw bears to us, which certainly we didn't. And here a small flash of woods thinking lit on me.

"I know! Let's put the brook between us and the food." I was pretty impressed with myself, as if bears don't cross brooks better than we do.

"Great idea!" Liz agreed. "But then, getting across that in the dark isn't really appealing, is it."

"I'll do it. I can make that." I didn't know if I could, but I was riding a wave of performative confidence. I snatched our plastic bag that still had the rope knotted around the twisted handles, grasped the clunky handheld flashlight one of us had borrowed, and started across before I changed my mind. Liz cheered me on.

I told myself these boulders were now my friends, my desire buddies, and that my feet would know where to land. In no time I was on the other side with our food and looking for a place to store it. It didn't feel quite right to leave it on the ground, so I strung the bag up about a foot off the forest floor on a small but strong enough sapling, though it did sag like a Charlie Brown tree under the weight of our ridiculous rations. I hopped back across without incident to find Liz yawning and unfurling her sleeping bag and pad. I pulled out my wool blanket and curled into myself for a night of the kind of sleep where I only knew I'd gone under because I startled awake every twenty minutes. Essentially no sleep, turning from one side to the other, my aching shoulders and arms contorted by the unyielding wood floor of the lean-to.

In the morning, I was bleary eyed, somewhat delirious, and definitely sore. I groaned my arms back into the loops and wobbled toward the brook. Across the water I could see that our food bag had persevered through the night. That minor victory got me back over, but the walk out was definitely tougher than the walk in under the circumstances of no sleep and bruised armpits. Branches were grabbing my hair, and rocks appeared out of nowhere to bruise my shins. About a mile from the trailhead we ran into a female forest ranger (who was this breed?). She took one look at me and offered Band-Aids. I would be fine, I assured her, I just needed a cup of dark roast. I was banged up, but we'd done it. We'd spent the night in the woods and made it out alive.

CHAPTER 7

BURROWING OWLS

(We move in together)

2007

Once the owls have accustomed to the changes and are found to be interested in the location . . . they are prevented from entering the old burrows. A simple one-way trapdoor design . . . is placed over the burrow for this purpose. If everything has been correctly prepared, the owl colony will move over to the new site in the course of a few nights at most.

—California Fish and Game, "A simple one-way door design for passive relocation of Western Burrowing Owls," H.O. Clark Jr., and D.L. Plumpton

Was it a coincidence that Jon and I were both in need of new digs at precisely the same time? Or was I right in thinking (hoping) there might be energy currents working in our lives—like air thermals, like murmurations, like the formation of rhyming lines out of the chaos of language—moving us toward each other and into our own right places on the planet? Or were we willful creatures, reading lease terminations and closing dates like tea leaves for the story we wanted to be true?

These were the facts on the ground: Jon's apartment building had sold, and the new owner was set to raise the rent exponentially beyond what he could afford. I was still living in my mother's house, and my sister and stepsister as co-owners had helped me to see that it was high time to put it on the market. I thought for sure I had months to figure out where to go, but it sold remarkably quickly. It was a process, always a process, the journey not the destination as I was reminded ad nauseam (though we were headed toward a destination, were we not?), but after many consultations with our respective people, Jon and I decided to give the grand cohabitating experiment a go (yes, I said that, too). He even took the lead on looking for a place.

Within a week he found a six-month rental for us to try as a test run. It was a house way out in a rural county across the river from the capital region where he lived and worked. I was in my final semester of grad school, so theory was that as a poet I was on the job wherever I went. The owners were going to a sun state for the winter and were looking for tenants who would not only care for the house but handle the shipping of rare and used books out of the store attached to the home. The physical store would be closed for in-person business, but they would still field offers for their inventory via the Internet. All we had to do was pack the books up and bring them to the post office down the road. The store itself was the location of the area's original post office, and its creaky wood floors and cramped nooks and crevices, now lined with shelves stocked with novels, memoirs, poetry volumes, original *Life* magazines from the 1950s, musician biographies, and histories of the Beats (the guy was a bit of a Kerouac fanatic), were undeniably appealing. Plus, the rent would be cheaper. And if in six months we found we'd made a mistake by jumping too soon, like having a meeting to go to at the end of our first date, we had an out. We said yes.

After that it all happened very fast. Consolidating, donating, divvying up, recycling, storing, packing, shipping, sorting all of my mother's things, her previously deceased husband's things, my own things, so much stuff and every last scrap of it felt like a piece of the person or time period associated with it forced through the crucible of the real estate market and its negotiations and timelines and signed documents and handshakes. It was an agonizing process. By the time Jon and I landed in the house with our two cats and put a few pieces of art up on the walls as one of the only ways to make their furnished space our own, I felt like I'd been whacked in the face with a shovel. Jon let me know that he did not appreciate the metaphor, especially as I proclaimed it loudly whenever I was asked how moving in together was going.

Even under less harried circumstances, settling into what turned out to be a quirky house that held the deep smell of its owners no matter how much incense I burned would have been a challenge. Ed in particular never got comfortable there. My fierce mouser, my alpha cat to Jon's beta Titi (though Titi, like Jon, had his sneaky ways about him), spent a lot of time hiding out in a laundry basket. And it wasn't long before the task of filling the book orders wasn't worth whatever discount on rent we were getting. The store was unheated, and we spent way too many cold hours hunting for titles only the owner could have known where he'd relegated them to. We'd sit at the long dining table at the end of the day with brown paper bags and envelopes, cutting the wrapping to fit the book, and taping the shipping labels to the outside like employees on an assembly line. It hung over every day, for Jon especially as he was the one commuting long distances to work and back. Of course that didn't stop him from skimming the contents of what we were handling, he couldn't help himself, sometimes sharing tidbits aloud, sometimes at a full stop in deep silence, his gaze penetrating the worlds between his hands, stretching the burdensome job out well past dinner.

There were other issues with the house. We weren't allowed to have fires in the cast-iron woodstove that sat taunting us in the living room as it was apparently "too finicky" for us to be able to use without burning the place down. The fridge was filled with their sticky half-used condiment bottles and unidentifiable packages with deep freezer burn. Getting to the washer and dryer required taking a few deep breaths before descending to the cobwebbed, downright creepy basement to hop across slate stones set into dirty, debris-strewn gravel. And if I wanted Internet, I was forced into using their computer, which was situated on a clunky desk positioned over a heat vent that blasted apparently all the house's warmth into cooking my feet.

But it was the place we returned to every day, where we returned to each other. Where we laid in bed together at night, taking turns reading to each other a handful of sentences before the snoring of the other let the reader know to put the book down and turn out the light. Where Jon put one of the shipping boxes we used for the books over the heat vent and wrote on it, "The comfort of my girlfriend's toes is important to me." It was the house that held the big fat tree we got for our first Christmas together, the tree that for some reason

I was determined to adorn with twinkle lights that were purple and green and only purple and green. Jon finally found them in a store fittingly called Wit's End, having searched all over the Capital District. I begged him to get every last strand they had in stock with an urgency that should have been a sign that something more than decorating was at stake. I spent too much money on a glittered star for the top and too much time looking up recipes so I could cook for Jon's adult kids the kind of holiday dinner that my mother would have made. I wasn't *not* a good cook, but I also wasn't typically the go-to person for this task in pretty much every crowd or relationship I'd been in, and then there I was, donning my mother's apron and wrapping a turkey in cheese cloth and stuffing my hand in its cavity for the first—and what will likely be the only—time in my life.

Though we were clearly trying, I'm not sure any of us ever came to feel at home in that house. The gift I suppose was that we were uncomfortable together. And we were learning and growing in our relationship, which was also uncomfortable, even if important things were happening between us.

There was the time I refused to admit defeat in an argument about god knows what. I'd certainly had years of admitting when I was wrong in all sorts of circumstances as an integral part of my recovery, but it is an entirely different matter, or feels as if it is, to yield to the other in the most intimate, and therefore the most intimately challenging, of relationships. Or put another way, in an ongoing relationship where something like a running tally underlies the relating (I can't be the only one in this). Jon had finally had enough and said, "Cara, you cannot always be right" in a manner that I could not evade, the way my mother had asked me about my drinking. I ran out of the room and dove face-first into the pillows of a scratchy couch crying out, "You're right, you're right, and I'm wrong, wrong, wrong," like a five-year-old. Jon quietly entered the room when I stayed in the dark, sucking through textiles, trying to breathe. He sat down on the couch and gently put his hand on my back. I told him through the fabric, "I'm sorry." I was learning that I could be wrong, that we could disagree, that we could even get fiercely angry with each other, but that we could still love each other. That he wouldn't hurt me even if he was upset. Or leave. Nor I him.

I wasn't the only one to regress into childhood. After one particularly ruffling scuffle between us, Jon retreated to an upstairs room across from the bedroom. He was in there behind the closed door for hours. I could hear what sounded like plastic blocks clacking against each other, repeatedly and in spurts. I pieced together that he was "sorting" his stockpiles of cassette tapes as a means of self-comfort.

"What's going on in there?" I asked after a time.

"Nothing." Also like a five-year-old.

Clearly not nothing was going on. My adorable man-boy. Six months into living together, and I was still smitten. As was he. Another phrase we starting using between us: *Not going anywhere.*

The house was another matter. The owners were coming back to live in it, so there wasn't an option to renew the lease, not that we would have. We had to get out, again. But now we'd become a little family unit. We wanted a place to make our own. And we didn't want to have to do it all over again in six months or a year. The only way to secure that, it seemed, was to take on what I came to call that other m-word: a mortgage (not marriage). We were going to try to buy a house.

The whole process was an invitation to obsession. Between scrolling the listings websites, driving randomly around the county looking over hill and dale for anything we might have missed on the Internet, calculating miles between a possible house and the locations we frequented, making dozens of pro and con lists, peeking in dark windows, hemming, hawing, and generally talking ourselves into and out of every property we were shown or snuck up on, we'd become driven, and discouraged. Then we looked at a renovated nineteenth-century house closer to the capital region but still on a rural county route of horse farms and wetlands and old barns. The house wasn't extravagant, but it was enchanting to us. So much so, it seemed too nice to believe it could be ours. We'd both lived for so long as scrappy renters, always barely getting by, never achieving our full potential (oh how addicts have so much unfulfilled potential). Surely if anyone found out about us, how rough and tumble we'd had it, they'd reject us before we even put in an offer.

Jon was particularly disbelieving. I was temporarily armed with some market confidence from having money for a down payment from the sale of my mother's home. I thought we could do it. Why not us? Why couldn't we be people who things worked out for? Who got to be in loving and committed relationships, who lived in nice houses, who enjoyed their work and were paid well (I was really going for it). I argued that we were. In trying to convince Jon, I was also convincing myself. And then, as always, I needed to back off. To give him room to come to his own decision, even if we were under the pressure of an open house the following day. It was clear he wanted it. His smile widened at each turning of a corner into the next room. It was a challenge, deferring gratification has never been a strength of mine, but we left the showing saying we needed more time.

We looked at one more house that afternoon that was disturbingly beyond repair, then drove north to the high peaks region of the

Adirondacks as planned. We'd booked a room at a bed-and-breakfast so we could get an early start on a winter snowshoe hike the next morning (things really were progressing!). That night, flopped out on the lumpy bed surrounded by faux paneling from the 1970s, our gear stacked in piles near the door, Jon agreed. That house could be ours. Well, the bank's, if they would have us, but he wanted to try. So with spotty cell phone coverage and no Wi-Fi, we squeaked a call through to the real estate agent and put in an offer.

After checking our phones, and rechecking them, leaving the number of the bed-and-breakfast and checking with the owners repeatedly, we amazingly received word that night that we'd been accepted. It was as quick as that. Look at a house in the afternoon, then by the end of the day legally commit to paying gobs of interest on the interest on the principal for the next two decades. We faxed the forms from the kitchen of the bed-and-breakfast at 10 PM, the owners having allowed us back into their personal space, all four of us standing around the whirring blipping machine in our pajamas. It was awkward, and there would be more to go through before moving in, but it was starting to look like the place we thought was too good to be true could be for us.

We hit the trail early the next morning. The sky was a crisp blue against the white cover of winter. The evergreens were loaded with perfect clumps of snow and rime ice, and we were out there among them, not another hiker in sight. We trudged in our snowshoes, the path crunching rhythmically under our feet, two souls fully alive for the adventure that our lives had become. Wasn't this what we'd both suffered the indignities of withdrawal and the labor of recovery for—to say a hearty "yes!" to it all, as Joseph Campbell, one of the thinkers I'd begun reading in sobriety, had advised? We were giddy. We were oxygenated. We were climbing together, on the verge of becoming homeowners of the loveliest place on the planet. The best, in fact. As in literally, the Best. As in, the route the house was located on was a road called Best. What could be better than that?

Best Road was a turnoff from the route we traveled into the Capital District from our rental. Every trip into the city, we passed a sign saying "Best → 4 miles." This tickled us to no end, especially because when we drove down Best Road the four miles we came to nothing but a small intersection of two county routes with one older building that was possibly a remnant of the now nonexistent hamlet. It was hard to tell. The only sign for Best was the one pointing in its direction, not at the supposed location. Just as "utopia" translates as "no place," there was no Best, but there was this road to it. And we were going to live on it if the rigmarole of inspections and financing panned out, which didn't *at all* seem like a given with our histories.

After the hike, we hurried back to get the process started. There were checks to write, appointments to make, and approvals to seek. Though it turned out we didn't need to worry (it was 2007 and the U.S. housing market was flooded with magic math), that didn't stop us from doing it. There were lots of calls on speakerphones as a soundtrack to this period. From my car. From his. From his office. My mom's house. From the kitchen island of Best Road while the home inspector poked and prodded the house as the mortgage brokers poked and prodded our bank accounts and credit histories. As a salaried worker designing buildings at a small architectural firm, Jon had a much better income than I did, which was a low bar as I was a freshly graduated poet at that point. But I had a surprisingly good credit score to his "still working things out with the IRS" number. I had a lump sum for down payment; he had a steady paycheck.

This conjoining was markedly different from throwing down crumpled fives and ones on a mattress to see how much weed or drink a partner in crime and I could get that night. Together, Jon and I apparently were worth the risk. We had become a team, which turned into another line we used between us: *We're on the same team.* Also shortened to *Same team.* As in *Same team, Bense.* Or *Same team, Jon.* Said as a reminder, an affirmation, sometimes an accusation when one or the other of us wasn't acting that way. We were approved.

We signed and initialed where all the yellow Post-it notes and sticky red arrows indicated in the hefty stack of papers that made up the document at the closing. The room was filled with fake plants. Our real estate agent gave us a bottle of cheap champagne, which I put in my trunk when she wasn't looking. We were handed the keys. Jon had to go back to work, but I drove straight to the house, the unwanted bottle rolling audibly from side to side in the back of my car.

I walked up the slate path to the front porch. There was a wood bin next to the door with a few logs in it. All the fires we would have in the fireplace! The fancy parties! The key was a little fussy in the lock, but I got it to work and entered. I walked through the living room with its historic wide-plank wood floors and into the kitchen, a bright room the previous owners had modernized. My footsteps echoed in the empty space. The whole house seemed to reverberate with my movements and with the traffic whizzing by. I was surprised to realize just how many cars were traveling Best Road, which was suddenly far closer to the house than I was comfortable with.

I went to the window to get a better look. Car after car shot by, each one increasingly agitating my nervous system. How had we missed the busyness of this otherwise bucolic road? Didn't we see the closeness of it to the house? Was this the buyer's remorse that I'd been warned might come up? I would later learn that it was trauma—all the violence and chaos my body had absorbed rocketing to the surface with each passing vehicle—but in the moment, I felt like I'd been sucker punched. I got out of the house immediately.

Back in my car, I told myself it would be better with all of our things in the home. With Jon and me and the cats, our smells and energy and routines filling the space. Plants and pillows, bedding and time. That first sacred cup of morning coffee. *Easy, Cara. Easy, girl.* Focus on moving in. On loving Jon and Ed and Titi. I did all of this, we did. We moved in over a weekend with help from friends, doing the predictable dance of *Shouldn't that be a bit more to the right? No, to the left,* the whirlwind of activity working as a diversion, but underneath the buzz of it all, my nervous system remained on high alert.

Come Monday, Jon drove off to work, and I was left with myself, our two cats, who were unwilling to let me squish them close in a death grip of self-comfort, and the seemingly unending stream of cars and trucks barreling by. I had no job, per se, except the impossible one of looking for work as a recently graduated poet, and the nervous system of a survivor. It was a perfect storm for despair.

CHAPTER 8

BLUE JAYS

(I go to any lengths)

Mid-90s

To counter the conventional notion of the blue jay as an obnoxious menace, perhaps it would be more fitting to . . . respect it for its continued ability to thrive in a changing landscape. . . .

—*Northern Woodlands* magazine, "The Curious Blue Jay"

I worked my ass off in early sobriety, and it was fucking grueling. There were moments of relief, like the magical night in the woods, but the periods between these were insufferable, and it took an exhausting amount of effort to talk myself into the motions of getting through each day.

I managed to do all the things, or most of the things, that were suggested. I got a sponsor in program. This was someone who was to help me through the steps, but initially she wound up mainly providing a couch for me to lie on in various states of hopelessness. While I called out, "I can't do this!" or "What do you people want from me?!," she calmly went about her business putting together bookshelves or cleaning her kitchen. At some point, she'd tell me to pick up one of the program books on her coffee table and open to a particular page. I'd read aloud the paragraphs she indicated. It was hard to complain when my mouth was full with recovery language, which I'm sure was her intention.

My sponsor also encouraged me to get a coffee-making position for a meeting. For this I was given the security passcode to a church and access to the meeting's storehouse of supplies. I'm not the first alcoholic to be utterly astonished at the bestowal of such trust on a ne'er-do-well like myself, and there have been many instances of this extension of faith going awry (god bless you, my fellow addicts who've made off with your group's treasury, I might have been you a few short months earlier), but it wound up being a source of pride for me that I showed up—*on time!*—week after week, making sure the coffee was ready to go before the meeting and having the books displayed at the ready for we acolytes to discuss and parse with reverence. Sometimes I hated it, the worship. And I was almost always initially resentful when Wednesday rolled around, and I had to leave two hours early to walk across town to fulfill my commitment. I was cranky and willing, resistant and desperate. I was told I was "right where I was supposed to be," as if that would be of any comfort, and wished a "long, slow recovery."

I was still without a license, let alone a car, so when Frank came across a bike that'd been abandoned behind a dumpster, he nabbed it for me. I rode that crotchety three-speed Schwinn, with its rusted bell and chain that popped off in uphill traffic, all over town, learning its quirks and moods that seemed to match my own, pumping hard or gliding, swooshing wide S turns across the width of roads, catching a delicious stretch of flow, or riding without using my hands, guiding my path with subtle pivots of my hips. These moments on my bike were some of the freest I'd felt without drugs, and I relished them as I pedaled between meetings and waitressing, between meetings and my sponsor's apartment, between meetings and Frank's apartment, between anywhere and nowhere and back again.

I also used it to meet my mother, I was so proud she didn't have to pick me up, when we got together at her beloved Victorian pool in the Saratoga State Park, home to a performing arts center, long stretches of stately pines, and multiple spigots of freely accessible spring water the town had been named for. It was hard not to feel out of place—still—among all the sculpted beauty. For chrissake, dancers of the New York City ballet lounged at the pool during their summer residency upstate. Their outward appearance contrasted greatly with my early sobriety edge, body unshaven and carrying extra weight like armor, shifting around on an outdoor chaise that left striped lines of its plastic rungs visible in my flesh as I did the walk of shame, between pool and snack stand for a soda and back to my chair, in rounds.

Toward the end of my first year, I began counseling. I'd heard there was state money available for recovering alcoholics to go to school, and I thought maybe that would catapult me out of waitressing, out of being "right where I was supposed to be." Unfortunately, one had to demonstrate in a verifiable way that the addiction was being treated by having a counselor sign off on the forms. I'd never officially completed film school, though I did attend the graduation in purple cap and gown, stealing out of the ceremony in

Washington Square Park to buy bottles of champagne I smuggled back in, one up each arm of the capacious gown, before devolving to staggering around Greenwich Village alone, crying, and drunk enough to be on the verge of alcohol poisoning. And now it seemed that the very cause of my incomplete degree might get me funding to finish. All I had to do was undergo some counseling.

I made all sorts of jokes about it. Couldn't Joe S., one of the most notoriously cranky, oldest of old-school old-timers in the rooms of Saratoga, vouch for me? He could not. I got my first appointment.

"So, what brings you here?" the counselor asked when I sat down across from her.

"Honestly?"

"We usually recommend that."

"Well, I'm kind of just here to get a sign-off for funding to go back to school. I've been going to meetings on my own since May. I think I did something like a 180 in 90," I said, referring to the suggestion to do 90 meetings in 90 days. "And no one made me go. I wasn't mandated or anything." Clearly I was pretty proud of myself.

"Great job," she said.

It felt good to hear.

"So, can I get, or can we work on those forms I need?"

She looked me directly in the eyes. I squirmed and tried to avert my gaze, but her stare was like a magnet. Then she broke into a huge laugh, patted me on the knees, and said, "We'll get back to that. First, let's do a history of alcoholism in your family."

I left that session utterly dumbfounded. This was going to take a lot fucking longer than I imagined, whatever I thought "this" to be, and that varied. At minimum, I wanted *not* to want it all to be over every day. I was desperate to stop the mouthy, constantly nagging, criticizing, cajoling, belittling, shaming, downright nasty voice from nattering at me every waking moment and even in my dreams. What varied was what I thought would do the trick. My lifelong go-tos were gone. The drowning of the noise with heroin, the drink, the numbing of the entire nervous system with whatever I could get my hands on, these mechanisms were no longer available to me. Or worse, they always would be.

At a meeting that night I shot my hand up when topics were asked for from the floor. I didn't so much as have a topic as a driving need to drop a ton of f-bombs.

"If any of you motherfuckers wishes me a slow recovery one more fucking time I'm going to lose my shit."

Most of the room started laughing.

"I'm not kidding. I can't stop the chatter. I don't think I can do this anymore."

The singular purpose of the rooms is that they got it. They understood the drive to snuff out the life to spite the mind, and by the end of the meeting I was saved from myself once again.

Not everyone was saved from me, however. Frank and I fought—*a lot.* In private and in public. The part of me that was changing was starting to suspect it would be in my best interest to be single and sober for a time, possibly even the dreaded year everyone was suggesting. The part of me that wasn't craved the engagement, the clashing, the making up, the doubling down, the backing away. I didn't want to be with him, and I didn't want not to be with him. He claimed that this was our biggest problem, though clearly he was a willing battle partner.

Finally, my counselor laid it on the line. One of the main causes of relapse, she said, was not being able to handle what comes up in relationship with a romantic partner. She strongly suggested either he and I do counseling together or I break it off once and for all. I wasn't quite ready for that, so I agreed to counseling. When I told Frank about it, he was surprised, I think we both were, but he seemed happy about it. The decision felt momentous. We made plans for after my waitressing shift that Friday night with an excitement that I hadn't felt since our early dating. I was actually looking forward to our date, and so, he said, was he.

That Friday night when my shift was nearing its end, I squeezed into the cramped manager's office next to the grill station in the kitchen to use the phone to call him as arranged. I stood there in my sticky polyester, the burgers sizzling and the deep fryer popping and roiling, waiting for him to pick up. Did he have an answering machine? Did I leave a message? I don't remember, but I know I didn't talk to him at all that night. I returned to the phone again and again, between closing out my final tables and doing the end-of-shift chores. Still no Frank. It wasn't until during my shift the following night that the manager had another waitress get me off the floor to take a call. It was Frank, calling to confess that he'd relapsed. A forty-eight-hour run smoking cocaine and I never found out what else, but I'm sure plenty. With my manager hovering and getting less patient by the minute, I pressed Frank for the details, most of which he couldn't remember or wouldn't say. I shouldn't have been shocked, but I was. Or hurt. But I was that, too. And then I caught myself feeling jealous, angry he didn't take me with him, wanting to say, "Come get me right now, and let's get so fucked up we don't remember our own names."

"Good luck, Frank," I said instead.

My manager was agitating in my periphery. The fry cook was eavesdropping. I could hear the other waitresses arranging to cover my tables.

"I'm so sorry, Cara. I promise I'll make it up to you."

A promise I, too, had made so many times over the years, and then broken, made and broken, until the moment when I sat down in a booth full of recovering alcoholics in that very restaurant, thus launching me on the improbable journey of recovery, the start of the process of learning how to keep my promises. And this was one I was making to myself and finally keeping. I would not let anything get in the way of my sobriety. I would do what I'd heard spoken about all too often in the rooms. I was going to step over the bodies, literal and otherwise.

"I wish you well, but I can't be with you anymore."

And just like that, another of my defective coping mechanisms was gone. With Frank's relapse I knew it was at last time to go without a relationship. More than that, to generally avoid men altogether. No flirting. No innuendo. No pursuit of the perfect romance or attempting to attract male attention. I was warned that letting go of these behaviors would thrust me into withdrawal as surely as quitting any other drug. The only crutch that would be left to me was smoking, but the days for that were numbered, too. I was in a blender. A whack-a-mole game. A vertiginous process of change. I was ready and not ready. I proceeded anyway.

This next phase of my recovery unfolded in spurts. After trudging through the monotonous tasks of each day I returned to my tiny apartment, alone, and sobbed voluminously and smoked, also voluminously. I bared my most vulnerable, ugly-cry self at women's meetings, then ran outside to smoke. I dug deep into my history in therapy, having learned that alcoholism is a family illness and that mine had not been spared, then lit up immediately in front of the building after every session. I started eating at a local health food cafe, then hid around the corner after my meal to smoke. I took up jogging, a truly unexpected turn of events, trotting first a very slow mile in raggedy cutoff black jeans and high-top sneaks, and returned to my apartment for a glass of water and a cigarette, not always in that order. I went to a doctor for shortness of breath, was diagnosed with exercise induced asthma, got an inhaler to use in conjunction with my runs, which were getting longer, my routes extending into sweaty oxygen highs, only to finish each one with a puff on the inhaler and then deep drags on a Marlboro Red. It felt insane. (It was.)

I've heard it said that addicts give up their vices in the order that they're getting killed by them. It's hard to say which of them for me was the most immediately fatal, but I couldn't deny any longer that my lungs were taking a beating. It was becoming unbearable, the hacking, gasping, and wheezing, but worse than those was the icky shame I started feeling with every drag. I was beginning to resign myself to the fact that I was going to have to let go of this one, too, this twenty-plus instances a day of stimulating the pleasure center of my brain via the added bonus of using means that satisfied an oral craving. In other words, I was still getting high by stuffing something in my mouth and sucking on it, and I was completely dependent on the "habit."

I wasn't sure I could break it.

I thought back to a time when I first quit drinking and was terrified of relapsing.

It was a typical day in my first year in that my whole focus had been on doing the things that would keep me from taking that first drink. I went to the early-morning meeting and talked with everyone both before and after. I helped put away the chairs. I called a newcomer to ask how she was doing. I went to the midday meeting and then to coffee with a bunch of women afterward. I went home to feed Ed and to change for the evening meeting. At some point, I was sitting on the edge of my bed, and I was struck with a terror that even having done all this, having devoted my entire day off to avoiding drinking, that I would somehow still find myself back at a bar that night. I called my sponsor in a panic.

"I've done everything the program says to do, and I'm afraid I'm gonna drink!" I wailed.

She paused. She was always one for speaking deliberately. It was infuriating.

Then she said something I did not see coming. She asked, "Did you pray?"

To be clear, my sponsor was not, at all, a practitioner of monotheistic religion. She was, however, an adherent of asking a power greater than ourselves, which we could define however we needed, for help with our drinking and also with our living. But that is not what I heard in that question, did I pray. *No, the fuck I did not pray.* She suggested I try it and then gently, but definitively, gave my surely coming petulant fit no room by signing off the call.

I looked around my bedroom, a tiny ten by ten I shared with no one but Ed and heard the words again. *Did you pray?*

Slowly I got up and went to the window. I looked outside to make sure no one was around, then twisted the blinds closed anyway. I went back to my sproingy twin mattress on its shin-bruising metal frame, dropped to my knees, and clasped my hands together in front of my face. I felt silly in that pose, but I was desperate. I whispered,

I'm afraid. Can you help? Are you even a you? I'm clueless, but whatever is greater, or bigger, or higher, whatever is this power they all talk about, please don't let me drink.

I don't know if that is what did it, but I do know that I didn't drink that day. Nor did I any of the following days. I began by asking in the morning for sobriety for that twenty-four-hour period. To that I started adding lots of other things. Could prayer help with letting go of cigarettes? I didn't know, but I resolved to try. It took nearly a year of praying every day for the willingness to quit smoking, but at last it happened, and I put out my final cigarette before I'd even finished it. Within months, I hit a depression so deep I almost didn't make it.

CHAPTER 9

RUBY-CROWNED KINGLET

(We fly off to Europe)

2007

. . . an extremely energetic songbird frantically going about while making twitchy motions as it moves through branches and shrubs of trees . . . they have this adorable nervous like energy as if they've had too much caffeine.

—Lesley the Bird Nerd

Within days of moving into our new house and finding that I was so impacted by the vibration of passing cars that I could not bear to be home without keeping busy busy busy while some combination of radio, washer, dryer, and ocean sound machine was playing in the background, I brought up the idea of going on a hiking trip with Jon. A big one. Like Switzerland big. A friend from grad school who lived in Basel had said we were welcome to visit, so wouldn't now be the perfect time to go hiking in the Swiss Alps? Aka can we please get me something to focus on to help manage the anxiety and PTSD, that infernal internal thrumming and throat-choking adrenaline that were being repeatedly aroused despite my already being on medication for it? Jon was initially reluctant, but same as with the house, I could tell he was actually excited about the possibility of traveling to Europe. And he could see that I desperately needed it, or something, and this was what I said I wanted. He came on board.

I threw myself into planning the trip. I bought maps and guidebooks of 13,000 and 14,000 foot peaks and spent way too much time in online forums. I made gear lists, tracked weather, and printed out screenshots of potential climbs to tack up on the walls of the office that I was supposed to be using to find a job because poets don't make money poeting, not that I was writing much, and I wasn't making anything to speak of teaching the prison class I'd managed to keep on with after grad school. Jon would come home at the end of his workday, and I would have the maps spread out on the kitchen counter, ready to run a variety of routes past him. I did my best to wait until he was fully in the door, but rarely did he get past me on his way to pee without me rattling off all sorts of itineraries and climbing combinations.

"I think we should go for Dufourspitze." I was in the bathroom door while he positioned himself over the toilet.

"Am I the first person you're talking with today?"

Valid question.

"I went to the gym. We need to . . ." I stopped myself. Course corrected. "I'm trying to up my workouts before the trip."

He finished, moved to the sink to wash his hands. I proactively headed for the kitchen island where the maps lay waiting. He came into the room and would have pulled out a crossword puzzle to fiddle around with on the counter to decompress after a day of high concentration at the office, but my agenda was in the way.

Finally, “Dufourspitze?”

Impressive, really, his spot on recall and pronunciation of the peak when he was only half listening when I spat it out to him.

“It’s the highest point in Switzerland.” I probably should have saved that. “But it’s not the most challenging one, by far. I mean, it’s not the Matterhorn.”

“That’s the bar? Not as hard as the Matterhorn?”

“Well, it’s in the same region of the Alps, so it gets compared. Plus, it’s higher so . . .” Stop. Correct. “There’s an alpine hut we’ll stay in! They’ll feed us, and we can hike up from there, so we won’t have to carry all our stuff, just what we need for the climb.”

And so it went, our usual dynamic of me talking us both into something out of our comfort zone, with Jon’s caution a tempering influence on my tendency toward recklessness, and my drive pulling him out of his resistance to risk. That is when our powers were used for good, as he always said. The trick was telling which was which. I don’t think either of us were particularly sure, but Dufourspitze became the plan.

To prepare for the trip, I signed us up for training with ropes and ice axes, and we spent almost every weekend hiking up in the Adirondacks, tackling increasingly lengthy and challenging climbs. Every hike had its rough spots and its rewards, almost always providing us with moments to laugh about afterward at a post-hike meal in one of our go-to restaurants up north. Or when we got out too late for that, once we were back in the warmth of the car and disrobed of the wettest of our clothes and safely pointed toward home, we would recall high and low points of each trek. There was the time I peed on my suspenders at a junction at 3,500 ft, which tickled Jon maybe as much or more than my car smelling like garlic on our first date. And then there was the hike when we were coming out well past dark in the cold winter landscape, and Jon, stunned by a stream crossing that seemed to appear out of nowhere, said, "What the fuck is that?" and the water got renamed as "What the Fuck Creek."

A definite highlight of our preparation was the day we trained with the ropes and ice guide. The morning was spent inside at the guide center, getting loaded up with gear and learning knots and hitches, how to tie in, harness up, and let rope out or lessen it between us. Though this was technically a refresher course for me, having roped up on previous climbs, I had retained very little of the specifics of the various figure eights, overhand bends, and prussik or taut lines. We practiced, fumbled, got frustrated (mostly me), but got some basic proficiency, enough that we could head out in the field.

That's when it got fun. Even though the Daks don't have packed snowfields that would replicate glacier conditions, we roped together and trudged upslope in near lock step, then simulated various falling scenarios we might encounter. We self-arrested in intentional free falls down the hill, throwing our bodies on top of our mountaineering ice axes to gain purchase to stop the glide. Then we switched axes for the shorter stubbier ones and headed to a wall of ice to climb. We took turns belaying the other, providing an anchor for whoever was hitching up the ice. Though we wouldn't do exactly this kind of climbing to get to the top of Switzerland, we thought it was a good idea to have some experience on steep ice with axes and crampons together, all while being responsible to and for the other via a length of rope. We kicked the toe points of our crampons and swung the axes into the sheer face. The climbing was intense and required every ounce of effort our bodies could put out, but we both reached the top of the pitch successfully, then down-climbed without incident. We weren't experts, by any stretch, but we'd come a long way from our tennis playing fiasco. We were climbing fucking ice, after all.

We continued hiking all through the spring and early summer while doing cardio and weight training at the gym. We were on a mission. It was hard not to feel like a power couple, or our version of one, both of us living our fullest lives as new homeowners and readying for a dream vacation in the Alps. Never mind that I was still harassed by the traffic and without any job prospects while draining my savings to stay afloat. Or that I'd never been on a high alpine climb as the one who had the most experience, or experience on a glaciated peak at all, as in Jon's case. We had trained, we had tickets, we were going.

In Basel, our hosts were gracious, if concerned, about our agenda to try for Dufourspitze. It would not be my first big mountain, I told them. And I'd developed what seemed like a reasonable plan. We would acclimatize by climbing the Breithorn, a lesser 13,000-foot glaciated peak. We had already reserved our bunks at the Monte Rosa hut, I'd declinated my compass for magnetic north on that longitude, we'd practiced with the knots and had our ropes ready to clip in, and we'd studied the route from the hut to the summit for months. We weren't not prepared. So after a few days of touring Basel, off we went by rail to Zermatt, the climbing mecca at the southern end of Switzerland, to begin our big mountain adventure.

The town itself sits at an altitude of over 5,300 feet at the end of a valley made by a branch of the Rhine. The train to the area dead-ends at Zermatt as there is nowhere to go beyond it but up even higher into the Alps and over a pass into Italy. The picturesque village is framed by some of the most notable mountains in the world, the pointed twisty pyramid of the Matterhorn being the obvious pick. We got out at this last stop and looked up. It was breathtaking and intimidating. I swiveled around to see if I could pick out Dufourspitze but couldn't see it from where we stood. Around us, the streets were teeming with tourists, families and climbers alike, and cows with gargantuan bells clanging from their necks being paraded through town.

We offloaded our backpacks at the hotel and headed right back out to the mountaineering store. Jon needed to rent crampons, so he was also going to rent boots to go with them. This had been part of the plan, and in hindsight it wasn't a very good one, but we didn't know that yet. He got fitted while I chatted with another staff person, doing my best impersonation of a confident trip leader. There was all sorts of talk bubbling in the store about the deaths of nine climbers earlier that week on the Jungfrau. There'd been so much snow that the Matterhorn was closed for climbing due to avalanche risk.

On the way back to the hotel, we went through the mountaineer's cemetery and quietly walked past the graves. There were ice axes and dead flowers. One of the tombstones of a young climber who'd died on the Breithorn, the very peak we were to climb the next day, read "I CHOSE TO CLIMB." (Really with the all caps?) We returned to the room and set about laying out our ropes and gear, practicing, packing, repacking, and shuffling items around as a form of nervous prayer.

This first acclimatization climb was to begin with an early cable car ride up to where skiers go right to glide back down and mountaineers turn left to trudge across the potentially crevassed glacier up to the summit ridge of the Breithorn that borders Italy. It's paramount to get off glacier before the sun softens snow bridges over crevasses and makes climbing sloppy and dangerous. This particular peak didn't require a middle of the night start as the Dufourspitze would, but despite obsessively going over our agenda for "day of," we didn't get to the cable car station until almost noon.

But the day offered an encouraging bluebird sky over brilliant sparkling snow, and we forged onto the glacier hopefully. We looked the part in our helmets and glacier glasses, even if the extra fifty feet of rope coiled over our shoulders was a bit much, the rest of it stretched between us and clipped into each of our waist harnesses. Fairly quickly we were huffing in the thinner air and shouting to each other to adjust the pace. I was the lead, yelling back over my shoulder for him to stop yanking on the rope while he repeatedly called ahead to get me to slow down and "hike like a regular person." I tried to institute the signaling system I'd learned on another climb, but it was hard to take it seriously when it was just the two of us. We kicked one step after the other upward, plunging our ice axes into the snow for purchase, eventually developing our very own distinct start, stop, rest, breathe, start-again pace as climbing teams were streaming past us in all directions. The sun became blisteringly bright, bouncing off the sheer white of the glacier. Sweating in multiple Gore-Tex layers, noses turning pink, we finally took our last steps onto the summit ridge.

The peak was bustling with other climbers, including some boisterous Italians smoking and drinking, and we weaved our way through the clusters to find a spot to rest. We plopped down in the snow and busted open our snacks (one of the best parts of hiking hard). We sat for a bit, munching in silence, before I grumbled about there being too many people or who wants to smell smoke up here or something about dumb Americans, aware of the hypocrisy of my comments, which only made me crankier. But the stunning vistas and the relief of successful effort eventually piped me down. I looked out along the ridge. One side was a corniced edge, like a wave of snow curling back toward Zermatt. The other slope flowed down into Italy and a blue-green glacial pool way below. Across a mass of mountains on the Swiss side we were nearly eye level with the Matterhorn. I was taking it in while also calculating logistics for the hike down and the next leg of our trip after that, always contending with a narrative and clock running in the background.

Jon spoke up. "Bense. My heels are bad."

"What? Like how bad?"

"Like *not good* bad."

The rented boots had been rubbing against his heels the whole trip up, and each step had become increasingly more painful. The sun was still relatively high, I immediately reasoned. Depending on how quickly we could descend, in theory we would make it down in time to get to the mountaineering store for a different pair of boots to keep us on a path to try for Dufourspitze. I didn't want to even broach the possibility that that would be off the agenda. But I didn't want him to be hurt, either.

"Can you make it back down?"

"I can, but I don't know about . . ."

"Let's just get off the hill first."

Our descent began. I was torn between trying to go slower to accommodate his reduced pace and revving up out of a sense of urgency to get to the store before closing. Fortunately, down-climbing was a bit easier on his heels, and we made it to the cable car in decent time. Once off the car at the bottom, though, I could see that walking was causing him discomfort. He needed to get out of those boots. We went back to the hotel to change. Jon showed me his heels, which were red and blistered.

"After swapping out the boots, let's get you better bandages and some really good goo. This is a mountaineering town. Surely they'll get you wrapped up right as rain."

Who was I, saying that phrase, ever Miss Chipper, European mishmash style, *Let's get you sorted, love, and we'll make that summit straight away, won't we just!*

Jon took me in stride, feeling the relief of having the boots off, and out we went to see what could be done about his troubled heels.

The staff at the mountaineering store were as helpful as could be, letting Jon try multiple different sizes and models of boot. It was clear none of them felt great, nor would they with his skin as compromised as it was, but he settled on the least aggravating pair. They pointed us toward the chemist in town for material for wrapping his heels, where we got what looked like surgical tape, gauze, massive adhesive bandages, and two different kinds of antibiotic gel. At the hotel he dabbed and taped, yelping occasionally, while I busied myself with staying out of his business. Eventually he got sorted well enough that we could have the talk about our plans going forward.

Getting to the base of the Monte Rosa massif, a hump of eight 4,000-meter peaks, which Dufourspitze topped, required riding a steep cog railway to just under the summit of the Gornergrat, a lesser peak across from our objective. At this stop the foot travel would begin down an Alpine meadow path, eventually descending roughly 1,000 vertical feet to the edge of the Gorner glacier and the metal bridge that would put us onto the valley ice. From there we'd weave around crevasses, rifts in the snow and ice that swallow hikers if not avoided, crossing the longest glacier in Switzerland to the base of the massive Monte Rosa massif. There we'd need to climb slabs and rocky glacial crumble back up to the height of where we'd gotten off the train to where the hut was situated at a little over 9,000 feet across the valley. And then the real climbing would begin that night, at midnight, up a confusion of boulders I'd read, before hitting the Monte Rosa glacier and a long trudge to the exposed rock crests jutting sharply up out of the cover of the snow and ice. This is where extra care would be needed, the trip reports had noted, as there would be some "mildly technical" climbing up a chimney and other rock features along the lengthy summit ridge to get to the highest spot, all with steep drop-offs and tremendous exposure looming.

Back in the States Jon and I had looked at the maps together, read all the reports. Studied the routes. We knew what was ahead of us, at least on paper. We'd made it up the Breithorn. And now here we were, in our hotel in Zermatt, facing whether to get on the railway to travel to climb far beyond a ski lift ride back to town if we ran into trouble. Should we do it? I suppose we might have faced this moment with a question even if Jon's feet hadn't been compromised by the first climb.

Jon put the new boots on with his heels bandaged and walked around the room. I said nothing. I could tell he was still affected by the wounds, but he was also definitely moving far better than he had been with the other boots and naked, raw skin. After a handful of turns around the room, he said he thought he could give it a try.

"You *think* you can?" I wasn't convinced.

"I want to. I want to give it a try."

"Please, honey, don't do it on my account." I meant it, even if I was hoping he wouldn't take this as an opportunity to change his mind.

He assured me he wasn't doing it for me and that he wanted it for himself. Or also for himself. That was as good a go ahead as we would get, so we decided we would go for it.

The next day we made it to the cog railway station in Zermatt in good time, an auspicious start. The open air railcar provided amazing views of mountains we couldn't see from down in town. The rest of the passengers were families and other tourists heading up to do casual walks or visit the restaurants with a view of the Matterhorn. Jon and I stood out for the white zinc cream on our noses and lips and huge backpacks. We got off at Rotenboden, the second stop from the top, and found the start of the trail down to the glacier.

Once on the path, I refrained from asking every few steps how he was faring. He wanted me to go first, so I had no idea how it was going for him behind me. We made it down to the metal bridge and the edge of the glacier without incident and faced a sizable gap between rock and ice. Here we stopped to put on our crampons. I looked over to Jon. He must have felt my gaze because without looking up he offered, "Hanging in there, Bense."

Out on the glacier, he was transfixed by the undulating expanse of the terrain. Of course he was. We followed the flagging that took us around all manner of crevasses, some crescents, some nearly S shaped, all glowing the luminescent blue that emanates from deep within ice. Jon had to be coaxed onward. He could have stared into some of the cracks in the surface of the glacier pondering their mysteries for hours. I was eager to keep moving. We reached the confluence with another glacier and then the rock where we would start up to the hut. Here we took our crampons off to scale the slab. After what was for me a really fun climb in the sun, but for Jon was a painful test of his will to hike, we arrived at the hut.

We checked in with crew, put our packs up in the bunkroom, and went back out to sit at a picnic table in the sun and have snacks. It was midafternoon and hikers were coming back down from either successful or aborted climbs of the peak above that we'd be leaving for that night if all went well. Jon took off his boots to assess. I let him care for his feet while I queried those coming off the peak about conditions. Many of the hikers were with guides, but some were solo or small private parties like us. The guides were less forthcoming with intel, proprietary info I suppose, but the other climbers were happy to share. The cairns, rock piles that act as waymarks on trails, were erected haphazardly throughout the boulder field we'd be climbing in the dark. It was apparently better not to trust them. And don't count on the fixed rope at one particularly exposed spot on the summit ridge either. The snow bridges over crevasses were definitely unsturdy on the way down, better prod with your ax before stepping. Not new information, but sobering hearing it firsthand on the eve of the climb.

Back at the picnic table, Jon showed me his heels. They were almost visibly throbbing.

"Jesus, Jon! That looks awful." I'd been through my own painful period of breaking my feet in as a hiker, but I'd never seen anything like this.

Other hikers looked over and grimaced seeing his exposed flesh.

"You still going to try?" one climber asked.

I waited for Jon to answer.

"It'd be disappointing to get all the way here, then not give it a shot."

"Yeah, but that looks rough," said another.

"Yes, it does, my love." My chiming in reclaimed the conversation as ours.

"If you can get in with another group," Jon said to me, "maybe you should do it."

I didn't want to. I wanted to climb with my guy but not if he couldn't, of course. Nothing was decided, so we wandered up the path a bit in our sandals to get a sense of how the trail was marked. It became too rocky for our footwear, but he was encouraged by moving much better when the air could hit his heels.

After dinner we got our gear ready with the plan to get up in the night as if we were going to climb and reassess then. We snuggled into each other on the huge bunk that was now filled with snoring and stinky hikers. At midnight our travel alarm beeped. We were the only ones getting up that early, the others were set for 1 AM, mostly with guides it seemed. Jon was up and dressing in the light of his headlamp. He'd pre-bandaged his feet so they wouldn't rub in his sleep. He was determined to try.

We made our way out of the dark, pungent bunkroom with our climbing gear and packs as quietly as we could. Downstairs, we put our harnesses on over our climbing pants but would wait to rope up until we were on the glacier above the rocky field we'd need to climb first. Outside the hut we started up the path walking in the small circle of light from our headlamps. Above us the Milky Way washed across the black velvet sky. We stopped and gawked. The night air was brisk, but the wind was low. We started up again and soon found cairns randomly crisscrossing the boulder field we were climbing, as the others had warned. We stayed on my compass bearing for a while, but it became disconcerting to see these rock signposts calling us in varying directions. I pulled out the map and checked my compass to reconfirm the bearing. If I was right, we were arcing up toward where we would get onto the path on the glacier. If I wasn't, we would come off the rock too soon onto the wrong section of glacier and have to tread an untraveled route to get to the trench the season of climbing would have forged in the snowfield to head for the Sattel.

At this point we'd been climbing for just under an hour, but it turned out to be an hour too long for Jon. I was about to show him the map and where I thought we were when he said he was in significant pain and didn't think it was smart to keep climbing—especially when he'd have to come all the way back down. I could tell he was struggling with feeling like he was disappointing me.

I'd like to think that even if I'd been more certain of our route and of our ability to make the summit, I would have been as readily supportive of him as I was, but I'll never know. What I do know is that I immediately said *Same team, my love. Same team.* And we turned back to descend to the hut in the dark. Before long, we ran into two hikers on their way up who were also confused by the route. They did not have a map or compass and were relying on finding the way others had traveled. They seemed anxious and queried us on what we'd found above. Then they recognized Jon from the day before and said they'd wondered if his heels would let him make the climb. The conversation was validating, but when they pushed ahead upward and we continued down, I felt some regret. My choice, I reminded myself, was to walk with Jon. Getting to the hut, down to and across the glacier, and back up to the train was going to be a bitch for him in boots. My job was to give him room but also to be at the ready if he asked for help, which he never did. I hung back and let him walk his own excruciating journey ahead of me while I took jaw-dropping pictures of him in the foreground of the Matterhorn that I hoped would help him to feel like he had something to show for his suffering when we got back to the States. He powered through utter agony for miles until we finally reached the train station. We rode the railcar in silence back to town.

We had half a week left before flying home, and we made the most of it, with him in sandals and bandages and me hiking solo here and there, lots of laughter, the occasional obligatory bickering, spending most afternoons tottering through museums and old castles and historic churches. I reminded him when it seemed appropriate that most hiking careers included at least a few aborted attempts and that I'd made those difficult decisions myself. He reminded me that he would never, not even once, describe his relationship with hiking as a "career." Fair enough. But did that mean he wouldn't hike with me anymore?

"Bense, give it a rest."

Also fair.

Back to Best.

CHAPTER 10

RAVEN

(I break. I soar.)

1998

As a talking bird, the raven also represents prophecy and insight. Ravens in stories often act as psychopomps, connecting the material world with the world of spirits. As a carrion bird, ravens became associated with the dead and with lost souls.

—New American Journal, "Exploring the Mind of the Raven and the Bird's Role in Human Culture and Evolution"

Quitting smoking left me with nothing. Worse than that. It abandoned me to depression. Anxiety. Startle response. PTSD. And at least one other disorder I'd never even heard of. But I didn't know any of this until after I'd suffered for far too long—sober!—and teetered on the brink of giving up. I didn't want to drink, I knew that wouldn't bring any lasting relief, but I couldn't bear the thought of continuing on in that state, either. I started entertaining thoughts that if reincarnation was a possibility, maybe it was time for a reset on my soul's path.

I didn't have a plan to execute, but I did have an idea of what it might look like. I thought if I were to do it, I would try to make it count for something. To use the attention it might get to make a statement about a cause I cared about but hadn't ever been functional enough to make a difference. Animal welfare. Global warming. Sprawl. The catchall *environment*. Depending on my method, I could have a letter tucked into my pocket or a sign hanging from around my neck. These images flashed in my mind while sitting on the edge of my bed in my sticky Friendly's uniform, trying to marshal the willingness to go in for another shift. While on the way to or back from a meeting. At coffee with people from the program. Perhaps I would do better the next time around, I thought, because surely this version had been a waste. The spite with which my thinking addressed me attacked even this notion. *How melodramatic you are, Cara. Self-absorbed. It's all about you, isn't it.*

Why couldn't I just be normal? Why did I want to destroy what I saw in the mirror? Why was I taking it all *so* personally? I was obsessed with answering those questions. I was stuck, and it was very, very dark. My thoughts were on a perpetual loop, like a scratched record, and I couldn't pick the needle up. Or when I did, it dropped right back to the same spot, on repeat. *You're ugly. You're stupid. Your skin is blemished. Body fat. Who gives a shit about your miserable, miniscule life? You're just a waitress. A hack. A wannabe writer. You're not even original in wanting to end it.*

There was a part of me that knew better, or at least suspected there was an alternate view to be had, and that almost made it worse.

What did it matter what I looked like? Or if I waitressed til the end of my days? My mind used these thoughts against me, too. The thinking itself had agency, it was a shape-shifter, wrapping a nugget of truth in admonishment, convincing me that castigating myself was how I would get better. *You think you've got it bad? Look at all the suffering in the world. Get over yourself. Why don't you help somebody else?*

Eventually I started sharing (some of) what was going on for me with friends and in counseling, even with my mother, who'd been doing her own therapy after the death of her husband, but this nearly always devolved into me seeking reassurance about the very things my brain was lying to me about. I could not keep myself from interrogating everyone on my appearance, on my writing when I had occasion to read it aloud, on my overall existence. Of course nothing anyone said could appease me, though bless them, they tried. I knew it was wearying to deal with, and I felt awful about that, too. And still, I couldn't stop.

My walking continued, as did counting my steps to give me something else to focus on, something to take up mental space. Numbers were neutral, they didn't provoke backlash the way language did, like praying or talking or trying to say something positive to myself as I'd been encouraged to do. I did try to interject counternarratives to the ones my mind was manufacturing. I even tacked the United Nations Universal Declaration of Human Rights up on the wall of my tiny apartment, which stated in the first part of the first article that "All human beings are born free and equal in dignity and rights." If this worldwide body declared *universally* that as a human I was equal in dignity, shouldn't that count for something? It did not. *Yeah, how's that going for the global south? Nice try, Cara.*

In addition to walking, I jogged when I could muster the oomph to chase after the endorphins. Then a group of coworkers at Friendly's were heading up to the Adirondacks to hike one of the peaks. Though some of the waitstaff were none too pleased with me of late because I'd long stopped pulling my weight as a team player (how could I tell them it was all I could do to walk in the door, let alone get extra buckets of ice or clear other people's tables?), one of the shift managers asked if I wanted to join them. While I had hiked a few of the smaller mountains with Frank after backpacking with Liz, I hadn't been out in the woods in any significant way since he and I broke up. Plus there was that quitting smoking weight gain. And the depression that I didn't know I was suffering from would have had me say no, but for some reason I said yes anyway.

The mountain they'd picked was Noonmark, not one of the highest peaks but apparently a rugged hike, gaining almost 1,200 feet in the last mile of three. The group of them were all younger and fitter than I was, and I was sure I'd lag embarrassingly behind. They were telling me the details as we ordered sandwiches and got water for the hike in the supermarket before heading north in two cars. When we got to our destination, I was amazed when they pulled off to park right alongside the road. How did they know this was where to start? Then I saw the opening in the woods, the path leading uphill at an angle, and farther along the trail a standing wood structure that turned out to hold the book to sign so that interested parties could track usage and rangers could search for missing hikers if someone didn't return.

On the trail, we were moving well enough for the first two miles that were relatively flat. They were joking and talking shit, the way restaurant shift workers who'd been in the trenches together do, while

I mostly said nothing. I was concerned about the climb they said was coming. *(You'll never fucking make it. Why did you even bother?)* Then we hit the junction to turn up. That's when the numbers they'd been rattling off became real. This part of the trail was seriously steep and quite rocky, requiring steps that were sometimes the height of taking two or more stairs at a time. Everyone seemed out of breath, a few of them were smokers and all of them were partiers, but I found myself powering uphill more strongly than I'd thought I was capable of. One of the dudes even commented on what seemed like my unlikely strength as a hiker. I should have been offended, but I was surprised, too. There was something so satisfying about exerting the effort required to propel the body upward on rugged terrain that jogging on the flat pavement never touched. Reaching the summit gave the whole endeavor purpose. Pick a height, grind yourself up to it, work your way back down, then call it a day. Where had this been all my life?

Back at the cars we were sweaty, bug bitten, hungry, thirsty, and exhausted. We piled in and agreed to meet a few exits down the Northway at the first opportunity to hit a convenience store. Driving in the dark through the Adirondack Park, with nothing around us but forest, we talked about all the different junk food we'd indulge in, feeling like we'd earned it. I got peanut butter–stuffed pretzel pieces and a diet soda and couldn't remember anything ever tasting so good. I knew right then and there I wanted to do it again, and as often as possible. I asked them about another hike, when would they be going? No one offered up anything definitive. I was going to have to take it upon myself to make it happen.

I now had something external to train my ferocious obsessive mind on. I would climb every mountain I could find out about and get myself to the base of. I still had no car and only makeshift gear. I'd climbed Noonmark with my water and sandwich in a green mesh bag that was one of the early alternatives to plastic bags, a pair of thin-soled sneakers, and all cotton clothing, which I eventually learned wasn't recommended for hiking as once wet from sweat or the elements, or both, it stays wet. None of that mattered. In fact, it became part of the equation, something to perseverate on instead of cannibalizing myself.

I worked it like a job, finding other hikers who knew more than I did and who could drive to the trailheads. I overheard a woman after a meeting talking about a hike she'd done in the Daks. I ditched the conversation I was in, mid-sentence, and zinged over to her. She was taken aback at first, the line of my approach, but when I explained I was eager to hike, she said she'd be happy to go with me sometime. I nailed a date down right then. On that hike, she had suggestions for how to find others to go with when I was already talking about setting up the next climb before we'd even reached the summit.

One hike—and hiker—led to another. I bought the map of the High Peaks region and saved up for a proper backpack, then boots. Before long, I found out that hikers like to make a mission of climbing the highest peaks in a range (state, country, continent, planet). In the Adirondacks, the goal was the forty-six peaks that had first been identified as over 4,000 feet back in the 1920s by surveyors and had since become a club with archivists, historians, correspondences, patches, and numbers given out for the growing number of people as they each completed all of the peaks. I was in. And I'd already climbed a few of them, so I had a head start on the list. Lying in bed or on walks between hikes, I would go over the names of the peaks, recounting their distances and elevations, shuffling around the order in which I might attempt them.

I got stronger with every hike. I pushed myself to the utmost speed I could manage, even if it was a nearly unmanageable pace. Once at a summit, I would deflate, briefly, then wait in an agitated state while everyone else wanted to take in the view before descending. I banged and scraped up my body, badly. I had to shave around all the scabs on my legs, and my back broke out in extreme acne from the new-found irritation against a backpack. My toes and heels were rubbed bloody raw, repeatedly, until they eventually calloused. I was always darkly bruised, somewhere. I lost toenails.

Late summer turned to fall, by all accounts a glorious time to be in the northeastern mountains. Even as I could be moved by the beauty of the hills while I pumped my body through them, I was still struggling with being myself. *(Look at the view like a normal person!)* Once November rolled around I learned I would need to dramatically shift my approach. Winter was going to change everything about being in the hills. My first cold, snowy hike was in jeans and a sweatshirt under a flimsy windbreaker. That's when I also realized just how much my pace had increased as I, out of necessity to keep moving, got frustrated with the others in the group who were going much slower. I resolved to get my hands on better gear and to find faster hikers to go with.

I signed up for trips I had no business attempting, like an overnight in winter in one of the more remote ranges of the target climbs. I was the only woman with three men. The only one with a ton of borrowed gear, most of it ill-fitting. The only one who hadn't ever camped in subfreezing temps. Once we were out there and I was falling behind due to carrying way too much unnecessary weight, the trip leader told me he didn't vet us because he'd assumed anyone who had the gumption to sign up for such a trip had to have something in them that would drive them to make it. In the end, he turned out to be right, but not without a fair amount of coaching and patience on their part and a maximum amount of stubbornness on mine.

The goal of this trip was four peaks, three on the first day, then back to camp, and the fourth on the following day before hiking out. On the way up the first peak, I found that powering uphill in deep snow required repeatedly stomping a snowshoe into the base to get purchase, only to find that often the snow wouldn't hold, causing me to slide back down below where I was trying to catch up to them from. It was exhausting and, to my mind, humiliating. *(What did you think, signing up for this hike? Jesus, what hubris.)* I'd found my faster hikers. But they were encouraging, even if the trip leader was fairly gruff. After watching me struggle with my cumbersome pack, one of the guys asked if I wanted help making some adjustments.

"No offense, but you look like you're going to tip over any moment."

I acquiesced by holding my arms out to the side while he tugged on straps that I didn't even know existed. This helped the pack hew to my body in a way that made it much more manageable to carry. I was still always the last in the group, but I made all four peaks and the overnight in negative temps. They were congratulatory when we got back to the leader's truck. Even he grumbled some approval. I was cold to the core, aching everywhere on my body, and had nearly broken down in tears multiple times, trying to gain ground on them on the trail, but patting me on the head like a "good girl" at the end of it all would get me every time.

Like any drug, though, I needed more and more to get right. More praise. More of the temporary relief a successful summit provided. More attention from a growing reputation as a rugged hiker.

Ultimately, none of this cured my self-loathing, and it always flipped to further internal recrimination. My mind was constantly seeking new and inventive ways to take me down. Another all-consuming focus that had likely been there for years under other layers surfaced. It made no sense, but I could not stop looking in a mirror to scour my face for blemishes. Seeking imperfections, I found them. I truly thought I was a monster. On the rare instances when I shared what I was thinking about what I looked like, my friends couldn't understand. They tried to convince me that they did not see me as I did, but it was no use. And wasn't this just more self-centered thinking anyway?

Talking about your face again? How vain.

Also: *How horrific, your face.*

At some point I realized part of why I was so drawn to getting out in the woods was because I had zero chance to see what I looked like, and it seemed to matter less out there anyway. Back in the world of buildings and public bathrooms, reflective shop windows and artificial light, I was obsessed. I was eight years sober, I'd done self-inventory and made amends, been through years of counseling, performed hundreds of hours of service, prayed daily to a higher power, and I couldn't see a way out of the misery. Correction. I saw one way out. The images returned.

I went for one of my walks. It was windy and cold, and I was bundled up, my hair whipping around my face, into my eyes, getting caught in my mouth. I started sobbing, nearly panting to catch my breath because I was crying so hard. I couldn't take it anymore. I blurted, *God, I need more help!*—and gasped. Inside me something broke, or spasmed, like a primordial hiccup deep in my solar plexus. I can't say precisely what it was that transpired. I only know that I'd never—not once, not for all my changes of consciousness that had led to my many surrenders: the drink, the men, the cigarettes, the lying, the cheating, the stealing, the everything I'd used to contend with all that roiled inside me for seemingly most, maybe all, of my life and possibly before it—experienced anything like what happened within me that day.

That afternoon at a meeting with my latest sponsor, she looked at me differently and said, "I think you're depressed. You should talk to your counselor about it." I hadn't said anything I hadn't already shared with her over the course of the months we'd been getting together, but apparently she sensed something she hadn't in all that time. I told her I would, that I actually had an appointment the following day.

At that appointment, before I got around to mentioning the conversation I'd had with my sponsor, my counselor cocked her head and said, "I think you're depressed. We can get you more help for that." Before I left, I was set up to meet with a psychiatrist for two weeks from then. I had many doubts and a lot of fear about taking psychiatric medication while also feeling like two weeks was too long to wait. How would he know? I wondered. Then, how quickly could a diagnosis be made?

I showed up early to my appointment at the Mental Health Unit that was part of Saratoga Hospital and fidgeted for twenty minutes in the lobby. I'd been to the in-patient wing on this side of the building to visit people in program who were there for various lengths of time, not always voluntarily. I was nervous. Eager. Embarrassed. My name was called.

I was walked back through double crash doors that only opened from the inside and led up a maze of stairs. Once inside the doctor's office, I took the indicated seat. His bookshelves were lined with diagnostic manuals and clinical textbooks. Among them I spotted *Man's Search for Meaning*. I burst into tears.

He began asking me questions. His tone was very gentle. After a few minutes he said he believed I was indeed depressed and that medication could help.

"But, like, *how* do you know?"

He repeated my answers back to him.

"You said you felt worthless. Chronically sad. Struggling with taking any pleasure in life. And that this has been going on for months."

Hearing my own words I teared up again.

"What will medication do to my brain?"

He was extremely patient with me, going to great lengths to describe the ways that the depressed mind operates versus the non-depressed one. The word he used was *fire*, as in how brains fire their neurotransmitters. He took down one of the clinical books from his shelf to show me images. The colors and areas of these brains that lit up contrasted starkly. The medication, he told me, would target the serotonin in mine by inhibiting its reuptake so that it would be more available for neurotransmission.

I stared at the pictures. The differences were irrefutable. I took the prescription he handed me and got it filled that afternoon.

It would be trial and error, he'd said, trying to find the right medication and the right dosage, and it would not be overnight. I spent the next few weeks weeping to Beethoven's *Ode to Joy* while walking, weeping in the cooler at Friendly's, weeping at home, at meetings, first thing in the morning, and while tucking myself in at night, as if now that I knew what I'd been fighting for so long set me free to let it loose. Slowly some of the heaviness lifted, the weeping began to subside, but I was not what could be described as easy in my own skin, not for a second. As I reported back on my state, my mood, my thoughts at each subsequent visit, my doctor tweaked the medication. Once the depression was somewhat contained, the anxiety, or GAD for general anxiety disorder as he called it, became something to target. And then it was the PTSD.

After two months of slowly increasing dosages and shifting medications to treat these issues, the mirror checking and anguish over what I saw were still plaguing me, and so were the images. I felt ridiculous *(Doc, I want to kill myself because I have a pimple),* but finally I told him everything.

"You have BDD," he said.

I was back in his office at the Mental Health Unit, a place I'd come to feel at home. *These, too, are my people*, I said often to myself in the waiting room. It was comforting.

"What's this one?" Come on, with the acronyms.

"Body dysmorphic disorder. It's a preoccupation with appearance that involves mirror checking and comparisons for something that appears very slight or not at all observable to others. It can cause significant distress, including suicidal ideation. Everything you're describing fits this one hundred percent."

That was all I needed to hear, and I walked out of there with a new prescription.

It wasn't long before the images went away. I had to work at it, but the mirror checking lessened, until I noticed I would go for hours, then days without thinking about looking at myself the way I'd been looking. I still startled, easily, and my adrenaline could spike to a nauseating amount more often than happens for those who aren't affected, or so it was explained to me. In other words, I was still me. I still had to do all the recovery work—the prayer, the self-inventory, the helping others, the meetings, the therapy, the mandatory monthly med-checks—but the difference was that all of this work now kept me in the game in a way that I wasn't without medication. The nasty talk was still with me, but the volume was (mostly) down. And I was more readily able to tell it to go fuck itself, which it would, at least temporarily.

I'd spared my mother most of the darkest parts of this period, but she'd been well aware of how much I'd been struggling with my face. She was relieved, once again, to see her daughter get the help she needed. She'd been having a tough go herself, grieving the loss of her husband, and she, too, now seemed to be experiencing a lifting of spirit. She became willing to let go of his car, and it was mine if I could clean up my driving record and get my license back, which I tackled immediately.

My world opened up in so many ways. Not having to fight so hard to get to the starting line, and then having a car once I got there, offered me options that just months ago would not only have seemed but actually been impossible. I drove myself to a local college to sit in on a poetry class and picked back up on the idea of finishing my degree, even considering the possibility of going to grad school for creative writing. And now I could give other hikers rides to the mountains! Which I did as frequently as they would go with me. I eventually started hiking solo when I couldn't find anyone. I was burning through the forty-six peaks, even as I returned again and again to climb a few favorites. Giant Mountain became a go-to when all else failed. A 3.3-mile climb straight up 3,300 feet from roadside to summit, on rock most of the way. I became intimately familiar with her boulders and bends, where a particular muddy spot would be or where the steepest pitches that required using my hands in a scramble were located. I never sat at the summit longer than necessary to refuel, always eager to get moving, only to think about when I'd come back to climb it again all the way down the mountain.

But the forty-six beckoned, as did some of the hiking community who'd become invested in seeing me finish, the gruff leader from the winter overnight being unexpectedly one of them. I got to the rest of the peaks and "finished" on Marshall on a gray, snowy November day. Many people make a big celebration of their final peak, inviting others on the climb or having a particular mountain as the last one, often throwing a party afterward, almost always with a ton of alcohol. For all my obsessing, it was total happenstance: Marshall, which at the time was considered one of the more remote peaks, without an officially marked trail but with a herd path that noodled back and forth across a brook that was easy to lose track of. I summitted with just two others, the gruff trip leader and a younger guy he knew from hiking in Colorado who couldn't keep up with us because the Adirondacks, many hikers from out West were quick to say, were uncivilized in their lack of switchbacks and intentionally graded trails. The Daks almost always took hikers straight up, erosion be damned. At the mostly treed-in summit, in grisly drizzly icy wet early-winter weather, gruffster handed me a patch, told me to never stop hiking—which I assured him would not be an issue—and that was that.

CHAPTER 11

AMERICAN COOTS

(Trying our hand at domesticity)

2007–2008

The coot has garnered many nicknames because of its behaviors: a mud hen, a marsh hen, a blue Peter, a spatterer or a pouldeau (poule d'eau means "water hen"). In the late 1300s, the word coot denoted any diving waterfowl. By 1766, it had come also to refer to a silly or foolish person. . . . When observing this awkward-looking bird, it is easy to understand how the word meaning transitioned from birds to humans.

—*Cambridge Day,* "American coot are birds that have the oddest feet"

We returned to Best and were right back into it, Jon to work and me to looking for work as a poet graduate while being battered by what I came to call the traffic trigger. Some days were so bad I curled up in the quasi-guest room at the back of the house with my head under pillows and humming to myself to ease the distress. All of the days I found zero jobs "in my field." I tried not to worry Jon, but occasionally I called him at the office and gave myself away.

"Hi, honey!" I said forcefully cheerily.

"What's up?"

"Just checking in. How's your day going?"

"Fine. Busy. Do you need something?"

"What time you think you'll get home?"

"Why?"

"Oh, no reason. Just . . . can you . . . I mean . . ."

"Are you having a hard time? The traffic?"

"Yes!" I blurted out and started sobbing.

"Do you need me to come home now? Would that help?"

"I don't want to make you miss work. But maybe, when you get home, we could play some board games tonight? Something to preoccupy me?"

"You got it."

He came home that evening with Indian takeaway and a big bag of goodies. A deck of cards. Monopoly. Risk. Scrabble (his favorite). Night after night we sat on the couch, with the letter tiles threatening to slide off the board between us, while eating out of takeout containers and talking about movies that were coming out or a band that was heading to town. I was so grateful for the distraction I didn't even complain when he beat me, repeatedly, with his ridiculous use of two letter words in just the right spot.

But the days were getting harder. The house became the scene of the crime for me. Our beautiful home of skylights and wide wood plank floors. Exposed beams from the original 1800s frame. Open floorplan. Bright and airy but also a cozy living room. With a fireplace! One we could use! The kind of place that I would have walked past in my early days of sobriety, wondering what it would be like to live in such a charming spot, with such a loving man, then I'd return to my small box of an apartment with Ed, and buck up for another shift waitressing. And now I couldn't bear to be in the home I would have longed for back then. I took to looking at real estate listings and began considering talking with Jon about selling the house and moving. I told myself that now I would know to look for a more remote place, one that was far from the road.

I knew it would be a hard sell to convince Jon to move again so soon. We were barely in the house six months; boxes were still to be unpacked (though likely they would remain taped up for years). And we'd just forked over thousands of dollars in closing costs and fees. Even if we could sell at the same price—not a given because we'd been so eager to get the house we overbid on what turned out to be an exorbitantly inflated price—we would be losing money. Neither of us were in a position to do that. Plus, Jon loved the house. He wasn't affected by the traffic, which was something of a misnomer anyway as there were never jams or clusters on the road. This was a rural county route that looked like it should see cars only occasionally but turned out to be a main artery for people living farther out in the county, a shortcut for those who worked in the capital city and its outskirts, which included Jon. I looked at listings anyway.

Without speaking directly to the situation, I began casually mentioning other houses on the market that I'd found that were what I described as off the commuter's path.

"Plus, this one's way cheaper. Imagine? Reducing our mortgage payment? That'd be great, right?"

"I don't want to live in the middle of nowhere, Cara. It'd make my commute an hour."

"Okay, I'll keep looking."

"But why are you looking? We just got here."

I said nothing, but I could feel my face reveal my anguish. And I could see on his face that he got it immediately.

"I'm sorry you're struggling. I really am. I definitely don't want you to suffer. But what if we go through all of this only for you to have the same reaction at a new place?"

"What do you mean?"

"I don't know how else to say this, but what if it's you and not the location?"

My beautiful Jon. He truly had learned how to confront me. It hurt, but I knew it was a gift. And that maybe he was right. Or at least in part.

"It might be both, you know."

"True. I get that."

I didn't want another diagnosis, but I didn't want to suffer anymore either. And I didn't really want to move, or mostly didn't. I told him I'd go for more help. And then I beat him at Risk.

Same as with previous interventions on my system, the added medication my psychiatrist proposed when I told him what I'd been experiencing wouldn't be a cure-all, at all, but it might tamp down the adrenaline spikes that took me hostage when a car drove past. But why was I suddenly so affected like this? I wanted to know. He had some theories. The battering by Tony, the violence I put myself through as an active addict, these had wreaked havoc on my nervous system (or, as I liked to say, my nervous nervous system), and this was still an issue all these years and medications later. But he also mentioned that perhaps I was a "highly sensitive person." That maybe I was biologically and/or environmentally predisposed to being hypersensitive to sensory stimulus, among other things. Whether it was nature or nurture that caused it, I told him, I did not care for the term, not one bit.

"That sounds like I'm just taking everything too personally."

"It's actually been scientifically researched."

"Yeah, well their language wasn't. It's a dumb name."

"If nothing else, Cara, your PTSD is getting activated, and this med has been shown to work on war veterans. I think it might help."

Of course I filled the script. As advertised, over time it tempered, some, my reactivity to the road. I learned to help this along by internally buffering my sensory connection with and attenuation to my environment. It felt unsafe to tune in to the vibrating world around me, particularly in my home, or to deeply relax in mind, body, and spirit, for fear that a disturbance would zing me back to that dark—very dark—state of wanting to find any means out of my own skin. In other words, I kept myself intentionally disassociated, to a certain extent, from my own self and from life around me. This I did within myself, as an act of preservation. I wasn't fully checked out. And it wasn't a matter of creating other noise around me or within me. I was learning to contain my awareness, so to speak, or to train it on something like my rib cage. Or to focus on what was immediately in front of me, like the computer screen. Or the dishes in the kitchen sink. It felt like I was treading water to stay above a certain level of consciousness or perception so I wouldn't get taken under. It was work, but I got pretty good at it. Or good enough, as the saying goes.

I also got a job. Not full-time, but some hourly work for an arts organization, and then a grant for the prison poetry class came through. Between me bringing in a bit of money, Jon nearing the end of years of monthly payments to the IRS to clear up debt from when he'd had a courageous if chaotic period of self-employment, and my ability to stay afloat synaptically, I started feeling like we could do this thing. We could be adults, in an adult relationship, as homeowners, with jobs, cars, cats. We had a home our friends and family could visit. His kids. My father and sister. We even had a party with a shrimp platter and other bona fide homeowner, party-haver accoutrements.

I began taking an interest in the flower beds that the previous owner had planted and that burst into surprising life in spring. I had no idea what was what, for the most part. Coneflowers—those badminton birdies of the floral world—sure. Daisies, definitely. Everything else was a mysterious jumble, but the yellows and pinks, the green green green, the way all the growth tousled together and invaded or retreated became fascinating to me. What would be considered a weed, something to pull, and what was to be cultivated or encouraged, was entirely subjective, as far as I could see. Much like how I geared up for hiking, I got supplies as I discovered something might be helpful. After a month of burrs, thorns, and permanently dirty fingernails and torn cuticles, I got a spade and some gloves and started wearing a long-sleeved shirt.

For Jon's part, the primary thing he wanted for the house was bird feeders. His philosophy was the opposite of being compelled to constant home improvement. He couldn't understand the drive others had to continually find projects around their houses in what he saw as similar to the motivating force behind capitalism, that an economy must always grow in order to function. What was so wrong with a happy stasis?

But the birds—he went out of his way for. He put a feeder up behind the house and one he could see out his office window and kept them both filled with the utmost dedication. At least twice a month he walked in the door with twenty-pound bags of seed over his shoulder. He got special mixes and a big container he could stir the various blends together in. The man was reluctant to spend money on new clothes for himself or furniture, but he had no problem investing a small fortune in keeping his avian friends fed. He loved to stand in the mudroom or bathroom, looking out the window, calling out the names of the birds he knew or going for his birding book when he couldn't identify one. He still had his boyhood copy of *Birds of North America* that was missing most of the pages on woodpeckers that he kept at the ready. Slate-colored juncos. Black-capped chickadees. Tufted titmice (he'd fake giggle like a boy). He could watch them all for hours.

I knew none of the birds but the most obvious ones. Blue jays, mainly. Cardinals, but only the red ones. I didn't even know that males and females of a species were often colored or sized differently. Or if I had known, I'd long forgotten it. But Jon's interest was contagious. His retention, stunning. I took to calling him my external hard drive. Or my walking Wikipedia.

"I know why you're compelled to do crossword puzzles," I said to him one Saturday morning in the kitchen.

He was leaning over, intently focused on filling one in at the counter island, and didn't take the bait.

I kept going. "Yeah, it's like you've got all this stored data, and you've got to get it out of you. It's got to go somewhere, right?"

I was sitting at the kitchen table over in the corner where I'd strung a few strands of the purple and green twinkle lights up as a canopy. This was where I did my morning routine with coffee, a candle, and a journal that I dumped into daily. Jon called them my "happy lights." My happy spot. The island was his, claimed via the tower of Sunday papers he let pile up and his beloved *National Geographics* that I'd gotten him a subscription to. When each issue arrived he dropped everything to go through it with reverence. He'd do a first read through, then back into it over the month for a deeper dive. He pored over them with delight and curiosity, and an ability to face some hard environmental truths that I was unable to absorb without becoming incapacitated by despair. Every time he tried to share with me something in the magazine I had to ask first if it was going to wreck me. I wasn't proud of it, but maybe I was the type of sensitive person my psychiatrist had mentioned, after all. The colorful pictures, foldouts of underwater oceanscapes or overhead shots of rivers winding through forests he held up for me to look at from across the room weren't a problem. I did resist with vehemence while doing one of his daily crossword puzzles he'd occasionally ask me if I knew a five-letter word for some ridiculously arcane bit of information in the rare instance he got stuck. I did not want to get sucked in to their mental shenanigans, I'd tell him.

This morning, without taking his eyes off the puzzle, he finally responded. "I'm staving off Alzheimer's, Bense. I'm keeping my mind active. This way in our dotage, you won't have to take care of me. I'll be sharp as a tack."

"You had me at dotage."

He looked up. His smiling eyes. Mine.

"What's a seven-letter word for . . ."

"Don't rope me in!"

We both laughed, and another phrase for callback between us was born.

As I stabilized in this new world order we'd chosen, as we did, I had energy to direct beyond immediate survival. This manifested in a number of ways, from writing more frequently and sending it out for potential publication, to getting involved with activist campaigns to get corporate money out of politics to give the planet some breathing room. My urge to save the world could be more consistently acted on.

I went to organizing meetings in libraries, in living rooms, and in community centers where clipboards were passed around with petitions to sign and with information on current campaigns. *Call the Governor: Say NO to fracking in NY State! Write your legislators: Support funding for clean energy in the budget!* I attended marches and rallies. I handed out flyers in parks. I posted links and articles to social media. I e-mailed my contacts. *I just called on the Department of the Interior to ban drilling in the Arctic. Will you join me?* I even crossed state lines to knock on doors and talked with registered voters when a politician came along who seemed to have promise.

Jon did none of this, protesting was not at all his thing but often said, "Go get 'em, Bense" when I was heading off to some event or other. (At some point, this turned into "Don't get arrested," another running joke.) He supported me in other ways, dropping me off at a midnight bus to go to DC, then picking me up at 1 AM the following night. Every now and then I asked if he would join me and got a hard no. Occasionally I pressed him further.

"But what are you doing about the things you say you care about?"

"Not everyone is a front liner."

"I get that, but . . ."

"Don't rope me in."

We laughed. I let it drop. I was going to have to get used to that. His resistance was growing stronger. It's what I'd wanted, after all, wasn't it?

CHAPTER 12

MOURNING DOVE

(Loving what I'm losing)

Early to mid-aughts

A graceful, slender-tailed, small-headed dove that's common across the continent. Their soft, drawn-out calls sound like laments. When taking off, their wings make a sharp whistling or whinnying. Mourning Doves are the most frequently hunted species in North America.

—Cornell Lab of Ornithology, All About Birds, "Mourning Dove"

At thirty-something years old and closing in on a decade sober, I went back to school to finish my abandoned degree. I worked hard at figuring out how to reorient myself to an academic mindset, to developing an *argument* (without sarcasm), sitting among all the eighteen- and nineteen-year-olds in classrooms with chalkboards, lecterns, overhead fluorescent lights, and those metal frame chairs with writing surfaces sprouting out of their sides. I was eager, as most returning students are, and would not let go of things I didn't understand, often asking the *no such thing as a dumb question* dumb question. I persevered, completing my program with panache by making my graduating project a short film I shot in front of an Irish bar on St. Patrick's Day, in the parking lot of a big-box store on a frigid Saturday morning, and in front of the public library in town. I asked anyone who'd talk with me if they read poetry. I didn't prove anything, per se, except that perhaps I should rethink my career choice, but I did have a lot of fun making the thing. And my mother came to the presentation when I showed the film to a committee. She was thrilled that I'd turned my life around. As was my father. Their daughter was no longer making the middle-of-the-night calls they feared. I was sober and getting a degree. This time I actually invited them to the graduation as a corrective—if awkward—experience. My father drove up from Long Island. My mother bought me a teddy bear in a cap and gown. They clapped and took pictures as I walked across the stage and shifted my tassel.

With my bachelor's degree in hand, I decided to go to grad school to continue to read and to write poems. Like many addicts, I hadn't expected to live past thirty, so why not take on debt as a poet? I was accepted into a program that seemed to value students who'd had circuitous routes in their education. Maybe my experiences, as people in program were quick to tell me, could become assets. I wasn't always so sure, but I'd come far enough not to let that hold me back. I bought an inordinate amount of books. I read and wrote late into the night. I recited lines I was trying to fiddle with on long walks. Was I finally coming into who I'd been meant to be before nearly drowning that person in a sea of drugs and alcohol?

I kept up waitressing. Going to meetings. Getting together with my mother. Her husband had died, so we were each other's dates most weekends. We were growing closer. We even did mother-daughter therapy, where I repeated the joke *You know if it's not one thing, it's your mother,* and she, being my mom, laughed.

"I have something important to tell you," she said one day on the phone.

"What's up?" I was rushing around to get ready for a shift at Friendly's.

"I don't want you to worry, if you can help it, but I have cancer."

I sat down on the edge of my bed. I didn't understand. Why was she telling me this?

"Worry?"

"No, not if you can help it. There are things we can do. There's a plan laid out."

She was working in oncology at a hospital, so she knew the ins and outs of various forms of cancer treatment and spoke about it like a nurse. Also, like my mother, who, when a bunch of us would be playing cards and one of us (me) was down by a gazillion points, would sing out, "It's anybody's gaaaaame!" to encourage everyone to stick with it even if it was logistically impossible for me to win at that point. She told me the plan.

"First I'll have surgery to help reduce what they have to go after with chemo."

"Surgery?"

"Yes, it's ovarian so they're going to remove my ovaries. It's good to get them out."

"Ovarian?"

"Yes, and they'll take my uterus while they're there, also a good idea."

"Take?"

It went on like this for much of the conversation, her explaining the steps moving forward and me only able to grasp and spit back one word at a time of what she was telling me. The surgery was in two weeks. The plan was to open her up and get as much of the tumor out as possible before she did a follow-up combination of chemo and radiation to kill off the rest of the cancer—or that was the hope.

My sister Donna came up for the surgery. We drove my mother to the hospital at some ungodly hour of the morning and accompanied her to a curtained cubicle for her to remove her clothes into a labeled plastic bag and wait to be taken. The beeps, blips, lights, buzzes, smells, coughs, gargles, false cheeriness, nervous laughter, hushed conversations, startlingly loud interruptions, and the squish of nurses' shoes and swish of uniforms surrounded us, surrounded my mother, who looked small and scared on the hospital transport bed. I wanted to be anywhere else, and there was absolutely no place else to be than here, with her, with my sister, waiting for my mother's body to be cut open. It was her time. Donna and I were ushered out to the waiting area as they wheeled her away.

We passed the time much as the others in the area did, being assaulted by the TVs, eating shitty hospital food, calling loved ones, pacing, and snoozing. I tried to read some of the texts I'd undertaken for grad school but gave up and resorted like everyone else to flipping distractedly through outdated *People* magazines. We went to the gift shop and spent an inordinate amount of money on a teddy bear, albeit the softest and most plush object I have ever touched. Finally, our beeper went off. We were to meet the surgeon in a claustrophobic private room off the waiting area.

His face was sobering.

"I'll get right to it. We're changing course in her treatment plan."

I felt suddenly silly holding the teddy bear, the eager, terrified daughter with the furry object that was now incongruous with the news we were receiving, like I was naive to have been hopeful.

"We opened her up," he continued, "and found one big mass of tumor in place of her ovaries and uterus. Cutting apart tumor from organ, or organ from tumor, would have been too tricky. So we took a sample to biopsy, closed her up, and we'll do chemo and radiation to shrink it first before going after it again surgically."

We asked all the questions. He gave many answers, as many as he had, and said he'd meet us in the room with her once she regained consciousness, which is when it dawned on us that she didn't even know yet and that we would most likely be the ones to deliver the news of what they'd found inside her.

Back in the waiting area, waiting again, this time for her room assignment, Donna and I hugged. We looked at each other with fear in our eyes, sadness, and then deep sighs, part resignation, part resolution. We discussed strategies, for telling her, for moving forward, for dealing. We repeated things the surgeon had said that we latched onto and manipulated to buck ourselves up. "They'll shrink it. They'll go after all of it. He didn't say there were no options. In fact, the opposite. There's a plan. They'll get all of it. That's the plan."

Up in her room, my mother looked like a little girl as we told her. We tried to be our mother's daughters as we did so, alternating between being medically matter-of-fact and ridiculously optimistic. When the surgeon arrived as promised, he showed himself to be the cowboy that most who take up the knife are, or at least that's what my mother called him later on, having decades of experience interacting with surgeons professionally.

"We'll get this thing," he said. "We'll shrink it, then I'm going to cut every last bit of it I can get out of you. And then we'll go after anything that's left with chemo."

We were so grateful, even if we didn't know if what he was saying would wind up being true, we needed it, his aggressive attitude toward the cancer, his dominant bedside manner. I tucked the teddy bear in next to her and kissed her. We would come back to get her the following day.

Donna went back to our mother's house, and I drove directly to a meeting. In the car, on my own for the first time since getting the news, the terror I'd kept at bay all day erupted. I couldn't see the road I was sobbing so violently, but I was compelled to get myself to the room full of support I knew would be available to me. Down in the basement of a church, on raggedy couches in the massive boiler room, when topics were requested I stuck my hand up. I blurted everything out. *If this is love, I don't want it.* I was just opening up to getting closer with my mother only for her to be taken away? It seemed cruel. I wailed like an eight-year-old. *Mama, don't go. Mama, please don't die.*

The room rose to the occasion. The meeting was filled with so many shares about supporting parents or loved ones through cancer, through end of life, through tragedy. The survival stories, the cycle of life, the camaraderie. I was not alone, not the only one who'd ever had a mother, who'd ever faced loss. And here they'd gotten through it and were still standing, even occasionally laughing. There was a handful of crusty shares, wouldn't be a meeting without them, that focused solely on "not picking up that first drink," which I understood. But I didn't want to know how to not drink, or not only. I wanted to know how to survive what I was feeling. I wanted to know how to live, how to show up the next day and then the following, how to support my mother through treatment while feeling like my heart was being ripped out of my chest.

Even the surgeon, when we met with him in his office later that week, said things like: "One day at a time. It'll be a matter of learning to live with cancer. It can be a roller coaster. Keep living your lives. Don't postpone things you want to do. When you feel good, celebrate it, because you're going to feel like crap right after each chemo treatment. But you'll bounce back before the next one. Take it. Take those good days."

I drove her to her first chemo appointment in a facility that was out in the middle of a rural area. In the main chemo room, there was a bank of chairs that patients sat in facing a window with bird feeders positioned for prime viewing while the caustic chemicals dripped down into their veins. Mainly, I watched my mother while she did her best to be charming. She got to know the nurses and all of the other regular patients, both the nurse and the entertainer in her kicking in, even with the needle stuck into her hand and while feeling like crap. She mustered it up, a cause to keep her going, focusing on others, a distraction, one that I also knew well (not the nurse, nowhere close on that one, but the entertainer). Still it was nice to see everyone light up when my mother arrived for each treatment.

After eight weeks of chemotherapy and my mother mostly feeling like shit, losing her hair, and all the things that filling one's system with chemicals to kill cancer cells that also kill healthy cells brings, it was time for her next surgery. My sister came back up. They wheeled my mother off, and Donna and I again sat in the waiting area. We got another teddy bear, this one a bit smaller. The beeper went off, and back into the consultation closet we went to meet Cowboy.

"Our plan is working. The chemo shrunk everything better than expected, and we were able to get her ovaries and uterus out."

I didn't throw myself into his arms or give him the teddy bear, though I could have, but I did cry and thank him profusely. Donna and I both.

"So she's good?" I asked.

"Well, yes and no. She'll still need to do treatment. It'll be a matter of living with it, like I said. We want to keep the cancer at bay, and yes at some point it's possible for her to experience remission, but we're not there yet. But this is good news, absolutely. As aggressive as her cancer is, it responded really well to chemo, which is a great sign."

We shook his hand enthusiastically, then headed up to celebrate with our mom, who commented on the decreasing size of the teddy bear.

"Hedging your bets, girls?"

We laughed. She was stitched up, bald, in need of more chemo and possibly some radiation, but still had her wit. This was a win. One of the good days in the loop-the-loop.

The next few months were upswing, if hard to trust. Her cancer continued to respond to chemo, and the days she felt better, more like her precancer self, were becoming more frequent. She even went back to work, learning how to schedule her chemo so the effects would hit her over the weekend. As she worked in oncology at a hospital, she was able to get her treatment during a workday. She'd take a half hour break to sit in the chemo wing with a needle in her, then head right back to her department to finish out the day. She'd lay out all weekend and be ready for work again come Monday.

Through all of this, I was fully focused on her appointments, surgeries, the vicissitudes of how she felt on any given day, and on her blood counts and CA numbers while squeezing in work for grad school, reading essays and poems in waiting rooms, next to her bed, in my tiny apartment with Ed. I was grinding it out, showing up, then falling apart at meetings to get put back together again so I could make it through another day. What Cowboy had said about taking the good days, about continuing to live our lives, had also been directed to me, but I was finding that easier said than done. I couldn't tear myself away, and it was taking its toll.

Then gruffster trip leader reached out to me about joining a trip he was putting together to climb "a real mountain." He was going to Pico de Orizaba, Citlaltépetl as the Aztecs call it, an 18,491-foot glaciated volcano in Mexico, the following January, six months away. I wasn't sure if scheduling something so far off in both time and place was a great idea, but he had my attention. I started considering it. The timing actually seemed perfect, between semesters and with no surgeries scheduled. I hadn't been doing any hiking since my mother got cancer, but I would have a few months to train. And borrowing gear was nothing new for me. I did have concerns about the altitude, but I was assured that we would do an acclimatization routine to get to 18,000 feet. So after checking in with my mother and sister and getting their blessings, I told him yes and bought my plane ticket.

Getting focused on trip prep proved harder to do than I'd considered. I was deep into the semester of grad school and still following closely my mother's day-to-day health and numbers, which began sliding back down. Cowboy said it wasn't time to panic, but that he was going to increase her chemo for a month to see if that would beat it back. She wasn't in dangerous territory, comparatively speaking, but this did spoil the feeling that we were in a stretch of good days, or having wins. My mother insisted I continue with my plans for the climb, and I did, even if I was struggling to give it my all.

I worked on the gear list through word of mouth, the biggest-ticket items being insulated mountaineering boots and an ice ax, but I also needed a sleeping bag, crampons to go with the boots, and a better jacket. I did manage to borrow almost everything I needed, but the boots didn't fit as they should have for such a lengthy and arduous climb. They were too big—better than too small, I reasoned—and the ax was apparently too long, but I'd never climbed with one before, so what did I know. Though I had gotten myself north for a few climbs in an attempt to get myself back into hiking shape, I only managed to do one hike in the borrowed gear before the trip. I slipped around inside the boots quite a bit, but at that point it was too late to try for anything else.

Once we got to Mexico, it became apparent fairly quickly that gruffster hadn't softened any. His lecture at the start of the first acclimatization climb to the training peak La Malinche only worsened my forming headache. I was wheezing my way up the nearly 4,500-foot climb to the rocky remnants of the summit crater at over 14,000 feet, but made it, and down we went and whooshed right off to get a jeep up to the Piedra Grande hut at just under 14,000 feet on Orizaba. On the nauseatingly bumpy and treacherous jeep ride to the hut, where we were all being jostled around on crumbly, narrow cliffside roads, gruffster turned around from the front seat and passed out a piece of paper for us to write down contact information in case of death.

Being at the hut was a blur. A lot of hydrating, climbing ladders up to the bunks, then down multiple times in the night to walk in the dark to pee, always a bit wobbly due to lack of oxygen to my brain. I was finding the acclimatization schedule he'd planned to be far too aggressive for me. Also that studying poetry beside one's mother's cancer bed wasn't necessarily the best preparation for such a trip. But

I was there, at the rocky dusty hut, and I was going to try. The first climb we did was over 16,000 feet to get to glacier, where we could practice self-arrest with our ice axes. I was a yellow dog, hauling myself up in full-body revolt, but I stabbed my way up the ice. I was so sick I didn't have to pretend to fall to practice the maneuver. I tripped all on my own as an unforced altitude sickness error. But my instincts were good. My body reacted perfectly with my gargantuan ax to stop my slide before it even started. It was decided. We would climb that night.

Back at the hut, on one of my many trips to the pee and shit shack, I looked up at the white covered peak, "Star Mountain" to the Aztecs, wondering if she would let me climb her, if I was up to the task. The midnight alarm roused us, and the group sprang into action getting dressed, boiling water, stuffing last-minute items into packs. I was dragging through all of this, just waiting for coffee to see if the caffeine would spark me. It got me out the door, in line with the others in the dark, making one effortful step after another upward in my clown-shoe boots. I quickly slipped to the back of the line and then dropped behind them farther. I realized fairly quickly that I had to let go of the climb.

"I'm turning back," I called out about fifteen minutes after we'd started.

There were a variety of replies. From "You sure?" and "Everything all right?" to the young dude who couldn't wait to get to it and kept looking upward impatiently, which could easily have been me on another climb. Gruffster acknowledged my decision ("Your call"), then turned the group back toward the climb. I hated them in that moment. And for the next ten hours I hated that hut I was confined to, waiting while they climbed. And I absolutely hated cancer. All I wanted was to get back to my mother, but I had another four days with them after their successful summit. Fortunately, I had some Spanish, which none of them did, and could navigate myself to Oaxaca for my own adventure for the rest of the trip. I even found recovery meetings and told my story in stilted Spanish. It was basic, *la lingua del corazón,* I called it, but it was close enough for the others to get me. This lifted me immeasurably, and I spent the rest of my time connecting with locals and ex-pats, playing street chess, and swimming in bahias.

Back in the States, I cried recounting the whole story to my mother, curled up next to her on her couch as she wasn't always up for going in to work. She listened and loved as much as she could. She kept up her mothering as often as her illness would allow, until she'd hit another downward slide, each one seeming to go lower than the previous. Then she would rally, put on lipstick and an attractive wig, and be back to work for a few weeks or a month, and we all would get a breather, an opportunity to rest in denial of what was happening inside her body. But it wouldn't be long before the bubble would be shattered by a call in the wee morning hours for me to drive her to the hospital because the pain was too great for her to bear. Some days I wanted to give up, to tune out, to not pick up the phone when she called. Once, I did let the call go to the answering machine, and I lay in bed, torn up on every level, listening to her strained voice apologizing that she had to do this, but could I possibly take her to the ER? *Mama, I'm coming. Mama, I'll be there.*

Finally, Cowboy scheduled another surgery.

CHAPTER 13
DOUBLE-CRESTED CORMORANTS

(We compromise, we try)

2010s

Cormorants have less preen oil than other birds, so their feathers can get soaked rather than shedding water like a duck's. Though this sounds like a liability, this is thought to be an adaptation that helps cormorants hunt underwater more effectively.

—Cornell Lab of Ornithology, All About Birds, "Double-crested Cormorant, cool facts"

For all our individual recovery and therapy, our combined efforts at negotiation and communication while dating and early cohabitating, it felt as if Jon and I had only now come upon what I called *the final frontier:* learning how to be in an intimate and committed relationship for the long haul. We were mortgaged up. Despite my crazy declaration after our ill-fated tennis match, our trip to Switzerland—what we might consider our actual honeymoon (not that we thought of it that way at the time)—was over. We'd survived my PTSD flare-ups. I'd finished grad school, and Jon was out of debt, or mostly. We'd done it. We'd found each other. We'd partnered. We'd stayed sober. We were us. In a house. Our house. Our cats. Our two cars. Our lives stretched out before us. What did we want from them—our lives? What did we want from each other?

"Are you happy?" I asked one night in bed. We were both reading, Jon more intently than I was. He was used to my interruptions to his reading by this point and rarely put his book down on my first query.

"Happy?" he said more than asked. It was a bit of a stalling technique, to see if I'd keep at it without his investment in the conversation. This was fair. It was late. A school night, as he'd call it. He lived for unwinding time. Reading time. Jon interior time.

"Yeah, happy. Satisfied. I mean, like, are you getting what you want from life?"

He took a deep sigh, put his finger in his book where he was reading, and rolled to face me. My hero.

"Have we ever talked about Maslow's hierarchy of unmet needs?" he asked.

"Unmet needs?"

"Well, that's how I look at it. Framing needs as a hierarchy, a pyramid to reach the top of, means once a need is met there's always another one that drives us upward. Always another level to achieve. It's sometimes used in corporate motivational psychology to keep employees striving."

This was pure Jon.

"Does this mean you won't go hiking with me anymore?" Pure Cara.

We smiled. I nuzzled closer and fluttered my eyelashes with his. He took up his book again, and I snuggled into his shoulder and fell asleep.

We weren't always so taken with each other, however, and a new level of needing to compromise was surfacing, even though we were working on it. We were going to have to because it finally came out that he *was* unwilling to hike with me, at least in a way that would satisfy me.

"Bense I know you gotta get your ups, and it turns out that that just isn't for me."

"So, no hiking, like, at all?" My face a pinched puppy dog's.

"I'm not necessarily saying no hiking, but I don't like being scared for fun. You see a 'danger do not go out past this point' sign, and that's exactly where you want to go."

I couldn't argue with that, but that didn't stop me. We hacked at it back and forth for months. He wasn't willing to hike peaks, even in the Daks, and I wasn't willing to let go of adventuring together. I insisted at minimum we take a summer holiday. Was there any place he wanted to go? Turned out, there was. The Midwestern boy who'd grown up landlocked wanted nothing more than to get to the ocean. I did the trip research, taking great pleasure in exploring options, looking at maps, and imagining the possibilities. He was happy to let me do this—in fact he seemed to prefer it—and then be brought in on decisions before any bookings were made. Occasionally he'd mention something that had caught his eye in the daisy chains of his enormous curiosity, and I would work to fold it in.

In his off hours, when he wasn't reading or staring out the window at the birds ("Bense, come here! American goldfinches on top of the coneflowers!"), Jon was often poking around in some creative pursuit or other, whether learning to play a hand drum or starting a project of tracing extinct species onto vellum. He almost always had some writing idea floating in his consciousness. Lately he'd been working on a story called "The Doleful Groan," a fictionalized account about Edmund Drake and his fanatical pursuit of drilling for petroleum oil in Pennsylvania. In Jon's story, Drake was tormented by graphic dreams of whale suffering due to the barbaric means the whaling industry used to derive oil from their blubber. The upshot was that now the whaling industry and whales generally had become one of the multitude of interests Jon stoked and stored inside him and in books and notes stacked all over his office and on his bedside table, even poking out from the pile of newspapers on the kitchen island. So most of all he wanted to go on a whale-watching trip. Other than that, so long as I wasn't trying to kill him hiking, he said he'd be good. We picked an island off the coast of Maine.

It didn't have anything anywhere near the highest peaks in the state, those were far inland (I'd checked), but there would be rugged coastal hiking on the island, which was small enough to navigate without cars. In fact, there were none allowed on the island, save a few worker's pickup trucks. I loved the idea of being able to walk out our inn's door and hoof it to the trails that circumnavigated the rocky island and webbed the forested interior that remained undeveloped because it had been designated as forever wild. When we first got to the island, Jon did hike with me on the wooded trails to a headwall on the far side facing the ocean. The bluff towered above the surf. I looked to Jon who was staring out to the water.

"Don't," he said without turning toward me.

"What?"

"Say what you're going to say."

Of course he'd nailed it. I was absolutely about to use this as an example of vistas that could be reached if only he'd go hiking with me more regularly. I pivoted.

"It's just nice to be here with you."

"It is, Bense. Don't ruin it." His eyes crinkled into a smile.

We walked back to the inn holding hands. But for most of the rest of the trip, we split up after breakfast and rejoined for lunch. I would put my boots and shorts on and bang my way around the island, up and down its craggy coast, five miles that ducked in but mostly out of the woods, with the ocean whooshing against rocks and gulls shrieking and laughing. Jon spent his time either in a rocking chair on the inn's porch or down at the wharf in a small café that had prime viewing of boats and ferries coming to dock. He was enamored with looking out at the ocean, writing snippets of scenes, listening in on conversations all around him, meeting the locals, tourists, and workers.

One afternoon I did convince him to take another walk with me, and we trekked down to the south shore of the island. There we became privy to the most spectacular avian display. There was a storm coming in, and the water was smashing against the rocks and spraying us. Most of the other tourists had retreated back to their lodgings, but Jon caught sight of what he later identified as a flock of northern gannets, sea birds that dive with aeronautical precision from some fifty or more feet in the air, forming their bodies into three dimensional arrows to ram into the water for fish, which we later learned would be swallowed underwater. One by one, sometimes two or three at a time, these magnificent creatures swooped, swerved, and plunged while Jon and I sat in astonishment. He, in particular, was awed. Back at the inn he took immediately to the library to hunt down information on what we'd witnessed.

And then there were the harbor seals, and the double-crested cormorants drying their wings in the air on the rocks, and porpoises swimming alongside our boat as we went out on our scheduled whale-watching trip where we saw not one, but maybe ten or more whales come up out of the water, some of them close enough to the boat we felt like we could reach out and touch them. The day was completely clouded over, so every surfacing was a complete surprise, oohs and gasps and squeals from all of us on board. Minke whales. Humpbacks. Rights. The whole trip we didn't know how lucky we were, from the gannets to the incredible showing of earth's greatest mammals. And I got to hike, though I'd have much preferred it if he'd joined me more than he did, even if it meant we wouldn't be going at the speed I wanted (needed). But all in all, we were doing it. We were figuring out how to get both our needs met, individually and as a couple.

This extended to other shorter trips and to creating a weekly date night of dinner and the movies on Fridays. We'd make it to the end of the week, and I'd go to the gym after being home working alone all day, then hit a meeting while he went to one in a different fellowship across the river after his day at the office. Then we'd text *where for dinner what movie?* and meet at the agreed upon restaurant before going to the theater. He also adored matinees, which freaked me out, going into the dark during the day, like waking hallucinations, coming back out in disorienting late-afternoon light. We negotiated that he would sometimes walk (not hike) with me and I would sometimes go to matinees with him. And come Thanksgiving, a holiday Jon called "the fourth Thursday of November where everyone acts weird," he suggested we go back to the bed-and-breakfast in the Adirondacks where we'd stayed when making the offer on the house so that I could hike and he could watch football and nap, then we would go to dinner together. We were creating our own family traditions and rituals. I was sad he no longer hiked with me, and he was disappointed I didn't go to matinees more often with him, though he felt freer without me there, he finally confessed, feeling like he didn't have to drag me against my will.

"Drag me! We'll drag each other! That's how it works in relationship."

"You know, Cara, if the poetry thing doesn't work out, you can always get a job with Hallmark."

"You funny motherfucker."

"Hey!" He didn't like being called that. Not that he never said that word or other rude, even crude, expressions—he just didn't want that edge of language between us. He'd always insisted on that with his kids, too. We could tease, press, be angry. But no fuck yous. No shut ups, even without "the fuck." Another concession, because who doesn't love to let rip a well-placed STFU?

But Hallmark would have to wait because I received word that the poetry manuscript I'd written for grad school, the collection I'd finished the day Jon approached me after a meeting to congratulate me, was accepted for publication by an independent press. It wouldn't necessarily bring in much money, but it was undoubtedly a step forward in my writing career, such as it was for what was often called *experimental* poetry. (Not only was I writing the least read genre (sorry, poets), but within that I was apparently targeting an even smaller niche.) Still, it was cause for celebration. And for supporting the book by giving a bunch of readings, a mini book tour, of sorts, including heading out to the West Coast, AZ, Chicago, and DC, topped off by two weeks in Colorado for a brief residency at a university in Boulder, to which I added a backpacking trip in the Rockies.

Unexpectedly, this put a strain on our relationship. Not due to my time away from home specifically, but because Jon became afraid that as I achieved more success I would leave him (had he actually read my weird book?).

"Yes, I read your book. Look, I'm not saying I don't want you to do well."

I knew he wasn't. I also knew that he'd been betrayed before and this was an acute wound for him. But so was dealing with a partner who felt threatened by anything I did outside of the relationship, which was a trigger for me. We began saying, "Our issues are dovetailing." Finally, we started seeing a couples therapist. "About fucking time." That's what I said. Then, "Sorry, honey. Sorry about the fucking."

We also went to a fellowship for couples in recovery, where we got a sponsor couple. This entailed sitting in chairs across from them in their living room every other week to confess our resentments and requests in the safety of witnesses. We also did stepwork together, creating written agreements we negotiated about all sorts of things, from parameters for taking turns initiating sex to agreeing on how frequently I could bug him about mowing the lawn, which, for the record, was never. This didn't come up because I cared about the lawn. In fact, before it came under Jon's purview in one of our agreements, I'd advocated for letting a large portion behind the house grow out, and Jon let me be me on that one. But it turned unwieldy, an odd trapezoidal shape that looked like a hotbed for tick infestations. One incredibly hot day, I ran at the thing with the mower and stalled the machine out repeatedly trying to chop at the knee-high grass. It took me a dedicated day and a half to beat my own experiment back. That's when that one got moved over into Jon's column.

So it wasn't so much that I had an issue with what the lawn looked like. What I cared about was Jon being engaged in tending to our home as a means of investing in us, of putting energy into taking care of the space we shared. What he seemed to care about was down time. Jon time. Chill time.

He loved sleeping late on weekends and said there was no such thing as a bad nap. But in addition to retreating from hiking, he was also getting to the gym less and less. That, too, was something I was supposed to stay out of, and I was hit-or-miss on that front ("I'm gonna go work out; you sure you don't wanna come?"), as was he hit-or-miss in celebrating my publishing successes ("You got invited to read where now?"), but we were trying. Jon described our efforts as the tithing of the poor man, proving he could still charm me with his wit.

One night, I came home flush with endorphins from a good trot at the gym. Jon was still at the office. Though I wished some things to be different, when would that not be the case? I was struck by how lovely our house was, how I had a guy who used his words, not his fists. I went upstairs to change out of my sweaty gym clothes. I stood in our bedroom looking out over the dining room that we never dined in but instead used for bookshelves and a massive plant Jon called Seymour. We were uniquely us, and it felt good in that moment. Then I heard a small thump at the bottom of the stairs and looked down to see Ed struggling up the steps. One of his hind legs seemed incapacitated and was folding under itself as he tried to put weight on it. I couldn't understand what I was seeing. He made his way over to me. My tough guy, my fierce mouser, my Ed. Limping. What had happened?

After carefully feeling his leg looking for cuts or wounds and finding none, I called Jon, who said he'd head immediately home. Then I called the emergency vet, who said it was up to me whether to wait until morning to see if he would get better, but they recommended bringing him in. I looked down at Ed. We'd be right in.

Jon drove. I sat in the passenger seat with the carrying case on my lap, hugging it to me, poking my finger in through one of the air holes to keep contact with my beloved. At the vet, they took one look at him, now he was mouth agape and panting, and whisked him into the back while we were told to wait out front. Jon and I sat down, squeezed hands, and looked around at all the other pet people in varying states of fear and anguish, their companions barking or moping or agitated in cages. After about twenty minutes, they called for us, and we were brought back into an exam room, but there was no Ed, just our empty carrying case.

"We believe Ed has had a heart incident. We've got him in an oxygen unit."

My lower lip and chin started to quiver. Jon put his hand on my back. I let him.

The vet continued, "We took a picture of his heart, and one of the chambers is misshapen. It looks like blood is gathering under a fold of tissue and most likely he threw a clot, and that's what cut off circulation to his hind leg."

"Wwwwill he, uh, will the . . ."

"He should regain full use of it once the clot clears. We've put him on an anticoagulant, which we recommend he stay on from here on out to prevent this from happening again."

We were taken back to see him in the oxygen unit, basically a cube cut into the wall with a plexiglass door on it. Inside the antiseptic box was my beautiful Ed, this ball of black and white fur with a pink nose whose existence had saved my life when I couldn't do it for myself those years ago in the subway tunnel with Tony. I'd gotten sober with Ed, which is to say I'd grown up with him, and he with me, and our bond was fierce. Primal. Beyond language. Creature to creature. Spirit to spirit.

It was recommended that we leave him there overnight. They made a follow-up appointment with the cardiac specialist on staff, had us sign off on the mounting costs of treatment and hourly oxygen, and sent us on our way. The ride home was dark and silent. Empty. Back at the house we comforted each other, Jon loved him, too, and Titi hovered, I think sensing an opening in the alpha cat's absence that he could exploit for connection. He jumped up on the bed with us, sliding immediately into Ed's nonnegotiable spot. I wasn't ready for that, so I nudged him gently toward Jon. Titi purred the whole time. Some cats are just like that.

When I got Ed home the following day, he was a bit gimpy, but the use of his hind leg was indeed returning to him. I now had a daily pill to get down his throat, directions to count his breathing in intervals, and a small contraption to monitor his heartbeat. No one had to tell me Ed would be a noncompliant patient. I had a few scars, as did Jon, from touching him the wrong way over the years. Some cats are like that, too. Bonded. Snuggling. Attack. Jon wasn't wrong when he accused me of being proud of how rough Ed could be at times. I'd relished Ed's reputation in my Saratoga neighborhood as a cat who dogs crossed the street to avoid.

Once he regained the full use of his leg, he was raring to go back outside. The cardiac specialist said in the follow-up appointment that it would be better to keep him inside if at all possible. I was clear that would not be possible without making all of us miserable, which might only stress him out further and create another cardiac event. Outside he would go, and I bought all kinds of cat gimmicks and funnels and crushers and soft, chewy coatings to try to get the pill in him without getting bloodied. It was quite possible, the specialist said, to think that Ed could have more time remaining if we stayed on top of his treatment. He still had quality of life, with the exception of all the hullabaloo that getting that goddamned pill in him required.

Jon and I made an effort to spend more time at home, having "family movie night" on the couch, with Ed between us, and Titi risking getting as close as he could. We had fires in the chiminea the previous owners of the house had left behind, and Ed would hang with us outside, then dash off to hunt something that caught his attention. We were consistent with his medicine and monitoring, and also knew when to give it a rest so everyone's lives didn't become unbearable. We were taking Ed's lead, for the most part, and he was consistently acting like the Ed I'd always known.

This went on for the better part of a year, though the pill got harder to disguise or surprise him with, and finding cat care people who would take that on so we could be away from home for even one night was a struggle. Were we crazy cat people? Maybe. Was this bringing up grief upon grief from our histories and, for me, my mother's cancer? Absolutely. Should we have handled what ultimately became his end-of-life care any differently than being fully committed to it? Definitely not. So when, with compromised heart, Ed confronted another cat in a raging fight that I nearly lost a pound of flesh trying to break up, and during which it turned out he had a second heart attack, we canceled what had become our annual summer trip. After an exquisitely painful month of tinkering with meds, letting him do much of whatever he wanted, which was mostly passing time in the front garden bed or catching the occasional mouse and eating it on the spot like a badass motherfucker (I could say it to Ed), he retreated to the corner of the bedroom upstairs. I brought bowls of food and water up and the litter box. I laid on the carpet and watched him. He didn't eat again, but he did stagger to the box, his legs wobbling through the heroic effort he was making to evacuate his bowels one last time in the designated spot. My brave Ed. He was done.

We wrapped him in a small blanket and gently slid him into the carrying case for the ride back to the emergency vet. Jon's car was on empty, so we had to pull in for gas on the way. I sat in the car, hugging the carrying case to me again, grateful for these last moments with the creature who had been my best and longest friend to that point in my life. With hushed tones and much gentleness, we were escorted back to the room where his life would end. I stroked him as they slid the needle in and plunged the sodium pentobarbital into his veins. It was immediate. The "good death," they said. Humane.

We drove back to the house with Ed's body in the carrying case. We would bury him at Best the following day. When we got home, Jon had the idea that maybe it would be helpful for Titi to process how home life was changing by giving him a chance to view lifeless Ed in the case. We opened the carrying case door and called Titi into the mudroom, where we were storing it until the next day. Titi dutifully responded to the call, took one look in the case, then seemed to skip gleefully back into the house. I don't think he ever looked back.

The following day I was shell-shocked, puffy faced, and dehydrated. I slumped in one of our outdoor chairs while Jon used a rock bar to break up the shale-laden ground behind the house to create a hole deep enough that Ed's body wouldn't get dug up or surface in freeze thaw cycles. We laid him down in the earth, covered him, and I assembled a small rock cairn to indicate a point in a journey, a junction. He was on his way. Then Jon and I went to a daytime movie where I willingly gave myself over to the dream of the story on the screen.

That night, again I nudged Titi back over to Jon in bed. I was too raw and simply couldn't bear any cat that wasn't Ed snuggling up to my body. In fact, for months I was too grief-stricken to let him close, to let him into my heart, even as he was intent on sneaking in there, that fluffy oddball (just like his person). But there was only so long I could resist Titi's insistent affection before he became as much my cat, in the way that Jon was my guy, signifying not ownership but connection, as he was Jon's. Titi was our cat, and we were his people, and we were each other's person, and life was hard and sweet, which I was reminded were inextricably linked, the hard and the sweet, in the way that poet Wendell Berry wrote, *The impeded stream is the one that sings.* (Not worth going into debt for, but thank you poetry for that one, all the same.)

CHAPTER 14

SNOWY OWL

(I'm right where I'm supposed to be)

2005–2006

It's a communicator. It depends on how you look on it. It can be the death of, not necessarily a person, but of something. For me it represented . . . a death of something that I cherished and, for me, my message was that it is going to be OK. That's the way I took it.

—Melissa Desmoulin (Luce), on a sighting of a snowy owl on a hydro pole, as reported by the CBC

The surgery revealed the extent to which my mother's body had been ravaged by the cancer. Cowboy did as much as he could, but her insides were being eaten away. She came out of it with a colostomy bag attached to her side for waste removal, the surgery partly serving to reroute her organs so that she could avoid the caustic and uncontrolled elimination she'd been experiencing leading up to the day of the procedure. She was fully bound to the bed and in constant pain and discomfort, except when it was time to press the button to release the pain med. It was hard to get any of her doctors' attention, Cowboy seemed to have retreated once it looked like his knife wouldn't be needed anymore, and her post-surgery hospital stay stretched through the better part of week, and then longer.

When I ran into one of the doctors on her team in a hallway, I begged him for help. *Why was no one on the team coming by more regularly? Was there anything to be done? Could we—should we—get her home? What are we facing?*

Both he and the woman who was accompanying him were so thoroughly condescending and unsympathetic as to be nearly anti-Hippocratic, insofar as that oath means to do no harm. True, I was agitated and emotional, my mother was likely dying, and it would have been easy to make them the enemy—the place to direct my anger about my mother's condition—but their response was cruel. They walked away after nastily scolding me on the inappropriateness of approaching them.

While my mother had been a dedicated advocate for her patients over the course of her lengthy career in the healthcare industry, she was far less willing to fight for herself. She didn't want me to cause trouble, either, so I refrained from recounting the interaction when I got back to her room. But I did press the nurses when it seemed like it might be helpful, both from my mother's bedside and out at the station. No one seemed to be willing to say what was becoming clearer by the day: She'll languish here indefinitely if we don't push to get her home. We didn't know if getting her home might help her to rally, but we knew for sure we didn't want her to spend even one minute more than was necessary in the hospital. So I pushed, and we got the okay for her release.

Through the enormous effort of a few of my mother's friends whom I'd entreated to help with her post-surgery aftercare so I could get a much-needed break, she returned home and got set up in her bedroom upstairs. This is when my sister came up, she and I were trading off care at this point, and she and a different friend of my mother's, who was a hospital colleague and had been trained as a hospice nurse, of all things, took over for the friends who'd gotten my mother home. My mother could sit up and was eating some, occasionally looking through mail with my sister, or so I was told when I called in from the short trip that had been planned months ago to a beach town I used to go to when I was a kid. No mountains. No climbing. Lots of crying with my sobriety sisters who went with me and walking by the ocean of my youth. Of course I'd considered canceling the trip or cutting it short, second-guessing it each moment I was away, but my sister and my mother's nurse-friend Cathy encouraged me to stay the course—my mother wasn't going anywhere just yet.

Upon return, my sister eased my reentry into the cancer bubble.

"Every day has been a little different," she said. "Sometimes she sits up, eats a little, seems engaged. Others, she's not interested in eating and is kind of checked out."

"And today?"

"Mixed."

We went upstairs. I opened the door to her bedroom gently. Entering felt like going through a portal into a different time zone where the only clock was my mother's state of being. At this moment, she was resting but awake. A cooking show was playing on the television on low volume. I got on the bed with her and put my hand on her legs.

"How are you doing, Mom?"

Without opening her eyes, she said, "How do you think?"

Wise ass. That felt hopeful.

Donna showed me the chart she'd created for disseminating the medicine. There was liquid morphine to put in ice cream to help with her pain.

"Well, you got your wish, Mom," I said.

She opened her eyes.

"You made nurses of us after all."

She closed them.

"Is there anything in particular you'd like me to get you to eat? What about a tuna sandwich?"

Donna had said that she'd responded well to those, when she did eat. But my mother was asleep or simply not answering. Donna pointed to the morphine, indicating that she'd recently given her a dose in a dish of vanilla. I watched her, looked at her moving chest, rubbed her legs tenderly. My beautiful mother. *Rest, Mama. Rest.*

The next day was my birthday, but what did I care? The thing I wanted most was something that no one could give me. No one could reverse the course of my mother's cancer. I was lying in bed next to her; we were facing each other with our heads on the same pillow. My sister came into the room, we were both staying at the house full time, and wished me a happy birthday. Pain came over my mother's face. She'd had no idea it was my birthday. She apologized.

"I'm sorry you have to be here on your birthday."

"Mom. Where else would I be? There is nothing that is more important to me than being exactly here, with you, at this moment."

So rarely did I feel like I was right where I was supposed to be, the saying that had tormented me from early sobriety, but being with my mother in what were likely becoming the final days of her life was the most sure of it I'd ever felt.

Later that day, or maybe it was later that week, the demarcation of days seemed unnecessary, the nurse who was assigned by the county to do home visits came by to do a check-in. She was a good friend of mine, another sister in sobriety, and during the visit, she, Cathy, and I stood chatting at the base of my mother's bed, saying things that were intended to include my mother in the conversation even if she wasn't taking the bait. Then suddenly the two nurses stopped talking. Their eyes rested on my mother's feet. I didn't know exactly what it meant, but the purpling of her heels was unmistakable. I looked to them. They whispered, "mottling" and quietly explained that it meant the blood was settling in her feet. No one said the words *death* or *dying*. No one had to. We looked at my mother in a hushed silence, taking in the reality.

"I can feel you looking at me," she said.

My mama. Still funny. Also telling us to give her room. So we did.

At this point, Cathy was staying at the house around the clock with us. How lucky we were to have her there, a trained nurse, a friend. The three of us became my mother's end-of-life care, her hospice unit. When my mother called out in pain, I learned how to get on the bed with her and move her legs around to help ease it. We all took turns sitting in the room with her, trying not to overwhelm her with our presence. I slid the ice cream with morphine off a spoon into her mouth until the moment she said, "No more." She thought I was still trying to get her to eat.

"Mama, this has the pain medicine in it."

She didn't have it in her anymore to take the spoonfuls in, so I started dripping the liquid directly into her mouth without needing her cooperation as it was half open already. It wasn't long after that that she started emitting a sound like a snore from deep within her throat, a phlegmy gurgling I later learned was called the death rattle. We could hear it from the other side of the door. We were solemn. We were focused. We were exhausted. *Go, Mama, go. It's okay to go.*

I wasn't in the room for her last breath. Donna came downstairs to get me after it happened. I went upstairs to look at my mother's body. No more rattle. No more pain. I opened a window. Donna moved the hands on a clock whose battery needed to be replaced to the hour and minute of her passing: 11:10.

We'd already been in touch with a funeral home and had procured a do not resuscitate order. All we needed to do was to make a phone call for them to come for her body. They wore subdued suits and soft shoes, carefully maneuvering her in a big black bag down the stairs and out the door.

The end-of-life dream became the grief dream. The August sun was too bright every time I went outside. I blinked and squinted often and misheard most of what was said either to me or in my vicinity. My mother was dead. The feminine cancer had taken her at the age of sixty-four. Donna stayed for a few days to deal with paperwork and the choosing of the urn for her ashes before heading home to Pennsylvania. I returned to my apartment. I sat on the edge of my bed. Ed jumped up next to me. A woman who lived in my apartment building was outside my window on the stoop in the process of relapsing, loudly. Her smoke and radio and outbursts and glass bottles clanking and tumbling down the stairs and "Nobody fucking cares you goddamned bitches you fucking sobriety hypocrites" poured in through my window. It was a hot night. My mother was dead. I went outside to talk with the drunk woman. Unsurprisingly, it did not go well.

"Can you please, *please*, take this somewhere else tonight. I really need rest."

"It must be soooooooooooooo difficult being you. So much energy spent looking down on me."

"I'm going to ask you one more time. I could really use a break right now. My mother just died."

"I don't give a shit about your dead mother."

I should have walked away. There's no talking to alcoholics under the influence and sometimes not even when they're sober. *You can tell an alcoholic, but you can't tell her much.* I clenched my teeth. I could feel my face contort. I took the bait. *Fuck you, fucking drunk, I'm gonna regret this later but right now I'm letting it rip, you selfish bitch.*

She met the escalation. I stepped toward her. Then stepped back. I left the scene. Back inside my apartment I sat down on my bed, listening to her continue to rant just feet from the head of my bed. I closed the window. It was a hot night. My mother was dead. I went back outside.

"I apologize for my comments earlier. That was wrong of me, and I'm sorry."

"Yeah? Well, fuck you. You think you're better than me, making your pathetic amends."

I said nothing more. She yelled at me as I walked back to my apartment. I turned out the lights and laid on my bed, staring up at the ceiling. I must have fallen asleep at some point. The next day, I gathered up Ed, some clothes, and my books for grad school and drove to my mother's house in the woods. I called my sister on the way. I would move into the house that she and I and our stepsister now co-owned. She supported the idea. She supported me. I arrived at the house. My mother's car was in the garage. All was quiet. I let Ed out of his case. While he sniffed around tentatively, I set up a litter box in the basement and my books near my mother's computer that I would now use for my papers and poems.

I went upstairs and entered her bedroom. The mattress of the bed she died on was bare; we'd stripped it after they took her. Or did they carry her out in the bedding inside the black bag? I found fresh sheets and remade the bed as my mother had always done it. The decorative pillows. A blanket draped over the end. This would be where I would sleep now. Where Ed would snuggle up with me. Where I would curl into myself and listen for a far-off train to whistle through the trees. I comforted myself with the isolation. I left much of her home as it had been, as she had last touched it. The rolled up ball of socks in her jogging sneakers. The hair in her brush. I wanted to be wrapped in the evidence of her material life. My mother was dead. Here, a tissue in a coat pocket. A scrap of a to-do list in her handwriting. The last load of laundry to wash in a basket in her closet.

I began wearing her clothes, starting with pajamas. My obligations outside of the house were limited—my grad program required me to be on campus only once a semester—so I wandered around in her robe and slippers for lengthy periods of time. I started watching her beloved cooking shows and made a casserole for myself to eat throughout a week. I wallowed. I avoided. I knew better. I broke open. I shared. At meetings. On the phone with recovering women. At a hospice group for daughters who'd lost their mothers. At my therapist's office where she had a vision of my mother's spirit embracing me as I sobbed convulsively. My mother was dead. I was sober. I would embrace my grief. I would withdraw. Coddle myself. Resurface. Hold back tears at the gym. At the market. At hello. I cried at commercials. *Mama, don't go. Mama, don't be gone.*

I bought mums for her back porch and a hooked rug for inside the front door. Ed was as eager to go out in the woods as he'd been in the residential side streets of the village where we moved from. I worried about predators, but he came back every time. The house was conducive to having people over, so I put it out to the women from the hospice group for a social evening after the final session. Then I had a gathering of my mother's friends for telling stories, laughing, and crying, and where everyone said my laugh, my smile, my mannerisms, my conversational rhythms were identical to hers. I invited a few select women from my inner sobriety circle to come for a meeting to support my rite of passage. The woman who'd been one of my sobriety sponsors but had moved drove in from Buffalo. There were five of us in my mother's family room. Candles. Quiet. My mother was dead. Her daughter's life would go on.

I bought a Christmas tree that Ed left alone and threw a small dinner party for no other reason than the time of year, and I made space in myself for celebration. Then I heard that Jeff, a guy I knew in the rooms, had successfully summitted Denali in Alaska earlier that year. I noticed how that caught my attention. I started looking to run into him at meetings. I didn't want to go for Denali, that was a full-month venture, and I was still in grad school, still grieving, and not up for leaving Ed or my mom's house and clothes and kitchen utensils for that long, but maybe there was another trip he'd be interested in. Rumor had it he'd also climbed Mt. Rainier twice, once with a guided group and once with a few friends. I decided I wanted to become one of those friends.

After a preliminary conversation when we crossed paths, Jeff and I started hiking in the Daks together to see if we'd be compatible on a bigger climb. Basically, he was sizing me up. After a few trips above treeline in high winds and subzero temps, he said he'd be willing to go with me to Rainier that summer. We booked tickets. I started purchasing things on the gear list he gave me with money my mother had left me. I kicked into training mode while balancing writing and reading for school. I was on task. I jogged and hiked and lifted weights and wrote poems and went to meetings and shared about it all. My mother was dead. I was going back at a glaciated volcano. I was writing for grad school. Then I finished the final poem of a draft of my creative project, and the man who would become my life partner summoned up the courage to approach me one night to say he could not have been more admiring of that fact. And so I added dating Jon to the list.

That July, my new boyfriend drove me to the airport where I would meet up with Jeff at check-in. Our backpacks with all the climbing gear and food weighed almost eighty pounds each. It was just the two of us carrying everything we'd need, so it was quite the haul. Once we arrived in Seattle, we rented a car and drove right to the edge of the park to get a motel room in Ashford. There I rented the last of the gear I needed but didn't want to buy, and we drove toward the park to get inspired for setting off the following day. "The mountain" is all anyone in the area called it, and driving up into the park for a view of it from that side made it obvious why. I called Jon from a payphone. "The mountain is biiiiiiig!"

The next morning, I drank way too much coffee and ate a huge pancake breakfast to fuel up for the climb ahead of us that day. I peed twice before leaving the diner. I was about to go one more time, worried I'd be starting with a full bladder, when Jeff assured me there would be a bathroom at the Paradise Visitor Center inside the park where we would get our climbing permit and start our trek. This wasn't a repeat of Orizaba, I told myself. I'd trained. I was ready. And this wasn't gruffster asking for contact information in the case of my death on the nauseating jeep ride to the hut. Jeff was in recovery. He wanted to help me have a good climb.

We drove through the immense forest and up to Paradise at 5,400 feet. I zipped right inside the center to pee, then joined Jeff in talking with a park ranger. He was getting intel on the current conditions while filling in our permit with our target camping and climbing itinerary. We were prepared to be on the mountain for four to five days, if needed, depending on weather windows and acclimatization. The ranger was informative and approving. Though there was potential for weather coming in over the next few days, when wasn't that the case on a mountain as big as this? We received our permit and went back out into the sunny day to load up at the car. We were in shorts and short sleeves to hike through meadows to start but would be up on snow by the end of the day, having climbed over 4,700 feet in about four and a half miles if all went according to plan.

The pack was the heaviest I'd carried, with the ropes, harness, tent, stove, all the food, and everything else we'd need to camp and climb on glacier for almost a week. I did a half squat to create a shelf of my upper leg and hauled the pack up onto my thigh. I took a deep breath and swung it the rest of the way up to my shoulders while shoving first my right, then my left arm through the loops. I staggered under the weight of it to get my balance. It wasn't graceful, but finally I steadied. Jeff took the lead. We were very slow with our steps, deliberate. I had no other choice.

The trail passed through wildflower meadows that thinned out to bunches of colorful clusters here and there in the dirt and rocks and along glacial runoff creeks winding down through the otherwise brown dusty earth. Few day hikers were out and about yet, but a guided group of younger hikers also on their way up to Camp Muir blew past us as we continued our slow but steady pace. As a guided group, they weren't carrying as much on their backs as we were, plus it was spread out among the six to seven of them. I felt like we'd never make camp at our rate. Jeff assured me we were doing great, that our pace was also good for acclimatization. That's all I needed to hear to settle in, that this would help prevent getting sick. We kept on.

We got to the edge of the Muir snowfield, which seemed as bright as looking directly into the sun. We donned glacier glasses and slathered our faces with sunscreen. We were still in short sleeves and shorts but added gaiters to cover our ankles and calves so snow wouldn't go down into our boots. We stepped onto the field. There were multiple snaking trenches in the snow, and we plunked one foot in, and again, and again, and again in one of the more pronounced routes. It was arduous and hot. After a solid hour of trudging, we pulled off the route onto a rocky outcrop for a rest. I was hesitant to take my pack off because I wasn't so sure I could get it back up, but I dropped it anyway. I felt my body rising from the shoulders with the release of the weight and floated over to the rocks to sit, drink, and eat. We still had maybe a mile or so to go and at least a thousand or more. It looked never ending, like a long tongue of snow with nothing to break up the distance, nothing to give accurate perspective, except for the growing amount of ant-sized-looking climbers who were now ahead of us on the trail. I braced for the inevitable and stood up. Here I could put my foot against one of the rocks to heft my pack onto my thigh and hoisted it onto my back without issue. We kept on, the theme of the day.

With the sun still relatively high in the sky we finally made it to Camp Muir and staked out a spot to set up our tent, even though there was a public hut with room for thirty. There was also a second hut for guides and some of their clients and for the rangers, as well as a few outhouses. All around other tents were erected. We got to work pitching ours, which involved a specific strategy for burying the stakes in the snow with the ropes knotted and wrapped around them. Jeff was intent on teaching me, whereas I would have been very happy just to be told what to do, but I watched, listened, and tried to commit everything he was showing me to memory, knowing full well I'd have to be reminded of it all over again at our next site the following day. We stuck a few wands with orange flags in front of a small crevasse in the glacier that was fairly close to our tent to keep us cognizant of the gap as we were moving about.

Not far from where we were camped was a group of tents of the younger, faster climbers who'd blown past us on the way up. With a potential snowstorm coming in the following night, their guides were taking them on a summit attempt that night in the clear. I started wondering if we should do the same thing and abandon our plan to hike the thousand feet up to Ingraham Flats the next day for a summit attempt that night. I asked Jeff about it.

"We can wait it out if we have to up on the flats. That's why we have the extra food."

My face must not have looked convinced. He continued, "I think it's better to sleep the additional night at elevation, Cara. We'll have a better shot at it."

I didn't really want to push a summit attempt that night anyway, so I settled in to our plan. We went back down on the snowfield to practice self-arresting with our ice axes until it was time to cook dinner. We were both still in shorts, though we'd added upper layers. The sun had been strong all day, even up that high. The Camp Muir ranger was walking around checking in with the different climbing groups. When he got to us, he was impressed that we were still in shorts. I was surprised at that, but then the sun dipped behind a rock ridge and the temp dropped precipitously. While Jeff was fussing with food, I dove into the tent for my brand-new down jacket and fleece pants. After wriggling into them, I maneuvered around to get back out of the tent. The view from the opening was breathtaking. Deep purple light was glowing behind Cathedral Rocks, the rocky prominence we would be climbing over the next day, and backlit the dramatic ridgeline to glorious effect. I climbed out of the tent into that big sky, on the big mountain, in my warm layers, and took a seat on my rolled-up foam pad to eat a hot meal with my sober friend.

"How's your breathing?" Jeff asked after dinner when we got into the tent for the night.

I knew he was asking how I was handling the altitude.

"Good! Thank god." Being forced to moderate my pace under the weight of my pack was working.

The next morning after coffee and oatmeal we packed up camp to head another thousand feet up to the next glacier above Cathedral Rocks. The day was clear, the morning chilly until the sun hit us. Then it was back into shorts and short sleeves, but now we would be donning crampons and helmets and roping up to travel on glacier. We got our last weather info from the ranger—yep, snow coming in the following day—then saw a few of the young climbers rustling around outside their tents. They still should have been higher on the mountain at that point if they were summitting. Jeff called over to them. Turned out none of them had been feeling well enough at altitude to try for the summit. I commiserated, telling them about how sick I was on Orizaba, and asked if they'd try tonight. They were heading back down, they said, and seemed glad of it. Jeff and I moved on, stepping into the groove in the glacier all the climbers had traveled that season to plod our way up the mountain.

Once over the rocks in the Cathedral Gap, we climbed onto the Ingraham Glacier, where there were some monstrous crevasses that the route veered around. It was unnerving to see the layers in the blue ice to the depth that could be observed from a safe distance. In many ways a glacier is a living, breathing entity. A movable being. It cracks and tumbles, creating large apartment building–sized blocks of ice called seracs, and stretches and accumulates and avalanches and thins and melts. Rock crumbles into it through constant falls. We could hear the spills throughout the day and night. At any moment the mountain could swallow a climber or bury her. Or shatter her head with scree. We plodded on more carefully now toward the area on the glacier that was relatively flat where we would set up our second camp at about 11,100 feet.

Not all climbers use the Flats as another point on their climb, so the amount of other tents here is typically less than at Camp Muir. There are no structures, either, only glacier. It looked like there was just one other group of about five tents, a guided group set up about 100 yards from where we would camp. After pitching the tent, we got to work digging trenches in the snow to block the wind for a cooking spot and a separate one for some bathroom privacy where we would shit into blue bags to be carried back down the mountain with us.

We had dinner early as we would be waking at midnight to start our summit climb. At 4 PM, in full daylight, we tucked into our sleeping bags in the tent. It was impossible to fall asleep. I rustled around for hours in my mummy sleeping bag, turning from one side to the other, trying to get settled, but couldn't. Finally Jeff's watch alarm went off, and the torture was over. The sky was brilliant with stars in the dense dark of night. No weather in yet, though likely we'd see some before the end of our climb. We readied in the light of our headlamps, roped up, and were off before 1 AM. We curved our way across the glacier to the next rock outcrop to climb the disenchantingly named Disappointment Cleaver. As we got closer to the Cleaver, my headlamp went out. I tried everything to get it going again, I had a spare bulb and batteries, but it was dead. Jeff had a tiny backup, basically a pen light, but it was better than nothing. He was in front, so technically all I needed to do was follow him. We continued on.

We reached the Cleaver where we would be climbing on rock, in crampons, roped up, and in the dark. I tried to make out my footing before stepping, but my light was too weak. I scraped along behind Jeff. At some point he went up and over a small ridge, and we came to a dead end. We couldn't see what was ahead or below the rock, but to keep going on the trajectory we'd been on looked impossible. We looked up at our other option, a nasty rock chimney, basically a narrow vertical tunnel in the rock above who knows how precipitous a drop as we thankfully couldn't see our exposure in the dark. *Oh hell no. Not in crampons.* I told Jeff I thought we ought to backtrack to see if we'd missed a turnoff. He agreed. Back over the ridge there was indeed a turn we'd missed, and we were back on course. I quietly rejoiced when we reached the glacier above the Cleaver at about

12,500 feet. I was still climbing in the dark as now the backup had also gone out, but I was less worried about my footing once we were off the rock.

The rest of the climb would be on glacier until the summit crater. This part would be long and very, very slow in the thin air. We still had almost 2,000 feet to climb at this point, but at last the rosy glow of dawn broke over my shoulder. The climbing was tough, but the light helped. The route veered north, then south, then north, crossing back and forth through seracs and around crevasses. We hit a spot with steep exposure that had a fixed rope clipped onto poles in the ice. Jeff said we should clip in, so I did. Past the rope, the climb was getting steeper and felt longer with every step. The rosy light was gone, and the sky had clouded over. Very quickly snow and ice created a wall of white around us. Here was that weather we knew might come in. We stopped to add full-face coverings and goggles. I already felt like the Michelin man, puffed out in multiple layers on top and bottom, but having any skin exposed was dangerous. In my huge mitted hands, I held my drink to my mouth and slurped, then quickly chewed a protein bar before we started again. The weather and wind did not let up. I couldn't hear Jeff if he called to me, so he instituted a communication system by hand signals that I struggled to remember.

Another climbing team of eight passed us, but mostly we didn't see any others on the route. I began to question if I could make it. We must have been about 300 feet from the summit crater, maybe less, and I was completely frozen over with a coating of ice over every surface of my clothing. I was doing the mountaineering rest step to catch my breath as best I could, but with every step I wondered if I'd be able to take another one. I called out to Jeff.

"I don't know if I can do it!" I shouted in the wind.

"We're so close! You got this, Cara. I promise!"

Sometimes all it takes is someone cheering you on. I thought of Jon. Of my mother. I took another step. Then one more, and kept on doing it until 8:10 AM when we reached the ridge of rocks that formed the eastern edge of the summit. We climbed into the crater and across the depression to the high point of the Columbia Crest on the far side. I stood in the slope of crumbly rock that was spitting steam out of it and felt like I was on the moon. The storm still filled the sky, preventing any view, but we were in the crater of a volcano at 14,400 feet. I'd always said I never climbed for the view but for the end of the suffering that is the climb.

We unclipped from each other for brief personal breaks, then clipped back in to begin our descent. About a thousand feet under the summit, crater the sun broke out and beat on us—and the glacier—unforgivingly. I started peeling layers and should have put on sunscreen, but I was pretty high on the climb and altitude, so I jettisoned that bit of caution. A pair of rangers on a short rope between them were climbing up toward us. When we crossed paths we discovered that one of them was the very ranger we'd gotten our permit from. He asked how our climb went. I told them we'd summitted and how amazed I was at the steam. *Holy shit! Rainier really is a volcano!* The ranger we knew laughed and clanked the shaft of his ice ax with mine, a mountaineer's celebratory gesture.

We still had a way to go to get back to our camp at the flats, so we pressed on. Our plan was to spend another night there rather than rush down to the car. Why not? The storm had passed. We'd successfully summitted. We had plenty of food. We took the opportunity to hang out on the mountain. After stuffing our faces with tuna, salty snacks, cheese, noodles, chocolate, and more chocolate, we tumbled into the tent in the afternoon and passed out until the next morning, when we packed up and made our way back down the mountain to the car at the Paradise parking lot.

At the Visitor's Center, I called Jon from the payphone. "I climbed the mountain!" I yelled into his voicemail. Then I bought a postcard of the first known woman to summit Rainier, spending the night in the crater in her wool skirt. We drove the rest of the way down the mountain back to the motel, where we both showered, and I started lathering my crusty sunburnt nose with goo. We spent the next day driving through the park, getting out of the car to check out one cool spot after another, from the gushing glacial waters to stone stairways and bridges, before turning in at the motel for another night of glorious rest on a bed and then flying home the next day.

After a few layovers, we landed at Albany, our home airport, after midnight the following night. And there was Jon, holding a homemade sign.

Cara Benson
Poet. Sherpa. Girlfriend.
Master (of Fine Arts).

We hugged. He wanted to hear all about it. And I couldn't wait to tell him.

CHAPTER 15

GRACKLES

(We get noisy with each other)

2014–2015

Ranging from metallic hisses to electronic yodels, . . .
[g]rackle songs evolved to carry through their nesting habitats—
dense marshes and brushy landscapes—where more
lyrical notes and phrases wouldn't carry well.
—*BirdNote*, "The harsh beauty of grackle songs"

Conflict, my recovery people reminded me, was necessary in a healthy relationship. If that was the case, I told them, then Jon and my relationship was brimming with vigor. We didn't have knockdown fights, for the most part—no slamming doors or screaming, we were both past that type of acting out—but we did argue, and the content and the frequency were escalating. If I had to sum up what the disagreements were about, I'd put it this way: I wanted more *from* Jon and *for* Jon than he did. And it seemed like what he wanted more and more of was to be left alone.

I knew how *extra* I was, right from birth and apparently even in the womb. My mother loved to tell me stories about how active I was in her body. Bam! An elbow to the ribs. Ooof. A foot on the bladder. I was constantly wriggling around, whereas my sister had been quite calm in comparison. My actual birth was also telling. The story goes that I was banging around in there, eager to bash my way out and to get on with things, faster than my mother's body could keep up. By all metrics, she was dilating at a normal pace, but normal was too slow for me, so I rammed my head into her pelvic bone, repeatedly. At one point, they were considering a C-section as they were concerned I was hurting myself in there, which seemingly I was. The story as I remember it is that I was born with a bump on my forehead. I shot out of there and never looked back is what they said.

A story from Jon's youth gives similar insight into character. He wanted to try ice skating or, if not wanted, was willing. But maybe he was interested in it, though not willing to do it in front of other kids. So he asked his parents to take him to a frozen pond out of town for him to give it a try. He got his skates on and was noodling around on the ice when out of nowhere a vehicle pulled up, and a whole bunch of kids from his school got out to take to the ice. Jon was unwilling to skate any farther. He sat down right where he was, took his skates off, walked in sock feet across the ice, and insisted he be taken home. He was done. No more skating.

My Jon, the refusnik. Me, the birth bomb. Our love for each other and especially our compatible senses of humor got us through most of our struggles, sooner or later, but it was getting increasingly difficult to get there. He started describing me as the ocean, relentless in my rushing at him, wave after wave, trying to erode his resolve to do things his way. In turn I said he was an impossibly rocky shoreline, holding firm, with more rock tumbling from cliffs on high, continually replenishing the line he wanted to hold, which kept receding from me. There was a little more play in our version of the immovable object meets an unstoppable force, but not much. He finally confessed that he was concerned if he gave at all, I would just want more. As in, if he went on a small walk with me, I'd ask for a longer one soon after, so why go at all?

Our conflicts were about more than hiking or walking. They were about a level of engagement. I understood that we both had different rhythms, different desires. I had listened to outside council about backing off, giving him room to be himself, but that had always been the case in our relationship. Something felt like it was changing. Was it me? Was it him? Were we still influencing each other for the better? Was I expecting too much? Was I overly focused on him and not on what I could be doing to fulfill me in my own life? I got sick of my own questions.

I kept at my writing, experiencing some higher profile publishing successes, from a few national publications to an unrestricted grant to support continuing to write. I kept protesting and organizing, going all in on fighting a proposed casino near Best that would clear cut green space to make way for an addiction-dependent business that extracts wealth from communities for the profit of a handful of shareholders (the usual suspects). I became a visible spokesperson for the cause, a go-to for quotes in articles and interviews on the local news. And we won, the announcement coming on the same day other activists I knew in NY State were successful in securing a statewide fracking ban. I kept hiking in the Daks, going solo or with others when I could rustle up some kindreds.

Jon kept at his job, always at his job, often going into work on the weekends and staying late on weeknights. He did get a therapist and also kept his hand in his creative interests, completely wowing the children of my friend who'd moved to Buffalo with a story he wrote for them about a hamster who fell into a tuba and arrived in the magical world of Hamsterdam. And he began work on a novel he referred to as the Viking raid story that was set on an unnamed island off the coast of Maine. He described it as an allegory for modern-day capitalism as a pillaging and looting force. He did try sending a few of his shorter pieces out for publication, but when he didn't experience any initial success he got deflated and stopped trying. I tried to encourage him, to let him know that—for no good reason I had ever found—rejection was an outsized component of writing if one wanted readers beyond friends and family. And also this, as with everything, was something I needed to give him room on.

We had let go of couples counseling, which actually seemed reasonable at the time, but we did continue our Friday night dates and meeting with our sponsor couple in recovery. In certain ways the letter of our agreements was being met, if not the spirit, but eventually his lawn mowing lessened dramatically and his gym going ceased entirely. The results of his lack of physical activity while increasing his eating became apparent. More concerning than all of that, though, was the fact that he was getting to less and less meetings and then not really any, at all. I adored him. I worried about him. I was mad at him. I could not change him. Finally I brought my concerns to one of our evenings with our sponsor couple. We were encouraged to renew our willingness to set aside a specific time to talk about the state of our relationship on a weekly basis. To *get current* with each other. We picked Sundays on the couch.

After saying some loving things to each other to open the conversation for our first session back, I started off with what I'd hoped would be seen as a joke and even a bit of a self-own.

"Currently, I feel like you're doing it all wrong."

It was not received as intended. There was this space between us, it was muddled and distorted. He was angry and hurt.

"It was just a joke, honey. In a way, I'm copping to my shit. I mean my stuff. I know I can come off like that. I know I've got my issues to look at, too."

"Too?"

This was not going well.

"Well, yes. Too. Do you think you've got nothing to look at?"

"I'm sure you have your list for me, so why don't you just tell me."

I didn't know how to break through. We sat in silence for a few minutes, Jon facing forward on the couch as I sat cross-legged on the cushions, looking at him in profile. Finally I spoke up.

"Jon. I'm really concerned."

He turned his head toward me.

"I love you," I continued. "I want you to be around forever."

"I take all my medications."

It was true. He took all the many meds he'd been prescribed over the years for his on-and-off health issues from carrying excess weight when he did. Again, this felt like the letter of the argument, not the spirit. And my goal wasn't to put him in a position of feeling like he had to defend himself. Or worse, to cause him to feel excessive shame. I knew those feelings, deeply. Feeling shitty about myself had led me straight into the fists of an abuser. Could I say something the way that my mother had when she asked me if I thought I drank too much?

"What would *you* say to someone who had stopped going to meetings?"

Instead of answering the question, he reminded me that he did have a therapist and also got together frequently with another guy in program and then listed a bunch of reasons why the meetings he used to attend had stopped working for him. I really, *really* did not want to be in a position of judging his recovery, but then who else knows better than another addict all the excuses we make for not facing our addictions? Also I knew, my mother aside, that friends and family are often the last people who are able to get through. I tried to find something as neutral as possible.

"I'm sorry for the issues with those meetings. What about others?"

Schedule, blah blah, work, blah, blah, couples recovery, blah blah blah. And don't forget even though I just brought it up a minute ago about how I have a therapist and that I meet with that one guy who yeah sure, I know I struggle with on a consistent basis because we fight about politics more than we do recovery work together at this point, but still we do it every other week.

I asked him if he would consider looking into another meeting.

"Just think about it, okay?"

"Okay."

We settled into a detente and back to the daily. We kept up date night, I kept on my writing, and Jon kept working late and most weekends. I worried he was being too Midwestern with his boss, that he wasn't advocating for himself enough. But when I considered saying something about it, I knew it could easily come off as me telling him that he wasn't doing yet another thing well enough rather than my wish for him for his own sake. Well, for my sake, too. I wanted a happy, healthy partner who stood up for himself. And there was the rub. Wasn't that, in a way, what he was doing with me by saying no, I won't do it the way you want me to?

"Relationships are messy," Michele, my friend who'd moved to Buffalo, said on the phone one night when I was lamenting, questioning, repeating myself, going over and over the issues between us, what should I be doing, was it all in my mind, was I wrong to want him to do it differently, was that just my controlling shit, what the what the *what?!*

"For the love of god, Michele. Please do not use the word *process* with me."

She laughed. We had it like that between us at that point. She wasn't my sponsor anymore, and even though sponsors shouldn't *really* be surrogate mothers, that doesn't mean that they don't fall into those roles or that we didn't sometimes still default to I'm going to be a big giant baby in a tantrum and say some cranky shit that she rarely took personally, which was to everyone's benefit, because we did. Usually, though, once I let all my hot air out I got back to a place of, if not acceptance, at least willingness. As in willingness to keep my mouth shut about what I wished he'd be doing differently and instead to appreciate all the things I loved about him. And even better—to tell him about those! Which I did. And also to find moments of simply being together, without an agenda. Which I did, too.

"My life is better because you're in it."

I'd joined him outside behind the house, sitting on a break from mowing the lawn. He'd taken to doing it over the course of days and in shorter segments, but he was still doing it, even if it took him longer to get to it.

He looked over to me and reached out his hand for me to hold. I took it.

"Same," he said.

We were sitting on our outdoor chairs, the only tip of the hat to backyard domesticity that we'd invested in, beside the lawn mower and the bird feeders, which Jon remained committed to keeping full.

It was a hot day, and we were under the shade of a gigantic black walnut tree, which was always a ton of work on the years it made its fruit and dropped them on us like golf balls. We were facing the feeder, watching the little songbirds take turns pecking at the seed, then flying off. Jon identified them for me. Nuthatch. Carolina wren. One of the many types of sparrows. And excitingly, sometimes we were lucky to see a few of the smaller woodpeckers.

"If I got some bee balm, would you plant it?" he asked.

"Of course!" I was ecstatic he wanted something for himself, for our home. "What's bee balm?"

"It's a really cool flower. It's a pollinator. And hummingbirds like it."

Aha. Jon was particularly fond of hummingbirds. He'd tried one of the sugar water feeders to entice them to visit. He'd sit for lengthy periods of time watching, waiting, with no luck. Fortunately, in addition to the many birds who did come to the feeders, he'd been blessed with getting prime viewing of bumblebees crawling into a patch of what we learned were turtlehead flowers that the previous owner had planted in front of where Jon parked. In summers, I'd hear him pull in but not come into the house for a good twenty minutes to half hour. I'd look out to see him sitting in his car in front of the winged critters climbing in and out of the tubular blooms. He often got out of his car to get up close, reveling in the buzzing activity. But the hummingbirds continued to elude him.

"You got it," I said. "I know just the spot." I was so glad there was something I could physically do to make him happy that didn't amount to merely leaving him alone. Oh how I hoped the flowers would bring hummingbirds to us. To him. How it seemed that he needed it.

CHAPTER 16

LINCOLN'S SPARROW; AMERICAN CROWS

(Jon retreats; I am all in)

2017–May 2018

[The Lincon's sparrow] usually migrates alone. . . .
It's very secretive in nature, to the extent that much of
its biology remains poorly documented.
—*Park Bugle*, "A Look at the Lincoln's Sparrow"

In all seasons, crows hang out with their family. . . .
[They] 'never do anything quietly. . . .'
—Oakland Natural Areas, "The case for crows:
bright, sociable homebodies"

In addition to the usual press of working in the high stress field of commercial architecture ("Imagine, Cara, that your job is getting yelled at by developers, engineers, and site managers always on a deadline, wanting everything yesterday and for a lower cost"), Jon was offered an opportunity to work toward taking over the firm when his boss retired. The industry never seemed like a good fit for him. He hated the grind, the constant output, the mentality of profit above all else. But he did love the problem-solving of building design and losing himself in the AutoCad zone, having taught himself how to use the software after having taught himself how to design buildings by actually building them as a construction worker after one semester of college. He didn't have a degree or an architect's license. He was an autodidact, and that had gotten him through.

Initially, he was excited about the possibility. Or if not excited, he was visibly pleased with the vote of confidence from the owner of the company. "An atta boy goes a long way," Jon always said. But to take over the business he would need his license, something he occasionally said he might feel more legitimate having, though he hadn't ever been particularly interested in doing anything about it. Now that seemed to be changing.

"I've got enough on-the-job experience to replace the need for a degree," he told me after work on the day he received his boss's offer. "I'll still have to take the exam, of course."

"I have *no doubt* you can pass that, my love. Zero." It was true. What wasn't true, or what I wasn't as sure about was if taking over the business was actually something he wanted. But I didn't want to taint the moment or to question his burgeoning desire to go for it. I'd been eager for him to be more involved in life, and now here life had presented him with an invitation to step up that he seemed buoyed by.

"Let me know if there's any way I can support you. I can be a study buddy if you want. Are there flash cards or something? I could quiz you."

He laughed. "Not sure that's a great idea."

"You're probably right."

"But thank you. Your support means a lot."

And that, in turn, was a lot coming from him to me, considering the impasses we'd been facing.

"You got it."

Then my job, as always, was to stay out of it, which I managed to do, or mostly (as always). This involved letting him be the one to bring up how his studying was going, though I did figure out on occasion how to broach the subject without it triggering the ocean pounding at the rocky coast dynamic between us. It's possible that was because I'd learned to ask without any agenda other than caring for him. And he did seem less defensive, probably due to discovering that he already knew most of what he'd be tested on. He passed all six parts of the exam easily. We celebrated every time he came home with the news. The best part of the whole thing was seeing him have a bit of pride in himself well up.

He was not, however, eager to complete the paperwork requirements to receive his architect's license. This involved going back through his decades-long career and documenting all the hours on the job in each specified category that completing a degree program would have covered. He was actively not eager, actually. Sometimes he was downright resentful. He didn't begrudge anyone their degree, but he was tired of getting paid less to do the same job when he was often so much better at it than they were. Not that he ever said that directly, but he did complain every now and then. "So many people with a degree couldn't draft their way out of a paper bag," he'd say. "They learn the software and stop there. They have no visceral experience of spatial relations. The computer is only part of the job. They forget that the actual building is the goal."

Another one of his favorite lines about the industry: "The code was written in blood." This meant that if there was a regulation in the building code, it was typically because someone had died as a result of cutting corners on a job. A floor collapsed. A fire broke out. Jon worked in high stakes situations where a mistake of his could not only cost millions of dollars but actual lives were on the line. He was all too often in a position of defending himself with aggressive clients who were angry about having to meet code. These were the same type of greedy bastards I often protested. Jon was his own quiet revolution, internally, trying to exist in a system that seemed intent on crushing gentleness, nuance, intellect, curiosity—qualities that were the very essence of him, crankiness and stubbornness notwithstanding. Again, I wondered if taking over the company would ultimately suit him, but I was concerned it might come off as doubting that he could do it if I asked him if he wanted to, so mostly I said nothing.

But now there was another reason for Jon to spend extra hours at the office evenings and weekends while still juggling all the other jobs he stayed late to work on so he wouldn't get yelled at. I did not want to add to his stress, so I reminded myself often that these added tasks had an end in sight even if I didn't know exactly when that would be. It did seem to be dragging on, though. He seemed to be dragging. He was tired all the time.

Date nights remained nonnegotiable, but the weekends were otherwise often consumed by his sleeping late—sometimes til 2 PM—and then heading in to the office for a few hours before it was time for dinner, then home to watch a bit of something together before going back to bed. Our Sunday check-ins were getting less frequent, and I, to his chagrin, eventually started doing some of the lawn mowing. Partly I thought it would help take pressure off. More than that, I was getting tired of waiting for him. Not just to do the mowing, but to—what? Delegate? Advocate? Finish those goddamn papers or admit to himself he didn't really want to run a company after all?

One night he came in from work looking particularly slumpy.

"What's up? You look upset."

"The guy I get together with for bookwork? He said he didn't want to meet with me anymore."

Secretly, I was pleased. Not that Jon was upset, but that maybe he'd replace that with an actual meeting where he could connect with more people in recovery than just one dude with a heightened amygdala ruling his politics.

"You have been saying how frustrating it was becoming to try to talk with him."

"That's kind of what's upsetting about it. I really hung in there with him, tried to make common cause. And he just dumps it. Dumped me."

He looked hurt.

"Oh, honey. I'm so sorry."

I didn't want him to take this personally, not for a second. I felt extra protective of him hearing this. His spirit had already been flagging lately.

"Is there anything you need from me?" I asked. "Any support you'd like?"

"Thanks, but no. I'll work it out."

With that, the door closed. It was fine, even good for him, for anyone for that matter, to want to work through an issue in their own way. I was afraid that this meant he would just hang onto it by himself. I hoped he was talking about it all in therapy, but asking about what someone worked on with their counselor? Not a good look. I let it go.

More and more Jon seemed to be carrying not only upset but anger. He'd always been particularly peeved by aggressive drivers—he disliked incivility of all kinds—but now he was saying things like, "I'm tired of there being no consequences" or "They shouldn't be allowed to get away with it." It was worrisome. I asked him about it.

"I've stopped giving way when they ride my ass," he explained. "Sometimes I even box them in."

"Jon. Please don't. Road incidents can get out of hand quickly. I don't want you to get hurt."

"Fuck them."

"Just please, *please*, be careful."

"I will," he said unconvincingly.

One thing he did do for himself was to follow through on conversations with his primary care doctor by undergoing an overnight sleep study. For as much as he slept, he said he never felt rested. Sure enough, he had sleep apnea, which meant he'd need to use a CPAP machine at night. He was worried I'd be put off by the mask he had to wear that forced air down his throat, but then I reminded him about the mouthguard I needed because of grinding my teeth in my sleep. *We'll be our own version of special,* I told him.

The mask looked uncomfortable, and Jon definitely wasn't happy about having to wear it. The whole system seemed like a complicated contraption that required dedication to pull off night after night.

But the diagnosis was validating, he said, and when he heard from others that they'd experienced miracles as a result of using it, he was initially encouraged. Unfortunately, he did not experience the kind of immediate relief that the people he'd spoken with had described.

"Maybe not everyone responds as quickly?" I offered one night when he was particularly disheartened.

"Yeah, maybe."

He was discouraged, but he kept at it. Kept going into the office, dragging his bag of meds around with him, filling the bird feeders, living for his reading or crossword time. He'd lie on the floor of our bedroom with a stack of crossword puzzles in front of him and Titi nuzzled up against his side. A man and his cat, two peas in a pod. Long-haired Titi, fluffy as a feather duster and equally as airy, as ungraspable. Titi had always been hard to figure out how to connect with, how to pet. He had to be scruffed at the cheeks from the side, never head on, and was impressively sneaky when trying to track him down or pick him up. He'd circle around and around, seemingly wanting to receive affection, but then be unable to stand still for it. It had always been part of his charm, but lately even he seemed to be less himself. Less interested in nudging in for attention. At first I wondered if he was picking up on Jon's mood, but when he stopped finishing his meals I brought it up with Jon that I thought something was off with him. Jon agreed. I got a vet appointment for the following day.

So began the familiar journey of caring for a beloved creature with a serious health issue. Titi, the vet said, had kidney disease.

"It's not uncommon in older male cats," the vet told me. "It's not curable; in fact it's progressive, but you can still support quality of life."

The vet explained that we would need to switch his food to a kidney-care diet and regularly flush his system by administering subcutaneous fluids—something they were doing with him at that very moment while the vet broke the news to me in the exam room. I could hear all the dogs and cats protesting their various forms of treatment beyond the door to the mysterious back of house. I looked to the door. As if on cue, it opened, and Titi was whisked in to me, wrapped in a towel. He had a shaved patch of skin exposed from where they'd drawn blood, but otherwise he seemed to have perked up substantially.

"The fluids will help him to feel so much better," the vet continued. "We can teach you how to do them."

My face must have registered squeamishness at the idea of having to do the needles because the vet continued.

"There is another option. I'm not saying this is what you should do, but some people do choose to put the pet down on diagnosis."

I was not having that, not one bit, unless, of course, Titi was suffering and it was time. But having been present to the end of life for two beings, I felt certain Titi was nowhere near done yet. The vet validated that immediately.

"You're absolutely right. With help, Titi can still live a good life, for a time. And I think you'll find that you'll get used to giving him his fluids. He was very cooperative, in fact."

That I believed. Thank god we didn't have to do this with Ed. Trying to get a needle in between that killer's shoulder blades and hold him still while the fluid dripped into his system would have required sedatives for Ed and full rubber bodysuits for Jon and me.

I got Titi home, and he popped right out of the carrying case, circled around and around, and was generally his fluffy self. I phoned

Jon to fill him in on what I'd found out. We'd give him fluids every few days and monitor him to see if that was doing the trick. If not, we could increase the frequency. We were back on duty, Drs. Benson and Lathrop, this time tasked with disseminating saline solution from vet-hospital-issued IV bags and creating a protocol for dispensing the used sharps, in addition to administering meds for appetite stimulation or nausea suppression as needed.

Initially, Jon and I bonded over Titi's care and over our love for him—his absolute vulnerability, his unquestionable desire to live, his pure joy in being with us, or so it seemed. How could we not be moved? How could we not want to help? To be in this life with another life who so clearly needed and wanted us? We rallied together as partners in the cause.

We rigged up a system with a hanger hooked onto one of the kitchen cabinets to hang the fluid bag that I would titrate while Jon handled Titi, tenting the skin between his shoulder blades where the needle slid in. Usually I was the one to give Titi his meds, that happening during the day while Jon was at the office, and I kept records of it all on sheets of paper I stored with all the supplies. The vet was right: We got proficient with Titi's care fairly quickly.

But it wasn't long before it began to hang over us and shadow the days we needed to give him his fluids. At the end of usually very long days for Jon, he would sigh deeply, then say, "Well, let's do it. Let's do the Q." While Titi was cooperative once we got him up on the counter for the treatment, he got smart to the drill fairly quickly and was remarkably elusive when it came time to scoop him up to get him there. Jon and I took turns tracking him down and bringing him to the kitchen. Nobody liked this part of the night, but the alternative didn't seem called for yet. Titi was still quite happy otherwise, mostly, though the every-few-days fluids went to every other day. The meds increased in frequency, too.

When he started having stretches of down days, Jon and I would wonder if this was it, but then suddenly he'd be fluffed out, what we called his livelier state, and the course we were on made sense again, even as it was hugely emotionally taxing. Jon, in particular, seemed to wear it heavily, not that I wasn't emotional about it all, because I absolutely wore that on the surface. Jon took it in, and in turn it seemed to take him down, but then he was still grinding at work, still up against it with getting the paperwork filled out for his license, still avoiding the gym and meetings, still *what*, I couldn't specifically understand, but best I could figure out to describe how I was experiencing him was that he seemed to be struggling in general. His gait was heavier. He rarely smiled. His shiny cheeks were dull. His overall physiognomy, dejected. Was it a gestalt effect of all the pressures? Was there something else underlying it all?

"I'm working something out, Bense," he'd say when I couldn't bear not speaking to what seemed to be so obvious and asked how he was doing or if I could be of support. In other words, he was saying, leave him alone.

I was heartbroken at being pushed out, and beyond frustrated. I felt for him, deeply, but also, *Goddamn it, Jon,* I wanted to shout at him. *Let me the fuck in. Or someone.* Life at Best had become really bleak. I was getting increasingly worried for him. How long could he go on this way? How long could we? And then I began questioning: How long could I? I couldn't imagine not being with Jon, but some days I wasn't sure if I could be satisfied in our relationship if he didn't start taking better care of himself, if he didn't step up again as I'd needed him to when we were first dating.

This was twelve years later, though. And I'd spent so much of my life teetering on the fence in relationships, always wondering if I was making the right choice, possibly even using the fact that I'd picked someone who wasn't up to it, who wasn't in my best interests, or was even downright dangerous as an excuse for why the relationship didn't work or last. Tony absolutely, and likely Frank—along with the many, many others both remembered and long forgotten—were men I chose because it would be foolish to commit to them.

None of this was that simple, nor was it new information. I'd been over it again and again in my mind, in therapy, in recovery work, at meetings and on the phone, and during long walks talking with the universe, but then there was something undeniably familiar in all of these situations. This time with Jon, though, it was different, wasn't it? We had progressed so far beyond anything I'd experienced with anyone else. The theory was that as I was growing in my recovery and healing, I'd become more available and willing to be in a relationship, and our twelve years together bore that out. My soul work, as I began thinking of it, was to stay with him. And if that was the case, something finally clicked in me, then I needed to accept him exactly as he was and to accept that he might never change. Some people in the rooms call this surrendering—emotionally, spiritually, mentally, even physically. It's a letting go of trying to control a situation or person through sheer force of will or by mentally obsessing on the issue. In a way, it was about being unconditionally in.

"I am fully committed," I told Jon one night while doing the Q. I was standing at the IV bag with my hand on the valve, ready to switch it off once the level hit the target amount. We'd been talking about Titi and what was clearly becoming his end-of-life care, but I was opening it up to include us. I wasn't telling him anything new, per se, but the tenor of it, or the energy, if you will, reflected my recent shift. I was done trying to get him to do anything differently.

Jon was focused on holding the needle he'd slid under Titi's skin, so he didn't look up. I don't know how I knew because he didn't respond verbally, but I was certain he got what I meant. I loved him and would be with him *as is*, until death do us part.

CHAPTER 17

SCARLET TANAGER

(The date night that wasn't)

May 25, 2018

Male Scarlet tanagers are among the most blindingly gorgeous birds in an eastern forest in summer. They're also one of the most frustratingly hard to find as they stay high in the forest canopy. . . .

—Cornell Lab of Ornithology, All About Birds, "Scarlet Tanager"

"TITI'S UP ON THE BED WITH ME!" I yelled down to Jon. I was still upstairs, the sun pouring in through the skylights and windows, and Titi had jumped up on the bed. That he'd done that was a huge win given how he'd hidden away from us for most of the previous days and we thought we were facing the end. But here he was, tromping over the ruffled covers to get to me, purring and nudging for attention. It felt like cause for celebration.

Jon was fussing around downstairs in his weekday morning routine before heading out. I could hear that he was saying something in response, but he wasn't lifting his voice enough for me to decipher the words. I couldn't understand why he wasn't more excited. It was a Friday morning, the sun was filling the house, and Titi was up on the bed with me. I called out again.

"No, really! He's purring and everything!"

Whatever he said back was still somehow muffled, if not the volume this time, the words themselves. I couldn't figure out what he was trying to communicate. I tried again.

"Titi is our miracle kitty! And tonight is date night! Hooray!"

Jon came up a few steps and stuck his hand through the spindles of the railing to gesture for Titi to come over to him, which he promptly did. While Jon scratched behind his cat's ears, he finally acknowledged the fact that it was Friday.

"Better than that," I said, "it's Friday of a three-day weekend!" I was clearly happy about what this new day was bringing. We even had plans for that Monday to go to dinner with another couple and then to a meeting in my sobriety hometown of Saratoga, where I'd get a coin for being twenty-four years sober.

"That's true," he said. "It is." He kept his hand through the railing while Titi circled around and back to him in his ritual of getting petted. "Well, I gotta get going."

"See you tonight!" I shouted after him as he headed down the stairs. I wasn't sure if he said anything back, but I heard the door close, and off for the day Jon went. I was disappointed he wasn't more encouraged by it all. It'd been *so* heavy lately. Titi jumped back up on the bed, still purring, and pulled me right out of worrying. Jon would come around once the workday was over. Of course he would. This was irrefutably good news.

I nuzzled Titi a bit longer, then got out of bed to start my favorite time of day—coffee and spirit cards and scribbling away in my journal under my happy lights in the kitchen. Titi followed me downstairs and went straight to his food dish. Another good sign! He was hungry. I opened one of the gazillion different types of food we'd been switching between to entice him to eat, and he dug right in. I stood looking at him in amazement, watching him take in the sustenance.

After finishing, he stretched into one of those full cat stretches and began grooming himself in a rectangle of sun slanting across the kitchen floor. As I shuffled around making my coffee, he finished his post-meal routine and then sauntered over to the stairs to head up for his morning nap. I got my precious mug of dark roast and took to my spot in the corner of the kitchen to begin my own morning ritual. As I was about to start writing, I heard the front door open in the living room, and in came Jon walking through the kitchen. He was already talking, entering the house mid-sentence, smiling, and going on about a call he'd just had with his oldest son. This was *most* unusual.

"Hey there, what's up?" I tried to be casual—I was instinctively reluctant to press him at this point—but clearly something was off for him to be home at this time. Something had been off for a while, and him coming home midmorning felt like confirmation. I almost said, *Now you've got to tell me what's going on,* but didn't.

"Nothing. I just forgot to do something." He was smiling and kept moving through the house to his office.

"Anything I could have helped with? Or could now?"

"Nah, I've got it covered."

I heard him shuffle some things around in his office. Then he started up the stream again about the phone call and how his son had the weekend off from work, and I'm not really sure what else Jon was saying, but it was befuddling. He was smiling. He was talking. It didn't make sense. What was he saying? He kept on and on, almost as if he didn't want to give me any room to enter the conversation. As he was going on about his son and hugs and petting Titi, he walked up the stairs, and I heard Titi jump down off the bed, and I imagined he walked over to Jon as he'd done earlier that morning to meet his person's arm stuck through the railing to pet him. Jon stopped talking briefly.

I was on pause, waiting for Jon to come back through the kitchen, when I might get another shot at finding out what was going on. After about a minute he started up again about his son and hugs and walked over to me to give me one while I was sitting at my happy spot. He leaned in and I opened, angling upward to receive his embrace. Then he was off, back through the living room and out the front door. I remained seated, facing my waiting journal and mug of coffee. On the surface it seemed understandable, I told myself. He forgot to take care of a task in his workday and returned home to see to it. What was so weird about that?

Titi thumped down the stairs—he had a remarkably heavy footfall for such a feather duster of a cat—and padded over to join me on the bench. That's right. It's sunny. The day is good. Titi is on an upswing, and tonight is date night. I'll talk with Jon at dinner. I began my morning finally. I had writing to do and e-mails to send and then would hit the gym later in the day before my recovery meeting. My usual Friday before Jon and I would text to connect for dinner and make a choice on a movie. I was twenty-four years sober and living in a home with a man I loved. Our cat was on an upswing. I was committed. I would see Jon that evening.

My day was unremarkable. The usual writing time balanced with e-mail time and proposals and searches and hustling for opportunities to keep the income coming in and the words going out. Titi remained buoyant throughout the day. The sun filled the house. Spring, the season of expansion and blooms, was fully underway, and for the first time in far too long I felt a sense of possibility that whatever had been so incredibly hard had taken its foot off our necks. I dressed for the gym.

The YMCA was a short drive from Best and my Friday night meeting was just a few minutes farther, so I had a habit of working out at the gym, then sitting through the meeting in sweaty duds before heading back to the house to wash up and change while texting with Jon to nail down the location and time. As the weather was getting warmer and the light of day stretched out longer, some of us would stand outside the building chatting after the meeting. This night I was particularly eager to get my evening going with my beloved, so after helping to put the materials away, I beelined for my car and phone to see if Jon had started the thread for our picks. He hadn't. I lobbed the first one out.

Hey there! It's Friday!

I drove to the house while keeping an eye on my phone for his response. We typically met for dinner around 8, sometimes 8:15 if it was a later show. My meeting ended at 7, so my job was to be quick about cleaning up so I could get to the restaurant, which was usually across the river to be close to the movie theater in the capital city. I got to the house and still no text back yet from Jon. We didn't always respond to each other immediately. In fact, this had been an occasion for me to panic a few times over the years when I didn't hear from him as expected. I'm not sure why that was a trigger for me, but once the switch flipped, which wasn't always the case, I was fully under siege and would text repeatedly until I heard back, which I always did.

He'd be apologetic. Phone in his car. Phone on silent. Something easy to understand. I was the one, truth be told, who was more apt to disregard the thing completely. *What's the point of having a phone, Cara, if you're not going to check it?* It was hard to argue with, though that didn't necessarily change my attention to my phone. But not on date night. If nothing else, we'd have the restaurant picked by 7:30 so we both had time to get to it and then could decide on the movie over dinner.

I brought my phone upstairs with me while picking out pants and a shirt. My first text had been at 7:19, and now it was nearing 7:45 with no word back yet. Come on, Jon. I started reminding myself of all the times I worried when he'd not responded yet but he always showed up sooner or later. Once I was fully dressed and still no text, I tried again.

Where you at?

7:56 PM

And again.

I'm getting worried please respond.

7:58 PM

Then:

What is going on?!?!?!

8:04 PM

This was definite cause for alarm. Not hearing by 8:04 on date night? Not in all our years of Fridays. I called his mobile, and it went to voicemail.

"Hey there, what's going on? Where are you? Is everything okay? Just call me as soon as you get this."

I tried him on his office number and left a message there, too. But maybe I should try the general line? I fired up my computer because we didn't have enough coverage at the house for my cell phone to load webpages and got the numbers off the company site. I tried his boss's extension first and then the general office message box, even though I assumed everyone else would have already been long gone for the weekend. Jon was typically the only one who stayed that late or worked on the weekends. I couldn't track anyone down. I went back to trying his mobile and again his extension at the office. Maybe he'd been in his car when his phone was in the office? Maybe he'd been in the office with his phone in the car? Where else could I call? Who could I talk to? Who'd seen him last? Had to be his boss. Surely he'd have more information. Something to explain it all. He'd sent Jon up north to look at a job where there was no cell service. Or the two of them were having a heart-to-heart about Jon taking over the business and didn't want to be disturbed.

After trying his extension at the office one more time and getting voicemail, I searched the boss's full name on the Internet, trying for a cell or home number. Through the babble, I was able to decipher his home number. A miracle, it felt like. His wife answered. Another miracle, someone was home.

I explained who I was, we had only ever met briefly in all the years. "Sorry to bother you at home. I'm looking for Jon. Did he happen to . . ."

"Funny thing. He never showed today. He didn't even call."

The blood drained from my face and rushed to the rest of my body as fuel for action.

"I have to go."

She continued on. I couldn't understand what she was saying. Why was she still talking when something was so clearly and extraordinarily off? When had I ever called them at home? When in the twenty-plus years he'd worked for them had Jon been a no-show? She kept talking. Phrases like "unlike him" were penetrating the flood of adrenaline my body was generating. I couldn't fathom how it was that she was so thoroughly impervious to the import of the moment, but more than that, I couldn't understand why was I allowing her to prattle on.

"I need to call the police," I cut in and hung up, then did as I said and dialed 911.

"My partner didn't show to date night. He didn't show to work. He's a no-show, no-call. This is completely and utterly unlike him. Something is wrong."

The dispatcher took my information and said she'd send an officer out to me. Why a car was coming to the house where Jon wasn't made no sense. Nothing made sense. We hung up, and I went downstairs to wait and pace. I called Michele out in Buffalo and left a panicked voicemail. I called our sponsor couple's landline. Another stuttering stumbling message. Finally I reached Dawn of the couple that Jon and I had plans with that Monday. "Jon never showed. Didn't call. The cops are on the way. Can you come over?" She said she would.

I watched the black-and-white car roll to a slow in front of our house, then pull into the driveway. I met the officer at the door and let him in. When I was supposed to have been sitting across from my beloved at a restaurant sneaking sips of his soda, I was instead standing with this tall stranger in an oversized vest with a gun strapped to his hip in the very room where Jon had closed the door behind himself only hours ago. This, our intimate domestic space where the night before we'd watched a movie together and our coats and shoes commingled near the door. The officer was intently focused on my face, on what he needed me to tell him and in what order, methodically drawing from me the story. Jon and I had plans for that night. I texted him as usual, and quite unusually, he never texted back. No, he would not be at a bar, tipsy and ignoring my calls. I didn't know where he was or what happened, but happy hour wasn't it.

The officer calmly ran through other options that were not options. No, Jon would not have forgotten. We hadn't fought. He'd hugged me that morning. He was smiling. The sun was expanding our home as if the house was filling its lungs with light. I sat up straight when he approached me to say goodbye.

I showed the officer my happy corner where the hug happened. The purple and green lights strung like a chandelier above my daily altar. My journal on the bench. The candle. The spirit cards for the day. I did not specifically point these out. They were simply there to be seen. The officer's radio interrupted. He twisted the volume down but not off.

Why was he here and not "out there" looking? Why were they not blanketing the streets with patrol cars? The officer I came to know as Officer Hotaling remained calm. He needed more information. Had anything unusual occurred that morning? I told him about Jon coming back.

"What did he do or say?"

"That he'd forgotten to take care of something. I don't know what it was." I don't know why, but I was reluctant to tell him that Jon didn't let me in anymore. That it was my job to let him work out whatever he was going through, which only underscored that he was, in fact, going through something.

Hotaling continued his questions. Where did Jon go in the house? How long was he here? Was I home all day? I told him about hearing Jon shuffle some things around in his office. Hotaling asked to be shown where that was. He remained calm. I was nervous. Embarrassed. Exposed. My private life. Our personal relationship. Jon's messy office. Our open floor plan home with the dining room that we never once dined in but housed books and the huge plant Jon called Seymour and the standing hand drum Jon had started to learn to play but didn't always follow through on. We walked through this spacious room into Jon's office. There were stacks of CDs everywhere. Books. Papers. Banker boxes stuffed full of years' worth of unopened bills, receipts, and all manner of correspondence, personal and professional. This office that he called "a comment-free zone." Meaning I was not allowed to comment on how he kept it.

There, amid all the CDs waiting to be reshelved and notes of ideas for stories and projects, in front of his antiquated home computer that he used to write and to play games was a stash of cash under three CDs. I felt a sting in my face seeing the stack of bills. Was this typical, this amount of cash on hand at the house? No, officer. It was not.

Hotaling asked if those discs meant anything in particular. I looked at them. Jesus, Jon had a thousand CDs, including some of the most esoteric shit out there from the sounds of whales humping, as a former roommate of his had put it, to cloying Finnish lounge muzak, as I put it. How the hell was I supposed to glean any information from these discs out of all the others? Hotaling asked me to listen to them when I got a chance. I said I would. What I would be listening for, I didn't really know, but that was the first moment the word "clue" entered my mind.

We continued walking through the house. It felt ominous. Was Jon somehow lurking in the shadows here? And if so, who was this Jon who didn't show, didn't call, and was possibly hiding in the guest room or basement? I felt I didn't know him, this Jon. I both wanted him to be there and was afraid to find him. Hotaling and I walked up the twisty back stairwell off Jon's office to the landing between a tiny guest room and my office, which led to our bedroom. Nothing to be seen there, but on the dresser in our bedroom was a little cut-out word from a magazine that I'd left out as an evergreen note to god simply stating "help."

"Ah, that's mine, actually," I said defensively when Hotaling caught sight of the word.

Who were these people who needed help? Who were on psychiatric medications? Who needed recovery meetings and prayed to be saved from themselves on a daily basis? Our lives viewed through a police officer's eyes looking for what was off. What was a tell. Where everything went wrong. How to say that we'd become functional stable citizens, but would, yes, always be vulnerable. Weren't we all, though? Wasn't this cop with his vest and gun protecting his own precarity?

The officer took me at my word and didn't question it further. We went downstairs and outside to go through the Bilco doors down into the dirt-floor, centuries-old stone foundation basement full of cobwebs and ancient furnace, deteriorating boxes of Jon's work life, black walnut shells scattered by critters who lived with us more to Jon's annoyance than mine. Jon, the would-be licensed architect who knew what damage rodents could havoc on a structure, set traps and banged on the walls. I, who wanted to avoid killing at all costs, let him do the dirty work even if I wasn't happy about it. Our ongoing push-pull. Balancing each other out. "Brutish and short," Jon had said when I first objected, repurposing the infamous line about the nature of life. "Oh, fuck Hobbes," I'd said about its author. We'd laughed. Now nothing in the basement but waiting traps, echoes, and no Jon.

We climbed the crooked steps back up into the light. Hotaling ducked his head while I babbled nervously about hiking. We walked around the outside of the house to the mudroom in back. Officer Hotaling was impressed with my hikes, possibly allowing me the tether to normalcy my comments gave me. The carabiners, ropes, and all manner of accoutrements from our early excursions were dangling on hooks in the unfinished mudroom with its walls of roughly hewn wood and insulation turned into loose stuffing the red squirrels used for nesting. Jon's backpack was filled with another cache of black walnuts. These remnants of our former adventures. On the way into the house I noticed that our ladder was missing from its hook. I did not mention it to Hotaling. Jon could have brought it with him to visit a job site, after all.

"What does your gut tell you?" Hotaling asked when we were back where we'd started in the living room.

I blurted out that I was afraid he was in a ditch somewhere having been run off the road in a rage incident. I told Hotaling that Jon had been taking on aggressive drivers of late, and then I unleashed a battery of questions. Would they put out an APB? Is that what they even call it? Where would they search? How far a net would be cast? And with all due respect, officer, but for the love of god, why are you still in my living room when Jon was out there somewhere?!

He brought the focus back to what I could do. My job was to reach out to Jon's parents, friends, and kids. To get word out any way I could. Social media. Phone calls. Texts. E-mails. Direct messages. And they would do the same through their networks. I was to stay here in case he returned, to let them do the searching. Before Hotaling left, Dawn arrived. She recognized him from his assistance with a situation at the YMCA, where she worked. They had a pleasant exchange. Background chatter. Hotaling gave me his card. He would be in touch, and if I thought of anything, anything at all that seemed like it might be helpful, to give him a call. He was working the overnight.

I messaged Jon's children. They reached out to his parents. His parents to his brothers. Text chains started. Questions upon questions. I repeated what I knew. Last I saw him was that morning. He left for work as usual. Then, unusually, he came home an hour later. It finally dawned on me that it was to leave the cash. My brain was slow. My body was running high and fast. Jon came home, then was off again. Over and over. That's all I know. My phone was blowing up, and none of the messages were from Jon. I checked it like a nervous tic.

As advised, I uploaded a photo to social media. I grabbed the first picture that had a full frontal showing of him from a decade-plus of JPEGs. I didn't mean to include myself, but there I was. We were smiling, with our arms around each other and the ocean in our eyes on one of our trips to the island off the coast of Maine, the warm hues of the sun and the glowing blues and greens of the ocean as background. Our shiny, pink cheeks. A luminescent glimpse of two lovers on holiday doing the work to grab attention on the overloaded Internet with words like *love of my life* and *missing*.

I filled in some details. Last seen. He was wearing loose-fitting jeans, a handkerchief hanging out of the back pocket. I couldn't remember his license plate, he'd only recently received a new one. The old one I could spot in a crowd, that lift of recognition, but I was dumbfounded trying to locate in my mind the current number. I was embarrassed when Hotaling had asked for it and I couldn't bring it up. What kind of partner doesn't know the license plate of her missing lover? I gave him the make and model. The color. He'd said not to worry, they could access it through the database. I described the most likely routes between his office and home. His usual rounds.

The alerts were in the works when I asked Dawn to help me with Titi's fluids. She took my role titrating the amount of liquid flowing from the bag as I grabbed a handful of Titi's flesh at his shoulder blades and slid the needle under his skin. Beautiful, fluffy Titi. On the counter in the usual routine in this most unusual night. That finished, Dawn and I sat on the couch. I texted Jon again.

We got Titi his fluids! Now we're just here waiting for you to come home.

11pm

Dawn showed me how to make an animated avatar of myself. The one and only gesture I designed for her, this digital me, was her wrapping her arms around herself as red hearts bubbled up to the top of the screen. We were playing with it past midnight. Anything to keep me occupied for even a minute, thirty seconds, an inhale and exhale. I was desperate for distraction. She said she would stay the night. We talked on the couch, running through options, running through possibilities. She mentioned that she had friends who were connected into other realms through the veil between the material and the spirit. Did I want her to reach out to them for insight? I did. Was this an act of desperation, this willingness to believe in the beyond? Hadn't that always been the case, my reaching for something greater than myself to save my ass, my soul, my sanity? Did that make it any less real?

I paced around the living room while Dawn texted her people. Then I went into the dining room of windows and skylights and books and plants, with wide-plank floors and exposed historical beams—a space we didn't ever dine in, not once, but whose tones, air, and light filled our home. I beat on Jon's drum. *Jon. Where. Are. You. Please. Come. Back. Come Back. Please.* At last I heard Dawn talking on the phone, a call must have come in. I raced back into the living room to listen to one side of the conversation. Someone had images of Jon walking through the woods, searching. Flashes of repeated apologies. I'm sorry. I'm sorry. I'm sorry.

Are you kidding me? He's in the woods? All these years I've been begging him to get back out there with me? Suddenly I was furious. *Fuck you, Jon. Fuck you for taking off.* And a new narrative of what might be happening started to form. Jon himself had said, *Fuck it. Fuck it all. Fuck architecture. Fuck the license. Fuck taking over the business. Fuck Cara and her demands. Fuck dealing with Titi's kidneys.* He was off in the woods somewhere or had indeed picked up some substance or other and was holed up in a motel room, blowing off steam.

I got bedding for Dawn to sleep on the couch and went upstairs to try to sleep myself. Before that, I called Hotaling at the station to scour the details. To run it over and over again outside my own head. Plus I wanted to keep them invested, afraid they'd forget about me and my lost beloved, that we would fade into the chatter of the next crisis. I sat in my office in the dark at nearly two in the morning on the phone with Hotaling. Never called, never showed—I couldn't comprehend it. God bless him, Hotaling never tired of letting me puzzle it around and around, injecting himself at various moments or seizing on a slightly different twist in my language, always with the purpose of the ultimate goal of finding Jon.

Finally, I exhausted myself. Hotaling explained who would be on tomorrow and what would likely happen then.

"When are you in next?" I asked. I needed him, this first person on the scene, whom I'd imprinted on like a baby duckling.

"Tomorrow afternoon, back on the overnight. But they'll be on it all day tomorrow. Try to get some rest."

I thanked him and hung up. I was left with myself and my terrible thoughts. Then Titi came thumping into the office. Beautiful, still alive, fluffy Titi. He followed me into the bedroom and up onto the bed. I took a picture of the two of us and texted it to Jon.

We're going to sleep now but please come home.

2:01 am

I put my phone down and turned off the bedside light. I closed my eyes, then immediately opened them. I checked my phone. No response.

Please take good care of yourself. You mean the world to me.

2:04 am

We can't wait for you to join us.

2:19 am

CHAPTER 18

TRUMPETER SWANS

(Replaying in my mind, on repeat)

The week before

Trumpeter Swans form very strong pair bonds with their mate. The pair will remain together under most circumstances. . . .

—The Trumpeter Swan Society, FAQs, "Do Trumpeter Swans mate for life?"

Date night the week before the date night that wasn't was a special one. Jon, often on the lookout for his favorite musicians to hit the area, had discovered that Vernon Reid was covering Jimi Hendrix in a small venue in Western Massachusetts, a scenic drive from our home at Best. He'd tagged me on social media with a link to the show. *@Cara Benson Will you go to this with me?* I'd responded with multiple exclamation points in the affirmative. Holy shit, would I. My guy had picked something out for us and was himself excited for it. That in itself was a win. I'd have gone to a full night of nothing but nails on a chalkboard balanced on a humping whale's back to see Jon enjoy himself after how heavily he'd been wearing things lately.

One of his continuing disappointments was that sleeping with the cumbersome CPAP machine every night hadn't produced the results he was hoping for, though he did think he was losing weight and possibly picking up in his energy. Earlier in the week of the special date night, we were standing with another couple after a meeting when Jon surprised me by asking us all if we could tell that he had lost weight. I didn't see it, but the others could. I wanted to see it and felt badly about letting him down with my answer. We all reasoned that it's harder to notice a change in someone you see every day. Still, Jon seemed let down. It was an iconically pleasant spring evening, and we were standing with this couple we knew well in the parking lot outside the church where the meeting had taken place. I was grateful Jon was talking about something personal so openly with these other people who loved him. Who loved us. And we them. I wanted so much for their care to penetrate his heart. The bushes were flowering all around us, and someone noticed a bunny, then another, grooming themselves under the bushes at the edge of the lot. What else to call it but that we were witnesses to something important—even if we didn't fully know to what.

That Friday was the night of the special date. I went back home after the gym so we could give Titi his fluids before heading out for the evening. When I pulled into the driveway, I was astonished to find Jon was already home and out back mowing the lawn. I didn't want to make a big deal out of it, but maybe his energy was improving. For him to proactively try to get some lawn mowing in on a Friday evening and not drag it out as long as possible over multiple weekends was indeed out of the ordinary. I waved to him on my way into the house to wash up and change. Jon came in not long after to do the same.

On the ride out through the Berkshire Mountains, winding and curving up over ridges and down through valleys, we said little. There was a weight to the silence I couldn't understand. On one dramatic hairpin turn up a hill, a restaurant was perched that boasted a view. We'd driven past it on previous road trips without stopping as it looked like an obvious tourist spot, but it was early in the season yet, so we pulled in on a whim.

No one was at the host stand when we first walked in, so we stood outside waiting with a few other would-be customers who informed us they'd eventually been told by a staff member that they weren't seating for another ten minutes. The place seemed barren and the faux paneling in the bar area should have tipped us off, but we were called in before too long and got seated on the patio, overlooking the valley and across to another hump of mountains north of us. Again, we sat in silence, mostly, though Jon asked if I had any idea of the elevation of the hills we were looking at. It seemed oddly effortful, our conversation. Words in the air, but not necessarily Jon and Cara words. Not us really talking, but making talk. Not unheard of in a long-term relationship, but not when it felt like there was something under the surface that could be shared between us, or should have been, and wasn't. I didn't know how high the mountains were, I finally said. I guessed maybe between one and two thousand feet. Jon took the opportunity to click into math spatial head and set to figuring it out. It felt like distraction while we waited for someone to bring us menus, to say hello, anything.

Finally an older woman who had the skin pallor of a long-term smoker and the terrified eyes of someone who'd never waited on tables before approached us. She led with this wasn't her usual gig, but the place was short-staffed, and her brother who worked in the kitchen had called her, begging for help. She wasn't quite sure the order in which she should take our order. We offered our drink preferences encouragingly, and she stared blankly for a moment. I suggested she might write that down. When we asked for more information about some gaping holes on the menu, she looked at us as if we should have the answers. We reassured her it was fine not to know and ordered as an act of faith. I again reminded her to write it all down, and she did, then stood a moment longer in silence looking from her pad to us, then walked away without saying anything.

Our drinks and food came out in an unusually creative sequence, all delivered by other staff.

The food was predictably awful, and our waitress never appeared again. We figured she was chain-smoking out back by the dumpster, hiding from customers and management alike. Finally, we paid our check with another server and left.

Back on the road, we agreed that the look on her face when we'd asked what the vegetables were was priceless and made the whole fiasco worth it. Poor thing, but I was so glad we were sharing a laugh. Then we settled in for the rest of the ride, again curving through mountain passes and down through flatlands winding beside rivers. Jon put the radio on to *This American Life.* The episode was stories about death, more specifically about people trying to make sense of secrets around certain deaths. A Facebook page filled with eulogies for a comedian who wound up being alive and posted a month after the comments had poured in. A Navy SEAL who attended a funeral for another SEAL he didn't know anything about on behalf of a friend who couldn't make it. Jon took my hand with his right and steered through the narrow turns with the other. He hadn't done that in ages. I was slightly unnerved by the precarity of the driving, but I held on. The ghost of a Facebook page, suddenly eerily come alive. A Navy SEAL discovering the cause of death of the fallen soldier was suicide.

We arrived at the venue in full dark and parked down the street. On our way in I grabbed some free earplugs to save my battered hearing, and we found a spot to stand not far from the stage. It was a small, casual venue, and we were ten feet from where Vernon Reid would play. I was excited for Jon to see one of his heroes so intimately. They took the stage and launched into "Who Knows." The crowd of maybe fifty started moving and grooving, Jon nodding his head as his most exuberant dance move, me noodling around, and one woman front and center before the band was throwing her body around in a way that could not be ignored. I didn't want to begrudge anyone their pleasure, but I became increasingly distracted by her performance through the night. I did my best to shake it off, but I was up against it, my history as a woman with a body that'd been objectified, judged, abused, assaulted, and savaged was fully triggered.

On the way back to the car I shared with Jon what had come up for me. It had been a long time since I'd felt I could go to him for help with something I was struggling with other than what was coming up for me in our relationship or with Titi's care. I was puzzling it out, uncertain about the permutations of my reaction. Jon jumped in quickly, angry on my behalf. I was surprised at the edge in his response. Mostly we drove home in silence, Jon cycling through various playlists without reaching out for my hand.

The rest of the weekend passed in much the way I'd come to expect. Jon slept late, went into the office, then back home for something to eat and a bit of TV. Come Monday, the routine was the same, save for the sleeping in. Jon dutifully roused himself from slumber and dragged himself into the office to start the workweek all over again, even though he'd worked the past two days when everyone else was off.

Tuesday we had a meeting with our sponsor couple at their house in the early evening. As when we were standing with the couple the previous week, I was glad for others in it with me, with us, with Jon. I'd been feeling alone in trying to get Jon to open up and was grateful for the opportunity to hear what was going on with him. We started the conversation with the Serenity Prayer, then each of us took turns checking in on where we were at emotionally. At some point, the seriousness of recovery—the excruciating slog of facing individual and partnership truths and traumas—cracked open into laughter, and the four of us cackled with relief. Jon, in particular, was hysterical, wiping away tears and gasping for breath. Oh how we needed that. How he did, and how I needed to see it.

After our session with them, Jon and I went for dinner at a favorite Turkish restaurant. As usual, Jon was so damn personable the owner would text him when they made the special Plateau soup that was on the menu but never actually available. Jon was so curious about other cultures, about people, that he was often served all sorts of special dishes that weren't on the menu. We got to the restaurant just before the breaking of the fast for Ramadan. Our waitress, who we were friendly with, assured us it was no problem to be there. Once our food was delivered, the entire staff sat down for their meal. Jon and I were the only two customers in the restaurant, and we felt it was a privilege to be present during this intimate time. They even served us some of the family soup. We whispered occasionally but mostly ate in a reverent silence, smiling at each other over what we felt was our good fortune.

We were done with our meals before they were finished with theirs but didn't want to interrupt, so we waited the twenty minutes or so it took them to finish eating. Once they began clearing up, Jon walked up to the register, and I could hear him telling them not to worry about it, not one bit. It was our pleasure to be in the restaurant that evening. He wouldn't have changed a thing about it. But it was time to get home, we still had Titi's fluids to do, so we thanked them and headed out. It had been a remarkable evening, we agreed on the way to our cars. The relief I felt underscored how tense things had been. *Please, let this be the lifting of our burdens.*

Titi was compliant when we got home that night, but Thursday morning he took a sharp downward turn. His back leg kept giving out as he walked, and he wouldn't take any of his meds or eat any food. Then he crawled into a hiding space and wouldn't come out. I asked Jon if he'd go to the vet with us as we might be facing the end. He said he would. I got the first appointment available for mid-morning. Jon called the office to let them know he wouldn't be in. One of the other guys who worked there answered, and when he offered some sympathy, Jon welled up with tears.

"Thanks, man," Jon said, trying to downplay his emotion.

Their office culture was not what one might call touchy-feely. Quite the opposite. The dude who'd answered was definitely rough around the edges and boasted about getting into fistfights in bars. He'd never been particularly kind to Jon, from what I'd heard over the years, and often was openly hostile. But he'd wished Jon luck, sincerely, and this unexpected kindness seemed to move Jon deeply. My Jon. Of course he would have wanted a better working relationship with the guy but instead was in a position of having to put up with the animosity and friction as best he could. Some days he came home really worn down from having to keep his guard up all day.

We had an hour to wait before the appointment. Jon sat on the couch, hugging Titi to his chest. He looked truly forlorn. In all our years together I'd never seen him that sad. But then, weren't we both? Adorable Titi. Our fluffer. This might be our last morning with him. This might be the end.

Jon drove, and I held the carrying case with Titi in it on my lap, same as we'd done for Ed four years previously. When we got to the vet, I stayed in the car with Titi while Jon went inside to check us in. I was so grateful to have him in it with me. Jon came back out to the car, and we waited for them to come out for us when it was our time. We made guesses, Jon standing outside the car talking to me through the window. We bargained and bartered and reasoned. Maybe he'd need a different med. Maybe the fluid amount should change. Maybe we'd have to let him go.

The vet tech called to us from the door. I took a summoning breath, and Jon offered to carry Titi in the case inside. We were brought into an exam room. Titi was not fussing much in his case. They took him in the back to check his blood levels while Jon and I stared at each other and various posters for flea and tick prevention and photos of other people's pets hanging around the room. Our vet opened the door, and I braced myself. We were clear, Jon and I, that we did not want to keep him around for our own sake. The vet said that Titi's levels were actually stable and that he was able to give Titi an anti-nausea med without issue. He said it was entirely reasonable to increase his fluids for a few days to see how he responded before making a decision. We questioned him, hard. We did not want to cause undue suffering. We did not want to be selfishly keeping him alive. The vet reiterated that word, *reasonable*, and said that seeing if increased fluids would help is what he would do if Titi was his cat.

We left with our plan.

Our mood was somber on the ride back to the house. Neither of us had eaten yet, so I asked if Jon wanted to have a meal together after we tucked Titi in at home. He did, but he had to make some phone calls first. Of course, I said. It was, after all, a workday. Inside I put the case down on the floor and hoped Titi would come out of his own accord. Jon went outside to make his phone calls, I don't know why he did that there, but he was out on the front walk talking about various jobs he was working on. Titi came out of his box. It was a waiting game at this point. Waiting to see if the fluids we could give him that night would make a difference.

After a while, I didn't hear Jon talking anymore. I wondered what he was doing but figured he needed some time before coming back in to make our plan. About twenty minutes later, I heard the door open, and he called in.

"What are you doing? I thought you wanted to go eat."

"I did! I do. I was just waiting for you."

"You were supposed to come out so we could get going. I only had a quick call to make."

I didn't remember him saying anything about that and said so. He was still a bit sore about it, but I got myself together quickly and met him outside. I felt badly, more than the situation merited, but then there was something to Jon's demeanor, his upset about it, that felt bigger than the moment. We'd had all sorts of miscommunications about comings and goings over the years, so why was this suddenly a thing? Must have been the squeeze of grief.

In the car I apologized again. Jon was fairly subdued in his response. We were winding through back roads in our county heading to a new rural bakery and café that we'd never eaten at before. It wound up being close to a half hour's ride from the house. I started feeling uncomfortable about how long it was taking, as if I was stretching the limit on how much time I could take Jon away from whatever he might do that day. And also about leaving Titi alone, though I very much needed the break.

At the café we ordered at the counter and were given a number to put on our table. They would bring our meals to us when they were ready. We found a table out on the deck. We sat in silence, mostly, waiting for our food. I had a new phone and wanted to get photos into its memory, so I took some shots of Jon sitting across from me. Even on the best of days, Jon barely tolerated his photo being taken, though he did have a side to him that loved to ham it up for the right person in certain circumstances, I being one of the lucky ones over the years to be privy to his adorable goofball poses. Not today. He had his arms folded across his front, and his eyes were deeply furrowed. He didn't seemingly have it in him to attempt a smile.

A woman at another table saw me taking the pictures and offered to get photos of the two of us together. I pulled my chair around to Jon and leaned my head onto his shoulder. We were both wearing gray shirts, him white-and-gray striped with his salt-and-pepper, mostly salty hair, and me with a gray v-neck. We looked tonally muted, Jon especially. Ever the Leo, I instinctively smiled for the camera. The woman did some kind of awkward press on the button, then handed me my phone. Both shots were "bursts" of a hundred pictures each, a veritable strip of the two of us sitting stock-still and gray.

I moved my chair back around, and our sandwiches came. We ate in silence, the breeze pushing our napkins around the table. After we finished, I said I was anxious to get back to Titi. Jon said he had errands to run and would drop me at the house so he could go take care of them. I was curious about the errands, but he brushed me off saying he wouldn't be gone long.

Titi wasn't hiding away, but he wasn't fully fluffed out, either. I attempted some work at the computer but found it impossible to focus. I managed an e-mail or two, a paragraph here and there, but when Jon came back home I turned off my computer and met him down in the kitchen.

After telling him that Titi seemed status quo, I asked if he'd gotten his errands done. I don't know why I was so damn piqued by them, but I was.

"I did," he said, walking away from me. "I think I'm gonna go lay down."

He seemed wiped out.

"Okay, I'm going to go to the gym. Want to meet back here tonight to watch something on TV after we do Titi's fluids?"

"Sure."

As much as I often lamented Jon's unadulterated commitment to napping, I was glad he'd taken the full day off from the office and was doing some self-care. He'd been so stressed lately, so down. And I was happy, then, that he'd be around earlier in the evening than he usually was on weekdays as he often went back to the office to work after grabbing dinner at a nearby restaurant. Sometimes I didn't even see him until 9 PM or later on weeknights, just long enough for thirty minutes of something mindless on the screen and occasionally not even that. Tonight he'd be there when I got back rather than me waiting for him to come home.

I made my rounds of the gym and library looking for a DVD for us to watch. Then I got it in my head that our kitchen could use a new plant stand to bring some leafy green life into our home, so I went to a garden store that was open in the evening. I took way too long making my pick and suddenly realized that I would be getting home almost too late for us to have any quality time together after getting Titi his dose of the increased fluids. I raced the roads worried Jon would be mad at me for leaving him sitting there, waiting. That was a sore spot for him. If we'd agreed to meet and I was late (not unheard of), he felt taken for granted. I ripped into the driveway and trotted up to the house with the plant stand. I walked in the door apologizing proactively. Oddly, he gave me no guff. In fact, he was remarkably chill about it, about everything. We got Titi his Q, then sat together in the dark on the couch before heading up to bed. I went to sleep wondering what the morning would bring as far as Titi's condition. Reasonable, the vet had said, but not guaranteed. Oh, universe. *Please.* We really need a win.

CHAPTER 19

WOOD THRUSH

(Searching)

Memorial Day weekend

[Often solitary birds hidden deep within the forest, wood thrushes are] one of the most prominent examples of declining forest songbirds in North America. Some of the steepest population declines have been along the Atlantic Coast and in New England states. . . .

—Cornell Lab of Ornithology, All About Birds, "Wood Thrush"

"Jon, is that you?"

It was dark. I'd woken up alone in our bed late in the night of the date night that wasn't and thought I'd heard someone in the driveway or at the door. I padded downstairs in a camisole into the living room, where Dawn was sleeping on the couch. I'd left the porch lights on as a beacon. As an act of protection. As a guide to call him home. The glow beamed through the front door and windows and slanted into the room. I woke Dawn up.

"Did you hear anything? I thought I heard someone."

She hadn't. I was ashamed to be unnerving her, to be the anguished woman hearing things in the night. The woman whose lover was the subject of a police search. I apologized and left her as sentinel in that front room. I was afraid of him showing up in the middle of the night after this day of disappearance. What condition would he be in if that had been him? I returned upstairs to lie down alone with what I should not have been able to bear, yet somehow was ticking my way through the minutes and hours after the shock of *never showed.*

Titi was still up on the bed waiting for me. I climbed back in to attempt to pass through the overactive panic-stricken thinking once again, hoping that even a fitful sleep would claim me. Anything but lying there motionless and powerless, waiting for the night to end. Titi walked around the bed purring for a few rounds, then adhered himself to my legs like a barnacle, pinning me in place until the sun came up.

Hi honey I'm here [photo of me on the bed with Titi]

7:06 am

I went downstairs and nervously jibbered with Dawn over coffee before she had to head home, back to her life of comparative normalcy. Oh to have a lazy Saturday morning! To sit in my happy corner while Jon snoozed upstairs. The moment the door closed behind Dawn, I was back at the phone. Some of my close people who I'd called the night before clearly needed nudging as I'd not heard from a few of the key ones. I was particularly surprised that Michele hadn't made a peep. I tried her. She answered with a cheery greeting. I cut her off sharply.

"You don't understand. I'm saying that Jon is missing. Never showed last night and hasn't been heard from or seen since yesterday."

She hadn't listened to my message yet. When she heard the words *Jon* and *missing*, she snapped to attention. She said she would pack up her minivan and hit the road within the hour. But Buffalo was five hours away. Whatever was I going to do with myself until then? Then the phone rang. And rang again. Messages and calls started accumulating as word spread among his family and our friends and his work people. The calls kept me busy, but they were wearying. How many times could I repeat the story? I took a deep breath. Began again. The last time I saw Jon was the previous morning. He was smiling. His son had just called and told Jon to hug us all. A trifling errand he needed to take care of. Nothing I could have helped him with. Not a thing.

I hadn't heard from the cops yet, so I called the precinct. As Hotaling wouldn't be on shift until that afternoon, I was patched through to a different officer. What were they doing? What could they tell me? What should I be doing? Where had they looked? He had questions for me, as well, and we spent almost a half hour brainstorming possible locations to check and talking about Jon's hobbies and skills. Could he have gone into the woods to disappear? The officer wanted to know. I didn't mention the late-night call of visions of Jon walking in a forest and sorry, sorry, sorry. I did tell him that all our camping gear was still here and that I would have been *really* pissed if Jon had taken to the woods without me.

"No, really," I said when the cop obviously didn't get the full context of my comment. "I've been begging him to go camping again with me for years. It'd just figure."

The cop politely indulged me, the terrified woman making jokes. Then he launched into specifics of the search. They had pinged his phone. He explained the technology and why it was sometimes difficult to pinpoint an exact location, but I had limited capacity for comprehension at the moment. Cell towers and bouncing signals was it? A media alert had been distributed, and television, radio, print, and online news outlets had already begun reporting on the disappearance of a man who could have been any man but was my most personal person. Anyone with information should call East Greenbush Police Department. The language and rhythms of local reporting so familiar, so excessively common. In addition, the Department of Transportation had programmed missing person alerts to flash repeatedly on roadside LED signs. MISSING WHITE ADULT MALE. Make/model. License plate. I saw none of these, pinned as I was to the house, waiting.

Still here! Sending love.

10:54 am

But of course it would be better with you here. Please come home k?

12:02 pm

One of Jon's brothers and that brother's oldest son had driven in the night up from Connecticut to join the search on the ground. The text chains with Jon's family, with our mutual friends, with Jon's boss, with my friends, with my dad and sister were now lighting up my phone nonstop. I avoided the news myself but heard reports that confirmed what the officer had said. I did check social media. My initial post had been shared broadly, and strangers on the Internet took up the cause.

Beside my initial concern that he was in a ditch or worse due to a road rage incident gone horribly wrong, for some reason that wasn't quite clear, the cops, Jon's family, our closest friends, and I all had the sense that he was intentionally trying not to be found. I kept thinking back to the time when Frank stood me up a day after I'd committed to counseling together by going on a twenty-four-hour crack run. And then early in my relationship with Jon, our weekend of moping when he'd begged out of dating me, and I let him go. How I needed him to step up if we were going to be partners, and miraculously he had. And now? Mere weeks after telling him that I was in it with him until the end? Is that what made him run? That and the business he wanted to want to own but didn't actually want? Was it Titi? Doing the Q? The eventuality of having to make the decision to have that last needle slid in? What, Jon, what?

Titi having a good day, fyi. [photo of Titi on bed in the sun]

12:57pm

I felt I needed to tread carefully with my words if I wanted him to respond. The Jon I knew would have been horrified to be the center of all this public discussion, so I didn't say anything about how I'd reached out to his folks, his boss, and not a peep about the police. I was conscious of trying to make it easy for him to return. No big deal, we're here. Love you whatever's going on, Titi and I are still your Titi and your gal, just as we were yesterday, when you left. For some reason, there's this skipped day, but we can click right back in if only you come home. I was texting him as if this were all just a weird misunderstanding.

Wherever Jon was, his phone must have been under assault. When Hotaling got in that afternoon, he took up the information from the pinging of the phone and followed a hit off a tower out into a field. He found nothing, he said when he got back to the precinct and reached out to give me the updates and to continue to generate hypotheses of what had—strike that—of what was or could be happening. Staying on top of my language took effort. Hotaling thought the data that sent him searching in the field was likely mistaken, but also we talked about the possibility that Jon had thrown his phone from the car and the spot where the tower pointed was in proximity to where it could have landed. But the location that pinged was nowhere near where he would have been expected to travel. Or maybe it wasn't even near a road, at all, and couldn't have been thrown that far? Everything seemed vague. Everything was misleading. I was moved to a quivering *Thank you for helping me find my Jon* to hear that Hotaling kept trying, following anything that might be useful. I pictured him wading through waist-high grasses in full uniform in the searing heat.

It hadn't initially occurred to me that Jon would get rid of his phone, but once the possibility was floated, I could readily imagine Jon with his window down, flinging it away from him. My mind was generating visions like a kaleidoscope on full tilt. I put the phone back in his pocket and him behind the wheel. I needed to bring myself back to my own immediate surroundings, again and again, to what I knew and to what I did not know, but most especially to whatever the next right action for me to take could be. Please, god, let there be something for me to do.

Finally Michele arrived. We clung to each other at the door in a face-to-face confirmation of the reality of Jon's disappearance. Yes, our embrace said, this is real. This is grave. She pulled back and looked at me. I was raw and red and had swollen, puffy eyes. My face was pinched and searching, my gaze pleading. She kicked into action. There were coolers to bring into the house, she came stocked to feed me for days, and she immediately took up the task of answering the house phone that never stopped ringing. She became a front line between me and the outpouring of support and offers of help, all the friends and neighbors stopping by to see how they could assist in the search. Also, the requests for information, for insight, occasionally for assistance with managing the other person's own anxiety and, I suppose they couldn't help it, some of them, satiating their prurient curiosity. There were many theories floated, not all of them created equal.

While Michele set to work preparing a meal, I added to my growing list of places Jon might be that the cops or family and close friends could try. I wrote things down, crossed them out, underlined, added question marks and exclamation points. I babbled out loud.

"Good! That's a good one," Michele would say while boiling water for eggs or washing lettuce, and I'd write down whatever I'd said last.

Phone calls and texts—between his family and me, his kids, my family, my friends, our friends—were filled with guesses, proclamations, and speculations. *Did anyone check movie theaters? Or libraries? Or what about* and the person would shout or write in ALL CAPS a place that no one had mentioned yet. The brother who had come up in the night with his oldest son was driving the streets, doubling back and forth between the house and Jon's work. Side routes. A favorite nature preserve. They were also in touch with the police directly and had arranged to meet them and Jon's boss at the office that afternoon. I was still operating under the logic that I should stay put at the house in case he showed up. It was hot and sunny. I was wearing the camisole I'd slept in but did manage to step into a pair of pants. I was sweating a rancid fear. I beat the drum. *Jon. Come. Home. Now.*

After the searching of Jon's workstation and the conversation at the office, his boss called me. I was standing in the living room, the sun filtering through gauzy curtains draping from the windows, and looking at the fireplace that had been nonnegotiable in our search for a home. Suddenly I began pacing. Or maybe I was already in motion. I was trying to understand what he was saying. What I was hearing. He told the police what?

"I only mentioned it to them because they asked if anything unusual had happened in the last few weeks," he said. "Didn't you know?"

I didn't. I had no idea that his boss was considering selling the company to someone else. Oh, my beloved Jon. My face flushed, another sting. How could I not know that? I felt embarrassed. Then, pissed. Jon had worked his ass off to help build that company, nights and weekends, always, *always* with deadlines hanging over him and never advocating for himself in a way that I had hoped he would do some day. And now this guy was going to cash in and leave Jon to work for someone else, with no equity in what he had built? Again, I couldn't get my head around what I was hearing. The boss was defensive.

"I told Jon he would be in on the meetings with the potential buyer."

"And when did you tell him about changing your mind?"

"I didn't change my mind. Well, not really. You have to understand, Jon wasn't finishing the paperwork. He needed to turn in the rest of the forms for his license or he wouldn't be able to take over the company."

That, I did know. I was becoming more certain by the minute that he didn't want the responsibility of owning the company, but he didn't see another option to continue on in his job. Mainly what he wanted all along was decent pay and acknowledgment of how hard he worked, of how competent he was.

"It didn't seem to bother him," the boss continued about the news that he was considering another owner of the firm. "If it had, I'm sure he would have said something about it."

Clearly, for all the many days, and weeks, and months, and years spent together at the office, on jobsites, traveling between them, even at a few rare social functions, this guy did not know Jon as well as he thought he did. It took a lot for Jon to speak up for himself, especially on the job. So no, dude. It is not a given that he would have felt like he could have approached you on this. Not that quickly anyway. I didn't say this. I don't know what I said, but the ground was shifting under me, my perceptions were reorienting to take in the new information, especially the fact that Jon had not come to me with any of it, either. He'd held onto this. Was he afraid of what my response would be? Ashamed? My heart broke to think of him trying to figure out his next move on his own.

I thought about how the police knew that there was a situation on the job before I did. I began to wonder how they viewed me. What they thought of our relationship. Did they ever doubt me? What was the language they used back at the station? On the radio? In the paperwork? Adult. White. Male. Missing. Domestic partner. Reported. Never showed up. Last seen. How did they describe the nuances, if they did? What were those conversations? She seems genuine. Clearly loves him. Didn't know his boss had considered selling the company to someone else. He's blowing off steam. He's hitting the road. He's in relapse. According to the partner they were both in fellowships with long-term track records of recovery.

I got out of the conversation with the boss. The last two weeks flipped around in my head. How did I not know? Oh, Jon. Why didn't you tell me? I wanted to go back in time and tell him to fuck the job. But I had tried repeatedly to talk with him about how affected he seemed to be by something. I combed over every last word I could remember that we'd uttered between us over the past few weeks.

"What's going on, Jon? You seem especially stressed."

"Just work stuff."

"Yeah, but you're always up against it with the job. This seems different."

"Working something out. That's all."

"Are you sure there's nothing I can do?"

"I'm sure."

Michele and I both agreed when I told her what I'd found out, it wasn't worth it, Jon! We pleaded with the man who wasn't there. Nothing was worth this, this . . . what? Disappearance? *Was* he in a motel room with books and snacks and the fuck-its? We worked all the angles, Michele and I, like two friends who were intimately accustomed to bettering the world in ongoing conversations for decades. Over the years we'd saved the planet and fixed the healthcare system, or so we would have if the powers that be would have just listened to us. We could spend hours on the phone, spinning fantastic theories for how things should be done, even as we knew we were professors, doctors, and ambassadors solely in our own minds. It was our joke, and one that Jon took to immediately. Dr. Benson! POET SHERPA GIRLFRIEND MASTER. It was 2 AM, and I was completely spent, my nose crusty and raw from sun exposure on the glacier on Mt. Rainier, but there was my beautiful man with this amazing affirmation of my personhood, humor and all. Yes, what's not to love. Where was he now?

It was time to change course in my texting with him. Instead of enthusiasm displayed to encourage him home—hopeful missives to myself as much as to him—I wrote as calmly as possible the truth as I knew it at the time. The breaking of the silence on the search was a turning point for me. A deeper recognition that my guy was in real trouble. I went over the wording with Michele. It felt like everything hinged on getting it right with him. Also I felt as if I'd betrayed him by going public, and I was nervous about letting him know. But the time had come to shatter the breezy performance.

> Hi honey, I just want to let you know that I am worried, and that I have contacted the police. We have been in the process of trying to find you to make sure that you are okay. I have reached out to your friends, your boss, and your family to cast as wide a net as possible to reach you.
>
> I hope that as soon as you are able that you will reach out to me.
>
> Love,
>
> Cb
>
> **5:13 PM**

I sent the text. The words were out of the bag. I beat the drum. I wanted to go back in time. He was walking through the kitchen, the sun was ubiquitous. I can hear the *shwoosh* of his jeans as he moved through the house. He was smiling. He was holding to himself a turning point in his life, the explosion of the path he thought he was on. That biggest *atta boy* he'd received on the job had been compromised, the one that was supposed to make up for all the ones he didn't but should have been given throughout his life, the way we need so much from each other and it seems impossible for some of us to get it. To reach out from a deep interior—*help. I'm in here.* I did see him. I knew but didn't know. These last two weeks. All the if only's. I beat the drum again.

CHAPTER 20

TURKEY VULTURES

(Circling)

End of the three-day weekend, the start of the following week

. . . these large birds spend most of their time soaring on rising air currents, called thermals, in search of food, or simply traveling from one place to another.

—The Peregrine Fund, Explore Raptors Series, Turkey Vulture

Best Road felt like ground zero, even as the scope of the search expanded. I was overwhelmed. Bleary-eyed. Stricken. Phone ringing. Knocking at the door. Cop cars pulling into the driveway a regular occurrence, Hotaling and another officer back to have a second set of eyes on the stuff of Jon's life and to talk with the person who knew him best and had seen him last. I'd been combing through his crowded office all weekend. I counted the cash. I listened to the music. I discovered a few of his filing cabinets were locked and became obsessed with finding the keys. Were there secrets inside? Had I forgotten anything? We were scouring everything for an explanation, a lead, a trace.

Hotaling said that they'd tried to access Jon's bank account to see if or where Jon was using his card, but they'd been denied. In another instance I would have rued the state's ability to gain entry to this personal information of its citizens. But then didn't corporate identities such as banks and social media platforms readily share all sorts of data, and now here was an actual emergency, someone was missing, and we couldn't get assistance? Was it that I was only one person without money and influence? Did Jon and I not count? I said none of this to the cops in my kitchen. Hotaling, my go-to, my tether to the possibility that Jon could be found, stood steadfastly going over options, detailing what would be done next. Then he left me to the house, to waiting, to perseverating, to staring numbly at food Michele put in front of me in random intervals.

A cadre of friends came every night to help with Titi's fluids. Someone made a schedule. Lists for places to call were divided up. Michele continued to screen for me, asking if I was up for this or that conversation or visit. When I wasn't, I'd hear her relating what was known and not known to someone on the phone or at the door. Then the latest person to arrive would get details from those who Michele had already spoken with, and groups would form on the porch and in the living room while I paced in the drum room or splashed cold water on my face in the bathroom. Though I was cocooned in our home, I had a sense of the commotion Jon's disappearance had triggered beyond my immediate circle, the way crisis becomes addictive, both in real life and especially on the Internet. I was grateful for the extended company in the trauma. The viral posts. The media reports. Friends of friends and strangers of friends all eager for my guy to be found. But I had to approach it all very carefully, to manage the onslaught of unfiltered suggestions, questions, and projections.

On a text thread with Jon's family, one of his brothers floated the theory that Jon was blowing off steam and would walk in the door when the holiday was over. There was a plausibility to the feeling that the three-day weekend somehow figured into the situation. Business as usual was on hold in the U.S., so the notion that the end of the weekend would bring him home took hold. That didn't mean we stopped calling places. Or worrying. Or disbelieving that sometime before Tuesday he'd be back. But it became a story we told ourselves, one of many we repeated like fingering prayer beads.

Another story I told, that Monday evening when Jon and I should have been out to dinner with friends, then celebrating my sobriety anniversary, was the one where I'd recently let Jon know I was in it until the end, and now it was on him to step up to the commitment. And if he wouldn't, then like our weekend of pouting and like Frank before that, I needed to let him go. I felt righteous saying it, bestowing on myself a sense of power in a situation that was so utterly beyond my control. Five of us were standing in the kitchen. The couple Jon and I had plans with came to take me to the meeting, it seemed the right thing to do, and the couple that Jon and I had witnessed the bunnies with was over to handle Titi's fluids. I reiterated to them what I'd said to Michele before she left for a short break back at her own home: I needed Jon to level up.

The three of us went to Saratoga while the other couple stayed behind to not only care for Titi but to be at the house in case Jon did return. Would he do that with them there? I even wondered if he would show to the meeting. Was he out there somewhere, worried how angry I was, and might lurk at the outskirts of the celebration? I was as anxious about him surfacing at the meeting as about him not showing up.

I looked for his car as we circled for a spot. The lot was full, as typical for anniversary night, but none of the cars that I could see was his. I was on high alert, actively scanning my surroundings on the walk to the building, feeling like someone could have been watching from behind a tree or from a passing car. I took one last look over my shoulder as I went inside. The space that held the meeting was the rare room that wasn't a church basement, rather an airy light-filled hall on the ground floor that the congregation used for fellowship after services. One wall was entirely floor-to-ceiling windows, and the walkway into the room was also made of glass. It was a fishbowl. I took my seat at the front of the room with the other celebrants, some of whom I'd known since I first got sober. I tried to focus on what was being said but kept looking at my phone. When it was my turn, I stood to speak.

"Please forgive me my divided attention," I began after saying my name and my claim to my seat in the room. "But if nothing else, sobriety has taught me to reach out to others and to be honest about what's up. Well, this is what's up. My partner has been missing since Friday, and I'm here to tell you that I'm still sober."

I spoke about my early days, about going to any length, and about what it was like now, including the search for Jon. When I was done, I sat down, face flushed, and read my texts as discreetly as I could during the next person's share. I put my phone down and tried again to be present to the meeting, training my face on the person speaking.

After the meeting, I was surrounded. People had seen the reports on the news. They were concerned, offering love and prayers, saying they were available if I needed anything, anything at all. I was trying to move through the crowd, feeling a sense of urgency to get back to the house, when someone came rushing up to me to tell me that there were cops outside. I ran into the parking lot. I whipped my head back and forth, and when I didn't see anything, I asked a guy smoking a cigarette if he'd seen what happened when the cops were there.

"Whatever they were after, they didn't stick around," he said.

I went back into the meeting room and grilled the person who'd come up to me with the initial message: Why did he think it was connected to my guy? Nothing specific, really. Just cops. Missing person. Maybe there was something to it? I chalked it up to him wanting to be helpful and possibly to an alcoholic's predilection for jumping into the middle of crisis. I thanked him and extricated myself from the crowd, which was starting to re-form, to meet my friends waiting for me at their car.

Back home, there had been no sign of Jon there either. I relieved the house crew of their duty and took up my role as woman waiting, only now I would be on my own for the first overnight since he'd disappeared. I beat the drum again. *Tuesday, please Tuesday, be the day he comes back to me.*

Whatever you need. We can work it out. Please just come home. Everyone we know is looking for you.

9:38 pm

Titi joined me in bed. I curled into myself, and he curled into my legs. I woke up the next morning to the two of us in the same position. Fluffy Titi, our miracle cat who had rebounded with the increased fluids, began purring the moment I stirred.

I reached over to the bedside table to grab my phone, ever on hand. Texts and calls and e-mails and likely multiple messages on all the social platforms, but no Jon. Something in me sank. I rolled over to look at the empty space in the bed next to me and faced his abandoned sleep apnea machine on his bedside table. I thought about the cash on his desk—the full amount of his last paycheck that he'd withdrawn would likely have been the lion's share of all the money he had. The missing ladder I hadn't mentioned to anyone but had nagged at me all weekend. It was too short for anything he'd need on a job.

Hotaling's first visit to the house that Friday night, he put the question to me: "What if Jon didn't want to be found?" *There was no law against that.* Others occasionally took up that line of thinking. "That's fine," I told anyone who asked. "If he's having a midlife needs to leave me and all of his present commitments phase, I will survive. Let's just make sure that's what he wants and it's not that he doesn't need us. Doesn't need help."

This morning, the morning of the Tuesday no-show, the end of the hope that he'd dropped out over the long weekend for a reset, something about the start of a new week that should have been business as usual but so very much wasn't, and considering the only material clues I had to go on—the cash, the missing ladder—all tilted the kaleidoscope again, forming a notion that I did not allow myself to engage with all weekend. I got out of bed.

The search was ramping up. Community members I'd been in the casino fight with in my town arranged a meeting at a neighbor's house for that afternoon. Someone made a MISSING PERSON flyer with his photograph that friends were tacking up in storefronts and on telephone poles. Detectives were now on the case after having been away for the weekend. A friend came by to pick me up for the search meeting up the road from our house.

My neighbor's living room was packed. It was a vision I knew well from our monthly, then sometimes weekly, gatherings to organize taking on the casino developers together. Now here were many of the regulars, our town supervisor, who'd been launched into office from our successful activist fight, a county legislator who achieved office similarly, the detectives newly on the case, some friends from recovery, and, of course, Hotaling.

After some side conversations and talk of who was hitting what locations, where flyers were going up, what calls needed to be made, I stood up to speak to the room. After thanking everyone for coming out, for their time and support, I made eye contact with Hotaling and reiterated the details as I knew them. Then I spoke one more time to the question of what if he's intentionally hiding out.

"I'm fifty years old. I'm a grown woman. If this is his way of leaving me and his life as he knew it, that's fine. I'll be sad, but I'll recover."

I paused, then said what should have been impossible to utter—but wasn't.

"I need to know he's not hurting himself," I finally said.

I looked around the room. There were fifteen to twenty people filling it, some were standing, everyone intently focused. The concern was palpable. I don't know why I continued. I have no idea why I said what I said next. Was it what I wished Jon knew before he went out the door after hugging me last Friday? Was it what I was sorry I hadn't said more often?

"Look at all this help available. It's here for all of us. Or could be. Maybe I'm lucky with this, all of you here for me, for Jon, but I want it for everyone. For people to go to the wall with their love for the other. For everyone to be cared about."

"We'll find him," someone said.

Others chimed in encouragingly. Then the detectives spoke. Continue posting on social media, making phone calls, distributing flyers. Everyone had their marching orders, and the meeting broke. One of the detectives approached me to say they wanted to have a look at our house themselves. Could the two of them come by now? They would give me a ride. Folks were still milling around as the detectives ushered me out the door.

Back at Best Road, I went over everything again. I showed them Jon's office, where I'd left the cash under the discs after counting it and listening to the music for indiscernible patterns. One male, one female, these detectives were clearly accustomed to each other's rhythms and thinking, cutting each other off, finishing sentences. The male got on the phone to call the bank to finagle a way in to Jon's account. The female interjected suggestions as he spoke, and between the two of them the conversation with the bank unlocked the needed information. After the cash withdrawal Friday morning, Jon's card had been used shortly after that at a convenience store. The night before there was a charge at a hardware store. But then, that Sunday, there was a deduction. My spirit soared. This was a good sign.

"Aha. I see," the detective said into the phone. He thanked her for her help, then hung up.

"It was an automatic bill pay," he said. He'd not actively used it since Friday.

I told them about his errands. Perhaps that was the charge on Thursday night? They said they would reach out to the hardware store. The male detective was sitting in my happy place, the female was at the kitchen island. I was standing in the doorway between the kitchen and our spacious light-filled plant drum books room. The sun was filling every nook and cranny through the skylights and windows. I was sweating. The detectives got a phone call. Their postures, energy, and countenance immediately shifted. Jon's car had been found.

They moved quickly for the door while explaining that his car was discovered at a parking area for a nature preserve across the river. They were heading straight to the location, but I should stay at the house. And I should not watch the news, they cautioned. Media would have crews and reporters at the site, and speculation would likely run rampant. They assured me they would be in touch as soon as they had more information and rushed out of the house. I watched them hurry down the walk and peel out of the driveway in their black SUV.

I called Michele in a panic. *What could it mean?* I started spinning scenarios, the kaleidoscope tilting once again, then blurted, "Can you come back? I can't do this. I just can't fucking do it." She said she would. She'd be there as soon as she could, likely after dark.

I launched into calling and texting his family and my friends and support networks. "His car has been found." I asked Dawn to come back while I waited for news and for Michele to get here from Buffalo. Dawn came right over.

We took up spots on the couch where we'd passed much of that first night. I popped up frequently, unable to sit still. We talked about the visions of him walking in the woods, searching. About I'm sorry. I'm sorry. I'm sorry. I asked her to reach out to her people again. I was desperate. Picking at my fingernails. Repeating myself.

Please. What do they see now? I need to know. She put messages out. We waited. Dark was coming. Another day ending. The black SUV pulled back into the driveway. I opened the door as the male detective approached.

"We haven't found him yet," he led with. "We had over a hundred people out combing the woods in a grid search and will start up again in the morning. What we did find were notes in his car."

"Notes?"

"Yes. But until we have the person, we don't assume."

"Suicide notes?"

"Again, until we have a person, we don't assume. We're going to hang onto them as this is still very much open."

I hadn't even thought of asking to see them.

"I want to remind you not to watch the news tonight," he said. "Law enforcement officers and staff know not to talk with the media, but to get that many people out in the woods we called in local search and rescue volunteers. They've been instructed not to talk to press, but . . ."

I knew about SAR teams from years of following various instances of missing hikers from all over the world. There are a lot of really good people who show up to help. Not everyone, though, is as altruistically oriented. I took his point.

"I haven't looked at any of it," I said.

"We'll be back out there in daylight. You will be the first to know the moment we have anything to report."

After he left, I looked to Dawn. All the years of dealing with things one day at a time, one craving at a time, one minute, one second, the training to avoid succumbing to a catastrophic future by clinging to life in the absolute present would have to carry me now.

"They do not have him, Cara," Dawn repeated.

"Have you heard back from any of your people yet?"

"Not getting any real hits out there."

I didn't know if that meant they weren't picking up new information—however it is that intuitives and psychics do it—or if she simply hadn't heard back, but I refrained from pressing further, much as I wanted to beg to hear anything that wasn't what my mind was spinning on hyperdrive. I was acutely aware of my immense need, an anguish so primal and raw that it must have been palpable, *oh my god, please tell me my guy is alive, please fix this, please work your magic* emanating from me like Pig Pen's cloud, only this was spiritual and emotional dust. I said nothing. Michele pulled her minivan into the driveway.

She'd driven in the dark, another astounding effort on the part of her in particular, but also everyone who was affected, who loved me and loved Jon, who were themselves terrified and traumatized but working to support his partner, his confidante and lover, his everyday person, his *I'm in it until death do us part* woman, with encouragement and prayer and tasks and meals and phone calls.

We hugged again at the door. I told her the latest about the notes and what the detective had said, that until they found him—he'd been careful to say him—what the notes indicated were not to be taken as fact. Michele took up that cause. She put water on for tea, the next shift of care was starting, and Dawn went back to her family.

I called Hotaling, who was still on the job. He'd also been at the search at the nature preserve after the meeting at my neighbor's house. We went over everything, him calmly talking me through how they'd heard from someone who noticed the pine needles collecting on Jon's car over the weekend and that the search team would get back into the woods again in the morning. He encouraged me to get some sleep. I was wrung out, but closing my eyes terrified me, so I went downstairs for tea with Michele.

She was both wired and spent also, but we spun out myriad theories, options, laments, "goddamn it, Jon," "fuck the job, fuck everything, just come home alive," until neither of us could keep our eyes open and would hopefully drop off immediately. I climbed up the stairs to the big empty bed. Titi hopped up after me. I didn't text Jon. I hadn't done so all day.

The next morning Michele was up making coffee and eggs. I padded downstairs like a car crash victim. The phone was ringing again, the texts were texting, Michele was intervening. Through the chatter it solidified that Dawn would come back over to wait with us. I huddled in the corner, taking in some blessed caffeine. I was wearing the same damn camisole and floppy pants I'd been wearing at the house since Friday. I had showered and dressed once to get out to the anniversary meeting, but otherwise I was getting by with sink baths and clothes that I didn't have to think about.

It was Wednesday. I had not seen Jon since Friday. I was sitting under the happy lights where he'd last hugged me. Michele sat across the table. My friend, in my house all the way from Buffalo on a weekday. I should have been journaling, getting ready for writing or whatever it was my days consisted of a lifetime ago at the end of last week. I had papers beside me on the bench, scratched out places to try, lists upon lists. We were talking. We were silent. Nothing made sense. My eyelids were heavy. It was difficult to focus. I was out of theories. Through the kitchen windows I saw the black SUV coming on the road toward the house. I stood and moved quickly into the living room to look out the front. Following the SUV were two black-and-white patrol cars. One by one they pulled into the driveway.

Both detectives and a handful of officers, including Hotaling, who wasn't in uniform but khaki clothing with a gun strapped to his thigh, came up to the door. I let them in. The living room filled with police. The male detective stood in front of me; I was still standing at the door holding it open as the crowd entered. Once everyone was in, I closed the door and looked to the detective. I knew. He confirmed. Jon's body had been found.

I have no memory of getting to the couch. Did I nearly fall over and someone helped me to it? Did an instinct for survival steer me toward a soft landing? I folded into myself on the cushions. The detective with his coffee and adrenaline breath positioned his hand on my right shoulder, Michele hers on my left, me in the middle, crumpled, the entire room of police noiselessly trained on my shuddering body. A tableau of grief broken only when one officer sharply shifted his stance, and the entire room looked to the disturbance. Dawn was at the door. She was let in, and the male detective made way for her to take his place on the couch. Her hand replacing his. My convulsions the only sound in the room. My heaving body the only motion. My guy was gone.

DEAREST CARA,

I'M SO SO SORRY.

I JUST DON'T HAVE THE COURAGE TO FACE WHAT'S AHEAD.

I JUST DON'T HAVE THE ENERGY TO FACE WHAT'S AHEAD.

I'M SO SORRY TO LEAVE YOU.

IT WAS NOTHING YOU · OR ANYONE ELSE – DID.

YOU DIDN'T CAUSE IT, YOU COULDN'T CURE IT, YOU COULDN'T CONTROL IT. YOU DIDN'T MISS ANYTHING.

I LOVE YOU CARA. YOU AND MY KIDS ARE THE BEST THING THAT'S EVER HAPPENED IN MY LIFE.

MY HOPE FOR YOU IS LOVE & COMPANIONSHIP, FULFILLING WORK, PUBLICATION AND RECOGNITION OF YOUR TALENT AND FOR HOW SPECIAL YOU ARE. I'M SO SORRY TO LEAVE TITI'S END-OF-LIFE CARE TO YOU ALONE. I'VE BEEN SO LUCKY TO HAVE YOU BOTH IN MY LIFE. THEY'VE BEEN MY MOST JOYOUS MOMENTS. BLESSINGS ON YOUR HEALING!

LOVE!

Jim

YOU ARE SUCH A LOVING, WONDERFUL PERSON!

CHAPTER 21

WINTER WREN

(The dream that is not a dream)

Interlude

A secretive little bird of dense woods. It often creeps about among fallen logs and dense tangles, behaving more like a mouse than a bird, remaining out of sight but giving an occasional kimp-kimp callnote . . . in spring in the northern woods, males ascend to high perches in the conifers to give voice to a beautiful song of long-running musical trills.

—*Audubon Bird Guide*, "Winter wren"

I'm walking in the woods. It isn't the particular preserve where Jon was found, but bends and twists in the trail feel similar. He'd taken me there, where he left, to walk together. Once in the summer, and another time we snowshoed up and down its contours. I have body memory of his final place on the planet. Of him showing me different trails he'd walked with his kids or paths he'd cross-country skied once upon a time, but that's not where I am now. I'm walking in the woods. Green, leafy canopy swaying to reveal patchworks of blue sky, of cloudy sky, catching the rain, blocking the beating sun, holding the heat, the cool, the oxygen, the carbon. The birds in the trees. I don't know them as intimately as I want to. How well do I really know anyone? Through the chorus floats a song I recognize. Hermit thrush, a trilling harmonica-throated song I queried all the hikers I knew to help me identify well before Jon died. I learned their song, if nothing else. All the music I missed. All that was to come. I'm walking in the woods. Jon is with me. I am alone. I'm talking to him. I'm talking to no one. I'm talking to myself. My body. Keep going. Where am I going? I don't know where I am. There is a path in front of me. I put myself here to have direction. Purpose. I walk to the end and back again. I loop. I stutter. I stumble. I cannot breathe through what is pressing on my lungs. Simple sentences. *I hurt. I miss you. Please come back.* I'm walking in the woods. The brook is talking to me. The leaves on the trees are waving. The breeze touches me, gently moving the hair from my wet face. A hawk shrieking in the distance. Jon had the keenest eye for red-taileds roadside. Predators surveying the ground for kill. I'm walking in the woods. The Louise Erdrich line he so loved won't let up. *Not enough is said about the repetitive nature of grief. Not enough is said about the repetitive nature of grief. Not enough is said about the repetitive nature of grief.* I'm walking in the woods. It's our town park. A few miles of trails through the trees. We walked it together one Thanksgiving before we established our Adirondacks tradition, but just that once. We'd had nothing planned for the day, and I was antsy. I looked up green shapes on a maps program. Found the closest one. How did we not know about it? How had it not been on our radar? So close to our house. Likely a tract too small and low-lying to catch my attention. We walked it that Thanksgiving. Its bends and twists in the trail now feel familiar. I return. Again and again. On the way back from the park to Best Road I see an owl on a fence post. He doesn't look away. I'm walking in the woods. There is no trail. I'm lost. Pushing through thick branches, needles catching in my hair and sticking to my skin. Forest so dense it's nearly dark in daylight. But then maybe it's night. I've lost all sense of time. I come out in a field of grasses as high as my chest. I try to determine direction based on the location of the sun. I drop down a steep wooded bank to a creek in the forest. There is a downed trunk across the water. I don't know which side I should walk, but following the water will get me somewhere, I reason. I cross over on the fallen tree. I'm forced back-and-forth downstream, finally walking directly in the water. It's getting dark. I second-guess all my decisions. I should have walked through the field. I should have stopped him from leaving. If ever I needed you, Jon, I need you now. I tear my pants. My feet are soaked. I am nowhere near where I entered. I'm nowhere near anything I know. I stick with the creek, which leads me at last past a house, then out onto a county route hours after the sun disappeared. I become an unexpected pedestrian dodging cars speeding by in the night. An unexpected widow. I'm walking in the woods. All the walks, all the deaths, all the sentences swirling, the kaleidoscope tilting. I'm moving in slow motion. I'm not moving at all. Everyone and everything around me going forward. But what do I know. I mouth the words. *Not enough is said.* I'm keeping to myself the extraordinary circumstances of my loss. The excruciating context of my longing. I hear the long line of a winter wren through the branches. His body shakes as he sings.

CHAPTER 22

MERLIN

(Bodies)

After

Ther is a Merlyon. And that hawke is for a lady.

—Book of hawking, hunting and heraldry, 1486

I did not go to see Jon's body. It wasn't required, and though I did have the opportunity once the funeral director got my beloved's abandoned coil into his care, I was advised against it. Jon had left no instructions, yet I knew to request a cremation. His remains were divvied up into a few small vessels for his family and kids, with the bulk of them coming to me.

I sat on the floor of the spacious light-filled room we did not ever dine in and pulled the bag out of its container. A loved one was with me, someone who needed to reckon with the remnants of what had been Jon for herself. She stared resolutely at the weighty bag of speckled ashes. I looked at it, briefly. A vision—not something I saw, exactly, but sensed—of looking down on us took hold. *That's not me anymore. I'm right here.* I lifted my gaze to nothing specific. I felt a lightness in the air, a presence. The heaviness of the lump in the bag. I wanted to tell her. I said nothing. This feeling became my secret. My fantasy. A grieving defense. A truth. It did not fill the space where he had been. It did not solve the problem of no Jon. He was agonizingly out of reach. He was there, but not there. A phantom limb.

I hovered in an in-between space. A trance. I said sentences like, "The veil is very thin." I thought he would "come through"—language that came to me unbidden. I lay in bed at night, looking up at the ceiling. *Let me know you're there. But don't scare me, k?* Nothing noticeable happened at these times, much as I willed it. Nothing alleviated the ache, the material reality that was impossible to ignore. How easy it became to fall to the ground wherever I was standing. Face down on the wood floor of his office, my sticky cheek pressed into the hard, wide planks. Curled into myself on the kitchen linoleum, hugging my heaving body.

CHAPTER 23

GULLS

(Funeral)

After

Bense, I think they're grieving.

—Jon, to me when we were camping along a seashore once, and he noticed a small flock of gulls squatted down on the ground around one of their own. He felt certain this had to be a ritual of some sort. Sure enough, the next morning the flock was gone, and the bird in the middle had passed.

On the day of the funeral, I was worried there wouldn't be flowers. I rushed to the nursery for pots of them. I sped around town on errands that suddenly seemed existentially consequential. I begged people in line at a dollar store to let me jump ahead—I was going to be late for my lover's funeral and desperately needed these frames. I needed to fill the room with designs he'd made. To show the world his talent. One of his sons made a playlist, carefully selecting songs from the immense collection of music Jon cherished.

There were so many flowers. There were so many people. The line extended beyond what I could see and kept coming. We could not speak with everyone. We could not shake all the hands. Receive every hug. Listen to each last anecdote. We were exhausted. Grateful. Parched. A friend handed me a breath mint as she came through the line. Another gently ran her hands down my arms and spine.

The funeral director approached me. A man Jon and I knew from recovery, a steadfast presence guiding us now, he suggested we move ahead with the service though there were still hundreds to greet. *All this help available, my love. All these people who care.*

His father, his children, his brother, his friends, Michele and her family, people who knew him speaking. The photo of him with the ocean in his eyes blown up on an easel behind the speakers. Behind the many flowers. A candle lit and flickering.

I spoke last. The grieving widow. The wounded writer. I couldn't and couldn't and couldn't write anything until the moment I did. The day before the words tumbled out of me onto the page. My beautiful man. My precious Jon. He rooted for the underdog. How he wanted kindness to win.

CHAPTER 24

MAGPIES

(Accounting)

After

Magpies can distinguish between different quantities.
This means they can tell the difference between more and less.
Studies suggest they can assess numerical values and
make decisions based on those assessments.

—Bird Watching, "The impressive birds that can count"

Jon left me with all the money that he had, with all the love he could manage. The note. The hug. Things he took care of in his final hours. He was walking through the house. He was smiling. It was sunny. He forgot to do something. The clatter of the CDs on the desk in his crowded office. Petting Titi through the spindles of the railing. The missing ladder. His body, his lover, his life. He walked out the door. He left it all behind.

He left story ideas, scenes, dialogue, poems, tracings on vellum, a guitar, a turntable, speakers, hundreds of books, a thousand CDs, floppy discs, hard drives, unopened bills, birthday cards, filing cabinets I finally found the keys for, a sleep apnea machine, faded blue jeans, handkerchiefs, the indented space in the mattress on his side of the bed, birds to feed, Titi's end-of-life care, loafers with worn heels, boots, sandals, sneakers, seventeen rulers, his leased car, molding boxes of decades of business records and architectural drawings in the basement, mortgage payments I couldn't afford alone, the rest of my life without him, his pain, his suffering, his unfinished novel, his albums that Titi had scratched the edges of the covers of, his hand drum, his African thumb piano, his rusting tools from his days in construction, his lingering diminishing smell on pillowcases, his coats, his one tie, his one suit, his collection of *National Geographics,* his dusty tchotchkes, his phrases and sayings—so eminently quotable, newspaper clippings that caught his eye, the collection of handwritten notes by the phone, clever rebus messages he created to tell me he'd cleaned the litter box, to tell me to have a good day, to tell me he'd see me later, until the night that he wouldn't, on date night, he left me on date night, he wrote his last note to me with all that he had in him, I can see the effort in his handwriting, he wanted to free me on his way to the sky, he left me with the burden of the heaviest grief, he left me without a chance to say goodbye.

CHAPTER 25

NORTHERN CARDINALS

(Space)

2018, Firsts

The male Northern Cardinal is perhaps responsible for getting more people to open up a field guide than any other bird. They're a perfect combination of familiarity, conspicuousness, and style: a shade of red you can't take your eyes off. Even the brown females sport a sharp crest and warm red accents.

—Cornell Lab of Ornithology, All About Birds, "Northern Cardinal"

I was a zombie, reaching alien limbs out around me, searching. Where was the body, the man, the spirit, the lover whose presence, whose sayings, whose opinions, whose snoring and odors, piles of clothes on the dryer, whose car I listened for, whose recalcitrance I pushed against, whose everything I was so habituated to that he became a source of locating myself in the world? The days were gauzy. Out of focus. Punctuated by acute stabs of *I can't do this.* Filled with hours of shuddering. Sobbing with sound. Sobbing with no sound. Dehydrating sobbing. Towels, not tissues. Encountering first after exhausting first, of so many more to come.

My first night alone in the house, after. Every minute sound in every room, accentuated. All the familiar noises that should have accompanied them, starkly absent.

My first day empty of the search, of the funeral prep, of his car to return, someone to notify, something to cross off a to-do list. Though his abandoned things throbbed for attention, I did nothing but move a dried leaf he'd found interesting from one shelf in his office to another, then back to the spot he'd left it.

My first trip to the supermarket—flowers and cards and meals and baskets of lotion and tissues and waters and more flowers and more cards and more food had been delivered to the house or left on the porch so there was nothing really that I needed from going to the market but to try going—I was afraid of being recognized. Of being approached. I flinched at sharp bursts of laughter, carts screeching on the floors. I squinted under the bright lights. I scurried home.

Jon himself was in none of this. Jon defined all of it. I looked for him in everything.

I closed my eyes often, opening them in drowsy intervals, filtering my perceptions. Scenes, life played out in increments, fragments. My sentences were simple. "The veil is very thin."

I believed I saw signs of him communicating with me in the material world.

A leaf stuck inside the handle of my car door.

A suitcase abandoned on the side of a road.

A turkey feather sticking upright out of the grass in the front yard when I pulled in.

It wasn't just any old item. It had to catch my attention in a way that cocked my head. I started to keep track of them all in a little journal. *Kittens in Space* were the illustrations on the outside of the booklet. I felt as one. A kitten in space. A cat floating. A creature with an atmospheric bubble around her head in order to survive.

Friends in recovery arranged for meetings at the house when I wasn't able to bring myself out. They called one another to gather around me in my time of need and brought readings and care. Other friends started a GoFundMe page. *Let's keep Cara in her home in this first year of grieving.* Every 10 dollars, 150, 20, 2,000, all the strangers and loved ones and anonymous, the comments, the money from poets, streaming toward me. I cried as each contribution came through. How I needed this love. How I needed the help. I got good at asking. I got good at alienating. I got good at repeating myself. *I hurt. I miss you. Please come back.*

My poet friend tc flew me out west to hike on a trip intended for healing. I arranged for Titi care and packed up my gear, my little notebook, my tender self. We stayed in Denver at a mutual friend's as a stopping place. Selah offered to give me a reading. Did I want one? I did. I'd known of her gifts with tarot, but I was wholly unprepared for what followed. I sat for an hour scribbling in my little book, taking notes from what ultimately became an unexpected straight-up medium's reading in which no one could tell me otherwise but that she had insight that can only be described as *vision.* She was privy to information that I was certain she hadn't accessed through earthly sources. A specific book. A particular Midwest heritage. A love of birds. She said he transformed into a flock of them upon his death. He would watch over me as if sprinkling coins and signs from above. Following the reading, tc drove us through big sky country to Yellowstone while I stared out the window at the clouds. At our campsite, right where we were to pitch our tent, two bald eagle feathers.

After that trip, on a writing retreat out of town that had been planned before Jon died where I did no writing, where I slept late and told no one anything, while walking rural dirt roads farther and farther from the lodging, I came upon a remote house with a flag of a male cardinal—the species most associated with communication from a loved one who's passed on—adorned with the word *Believe.*

Clues, if not guiding my path when I didn't have one, as signposts that a path would appear if I kept going. I thought about taking big treks. Should I walk El Camino? The Continental Divide? Move to Montana? I went nowhere for long. I had beloved Titi to care for and our house to cling to. The GoFundMe money bought me time. I huddled in his things the way I huddled in my mother's things in her house when she died. I hugged his hanging coats. I laid on his side of the bed. I ran my fingers over the spines of his books. Our home held my days as it had done when he was here, and when I couldn't bear to be still with the grief, I walked.

I sought out parks and nature preserves (not that one) and conserved fields and forests. Anywhere I could be on a path in a short amount of time. My walking was stumbly. Halting. Trancelike. I was caught up short. He'd been traveling beside me when at once he disappeared as if a trapdoor opened below him, yet I kept on going. I returned again and again to circling the trails in our town park, blurry eyed, angry, hurt, so fucking hurt and angry. He was so, so sorry.

Well, I'm sorry, too, my love. I'm so sad you couldn't stay. Why couldn't you stay?

These questions I learned were particular to survivors of suicide, some of whom I came to sit together with on couches in semicircles and small groups as part of hospice bereavement counseling. Once a week was it? Once a month? It was too often and not soon enough. Daughters. Brothers. Fathers. Widows. Best friends. It was uncomfortable. Awkward. Important. I read books. Not whole books. Paragraphs, when I could. I was given copies of literary works on loss. Joan Didion's *The Year of Magical Thinking.* C. S. Lewis's *A Grief Observed.* Also therapy books. *It's Okay You're Not Okay. Unfinished Conversation.* I myself was drawn to Theresa Caputo, the Long Island Medium, though I'd never seen her on television. Her book *Good Grief* comforted me. Gave me simple exercises to do. Affirmed the signs. I bought myself a special journal to accompany *Kittens in Space.* My grief notes. My sightings. My secrets. The circumstances of my excruciating longing. I wore them on my face.

Jon was my Viking. My lover throughout history. I'd known him before. I would again. I wrote in my notebook. A leaf sticking straight out of the tread of the front left tire of my car. Another suitcase standing in the only remaining parking space pulling in to hospice for bereavement counseling. Titi, sweet Titi, alive and going strong. Seeing me through. Someone to come home to when he'd been *so* close to departing himself, rallying for months without flagging.

I began to watch the birds at the feeder, standing for good long stretches, holding Jon's well-used guidebook he'd held onto since childhood, flipping through its pages to identify who I was seeing, the names I'd heard him call out over the years coming to me. American goldfinches. Carolina wren. Black-capped chickadees.

One evening in particular I was keen to name the small songbirds pecking at the seed on the ground. I needed my glasses to read the book in the dusk, so I rushed for them, hoping the birds wouldn't fly off. Returning to my perch, I switched between my glasses to read, then lifting them to look at the finches, or were they sparrows? Back and forth intently when what I later settled on as a Cooper's hawk swooped in to suffocate one of the little birds right in front of me with his talons. *Jesus, Jon! Really? You know how much I love animals.* I could hear him remind me that the hawk needed to eat, too.

Then the female cardinal obsessed with herself in the windows of the room we did not ever dine in. I'd entered the house one day after retrieving from the mailbox a hospice flyer offering memorial ornaments with the option for the deceased beloved's name under the image of a male cardinal on a snowy branch. I knew I would get four, one for me and one for each of his kids. I read through the brochure as I walked distractedly up the slate path to the front door. Once inside I heard the most insistent tapping coming from a corner of the house. I followed the sound into the not-dining room to find a female cardinal flapping up and down at the top of the nearly floor-to-ceiling windows of the open two-story space. The room always felt like an extension of the patch of woods outside that part of the house with its wall of glass and monstrous plant mirroring the trees from the inside. Here she was, the muted yet luminous purple brown of the female so alluring to me, even preferable to the bright eye-catching red of the males, hovering and pecking and riveted in a way that I'd never seen. She would not let up for over a half hour. Finally, I left the house and while driving away looked back at her through the trees to see her still insisting on interacting with the glass.

For over a week she was after the house. She returned to the big windows but also did flyby's of the front door. She must have been nesting nearby and felt her own reflection to be a threat. And yet, in all our years in the house with these very same windows and these very same trees and the very same feeders supporting all the many birds, we did not experience once any of these birds reacting like anything resembling her unrelenting response to our dwelling. Not even close. When recounting the details to select loved ones, I always mentioned not only the timing of the hospice flyer with the cardinal on it but that Jon had been aware of how I was particularly drawn to the coloring of the females.

I made my way to the mountains. I returned to the hill I'd hiked the day he'd asked if I wanted to meet in real time and I couldn't contain myself. The very mountain he first hiked without me while I worked on a paper for grad school, wondering how he liked my friend. If we would hike together. If we would go the distance. Toward the top of the hill, I came upon two women I'd hiked with when going for the forty-six in the Adirondacks. We sat at the summit talking for a while, reminiscing about the many hikes we'd shared. I said nothing about Jon. Nothing about my tender insides. At times I was afraid if I opened that space to the outside, I would not get put back together. They invited me on a birding walk the following day and pointed out particular flowers on the way down. Blooms I'd seen but not seen. Trout lilies. Trillium. Dutchman's breeches. Colors and shapes that had blurred beside the trail as I powered my body uphill year after year came into focus as these women described identifying features. "See how the leaves look speckled like the fish? Look at the three petals of the flower. And those baggy undergarments!"

The next day I met one of them for the birding walk. She brought a pair of binoculars for me to use. Everyone had them. Many of them also had field guides at the ready. Phone apps. I had electrolytes in my water and was dressed to layer down once I got moving, which never materialized in a way that I recognized. We shuffled along, listening, watching for movement and flashes of color in the trees. We whispered. The walk leader put his finger to his mouth more than once, then pointed to a specific area in the branches. I was always the last one to locate the treasure. A vireo. One of the warblers. And toward the end of the day, two bald eagles, circling on thermals some seventy-five feet in the air above us. All told they identified fifty species that day. They said I had beginner's luck, getting eyes and ears on that amount my first outing. The day was celebratory. These tiny miracles. Such beautiful, vulnerable creatures, so many of them surviving incredible distances. No one spoke of loss. Nobody mentioned grief of any kind. Not personal, not environmental, not even a missed connection.

When in her unexpected straight-up medium's reading Selah said that Jon turned instantly into a flock of birds, she indicated a dropping down and immediate transformation into instances of flight. My hospice bereavement counselor confirmed he would have researched his method. It would have happened very fast. My guy, no longer suffering. He was done. He'd been weary. The world had taken its toll. He broke into a million birds.

My next hike I tried to zero in on one bird, counting its notes, repeating the song to myself over and over again. I had no binocs. No app. It was five beats. The first three were the same, then the next one lowered, and the final one lifted. I whistled it to myself. I traced my eyes along the branches but couldn't find him. I whistled again. Was it five notes? Six? Sing again, my friend! Sing again. It was five. How

I would ever find who was singing from my memorized whistling, I didn't know, but I committed to holding his song in my chest.

I signed up for more birding strolls. Flower walks. Forays ambling through nature preserves I'd only recently become acquainted with in my very county. I drove rural roads I'd rarely had occasion to travel. I meandered and wandered. I let myself be aimless. I let myself be lost. When I passed a parking area for yet another community forest, I pulled in and walked the trails. I never knew when a wave of sorrow would hit, when I'd gasp from the shock of it. I panted on walks that would never have winded me previously, sometimes requiring me to stop to lean against a tree, my grief taking my breath away. *Why couldn't you stay?*

I craved Jon. I was burning for more contact. Was he still a million birds? How did that work? I asked Dawn if one of her people could be what the unexpected reading had been. Could they connect me—with him? She said she'd ask around. A few days later she came back to me with a name and number. I sat in my corner under the green and purple lights, took a deep breath, and called. Could she help? She gave me a date and a time. Somehow I filled the days until the moment when I laid out a fresh yellow legal pad before me to take notes and waited for her call. Was I the desperate widow looking to believe in a fantasy? I didn't care. The phone rang. I swallowed. I answered. What I heard confirmed what I'd already come to believe. There was more to being than what met the eye. And yet, it was right there to be seen in all the many sightings. In all the uncanny occurrences. This did not take the pain away. It did not end my grief. Everything was bittersweet. My beloved was gone. He loved me still.

This also did not solve the problem of what next in my life or where to move once the donations ran out, though she mentioned a big building with a high ceiling. She described it in great detail, the exterior, the capacious interior. Not Best. Bigger. Taller ceilings. Something sacred. Maybe a wedding would take place there. Or had. Jon would be with me. This place would become very special to me. I wasn't particularly moved by the information. I didn't want to marry anyone that wasn't him. I didn't care about a big boxy building. If we were talking about locations, I wanted to know what town. What state. Was there anything else my guy was telling her? Did he know how much I missed him? A silly question, I knew, but what else was there to say? *I hurt. I miss you. Please come back.*

Yes, he did know, but then, that I had already experienced for myself. I'd seen all the signs. They were everywhere. They were never enough. I could not force them to materialize, much as I tried. They happened—or didn't—no matter my effort, and also, wasn't I looking? Wasn't I required to participate in the seeing? I thought of the Rumi lines. *I sought the Beloved with ten thousand hands. He reached out and grabbed me by the feet.* (Okay, poetry. You win.)

CHAPTER 26

EASTERN BLUEBIRD

(Loss and loss and love)

Late 2018

It is hard to imagine that this species nearly went extinct in the early 1900s because of a deadly combination of management practices that removed the dead tree snags that bluebirds depend upon for nesting, the introduction of exotic species that competed for nesting cavities, and the detrimental effects of pesticides. The recovery of populations across the eastern United States is an example of how everyday citizens can play a role in conservation. The major factor in the bluebird's recovery was the establishment of nestboxes by private landowners across their range.

—National Park Service, Species Profile, "Eastern Bluebird"

I fantasized about somehow being able to stay in our house, keeping everything as it was when Jon was alive, shuffling through the rooms, talking with my lover who was there but not there. Coming home to my dream of him. Lying in bed looking to his side, imagining his presence. My continued secret. But the GoFundMe donations had dwindled to a trickle and then stopped altogether, understandably, and my own earning remained nonexistent. I hadn't been able to focus on writing or any writing-related work since he left. My mind was still too scrambled. Too stunned. I had to face it. I needed to move.

I did not believe I could live anywhere near Best, where the proximity surely would break my heart on a daily basis. Occasionally I had notions that I would completely reinvent my life rather than viewing relocation as something I was forced into as a matter of survival. I floated thoughts of Vermont for its mountains. New Hampshire, same. Even back to Saratoga to be closer to the Daks.

I looked at listings. I drove through small towns. I did day hikes and backcountry overnights, groping for a feel for what it might be like to live in Manchester, Vermont. To live in Hadley, New York. To live anywhere near the White Mountains in New Hampshire. Keene Valley. Plattsburgh. Bennington. I went to recovery meetings in some of these locations. I would try to imagine myself starting over in that particular town. After an initial glimmer, a feeling it could be possible to go on, to build a life after, I would always constrict in grief and panic, racing home to where I'd last seen him, and rush in the door to the familiar, to Titi, who I would hug fiercely, sobbing into his fur. How could I leave where I'd had my life with Jon? How could he?

I'm so sad you couldn't stay. Why couldn't you stay?

But he hadn't. The bouts of grief and vicious sorrow often landed—how could they do anything but, eventually?—in the stark reality, the absolute truth that, in fact, my guy was no longer on the planet. That it was me, here, with our cat, living on my own in a beautiful but too expensive home, filled with my dead lover's stuff that every last bit and parcel of were now mine to contend with. The expletives that Jon would not tolerate while he was alive he would have to accept in his death, because I launched them, with greater frequency, as the months without him added up.

Motherfucker. You left me. We do not abandon each other! We said it! It was one of our agreements!

I knew he knew. Also, I knew it was oh so understandable, predictable even—of course I'd get angry. Of course I'd curse him out, let it rip, spitting as I ranted, and then feel awful and apologize. Feel contrite. Beg him—again. *Why did you go? I hurt. Please come home.* Which of course he never did.

His office was filled with land mines. I never knew when I'd come upon a card I'd written to him that he'd kept wedged between unopened bills, takeout menus, and napkins with ideas he wanted to pursue scrawled in his handwriting. I sat on the floor, uncomfortably cross-legged, in a small clearing I made, and went through every last paper, every last box, all the drawers and cabinets, all the notebooks and calendars. Friends helped me with the rest of the house, tending to all those tedious tasks that real estate agents recommend before putting a home on the market. Michele caulked and scrubbed. Diane cleaned windows and sills. Rebekah and John wired a hanging lamp. Michele's whole family came. They spackled. They painted. They replaced doorknobs and handles. I sorted and sobbed. Blubbered thank-yous and bought pizzas. The emotional labor alone was exhausting.

The house was getting readied, but I was as lost as could be about where to go next and about how to leave. Even as Best transformed to the type of personality-free space that's apparently required for buyers to consider, I still couldn't imagine living anywhere else. Titi and I cuddled together in all the same spots in the house that we'd always done, my cat and me against the cruel world of real estate. *Don't make us move!* I was a five-year-old. A wounded little girl. Ready to put up a fight to stay, almost, when Titi took the most significant turn he'd done since the day before Jon's death.

Sweet, fluffy Titi, my savior, my companion, my roommate when I'd lost my most important one, started hiding away, and I knew. But did I? He'd rallied so many times, notably six months prior on that last day of Jon's on the planet. I'd been through this with Ed, making the impossible decision. But then I'd had Jon with me. Now it was to me alone. I called Michele. I took a picture of Titi under the bench in the corner of the kitchen and sent it to Jon's children who'd been teenagers when Jon adopted this scruffy, odd kitty who unexpectedly turned out to be long-haired once he grew up. Titi surprising everyone over and over throughout his life. Sneaky Titi sidled his way into my heart and stayed with me through the days and months after Jon's death, now hiding under the bench.

I did not have it in me to take him anywhere. I did not have it in me to make the decision alone. I did not have it in me to kill my cat. I did not have it in me to let him go. I made the call. A home visit. I was a wreck. Gasping and sobbing while answering the door, begging. *Please tell me I'm doing the right thing.* The gentle man who came to the home asked to be shown where. I walked him into the kitchen. Titi could be seen under the bench. Yes, I was. Doing the right thing. And I nodded my head for the man to do his, which he did.

After the respectful silence with Titi's now lifeless form, there were decisions to make. Should the man take Titi's body with him?

Or would I arrange something? I would not be digging a grave as Jon had done for Ed, that much I knew I was incapable of. I belabored and fretted. What was right? I had the man leave with me Titi's body wrapped in a prayer shawl someone had given me after Jon's death. The man left. I panicked. I called him back to the house. He graciously accommodated the grieving cat person in her stricken state and returned, gently picking up and removing the body of the last living creature—save me—who'd resided in this home together. I shut the door behind them. The emptiness of the house was now absolute. There was no one to listen for in the other room. No beloved stirring or purring or humming or snoring or coming down the stairs to greet me or leaving a book tented on the kitchen counter or nudging my leg or taking my hand on the couch or nuzzling up to me in bed. It was a Friday evening. It would have been date night, transformed into movie night on the couch with Titi, now not even that.

I called a friend. I washed my face. I left the house quickly and would not be back that night. There was no Q to rush home to do, so it didn't really fucking matter where I went or when. My friend offered me her couch at her place in Saratoga for as long as I needed it. I drove north. We watched a Whitney Houston documentary on her laptop in the dark until I finally fell asleep.

The next morning she left early for a commitment. I made myself coffee, not knowing what next. Sitting with a mug and her two cats, I had a flash. I'd never been a person who thought a cat could simply be replaced with another cat upon death. What I did know in no uncertain terms was that I could not be in that house alone. Not even for a day. I arranged to sleep over at another friend's house that night, and then thought I might stop by the pet store that had been so helpful to Jon and me when we were trying to feed Ed, then Titi in their finicky end-of-life eating. I just wanted to see if there were any cats or kittens in the rescue room. I didn't have a plan. It wasn't premeditated, per se. I instinctively drove directly from my friend's place in Saratoga to the pet store without passing go and asked if I could say hi to any kitties who might be hoping for forever homes.

A volunteer took me into the room. It was alive with cats. They were curling in and out of my legs, swatting at toys, jumping up on the windowsill, meowing and chatting and purring. It was perfectly raucous. I stood in the middle of the brood, letting the activity swirl around me, when a small orange kitty high up on a perch woke from her nap, yawned, stretched the way only cats do, leapt directly into my arms, looked me in the eyes, and farted.

"This one," I said to the volunteer. "I'd love to adopt this one."

"She comes with a brother. Will that work for you?"

"Absolutely."

The brother, Murphy, was at a foster home getting treated for a bladder infection, but I was assured if I thought this little one was snuggly, then Murphy was bound to be a hit. As I told the woman about Titi and doing his subcutaneous fluids, the little one was curled into the crook of my arm, purring, during the entire conversation.

"She adores you."

Things were looking good. I was thinking I'd have this little love home with me possibly that day and her brother as soon as he was ready, when the director of the rescue came into the store. Suddenly there was competition. Other potential adopters had apparently indicated interest and had already filled out the application. She handed me a copy, which asked for references, the info of which vet I used if I had previous cats, and how much I'd be around to give them attention. She was not fooling around.

I filled out the form. I had cat experience and vet relationships galore, but there were already other applications. The volunteer who'd seen the little one they called Becca and me bond said she'd work on the director to help steer it my way. But I knew. That little one was mine. I was hers. It was merely a matter of time. The director said she'd be back in touch with me once she could check everyone's references on Monday.

That left the weekend to fill. Fortunately, I had a plan for that night—a commitment to speak at a recovery meeting and then I'd sleep at a friend's place who was also going to the meeting. I reluctantly drove back to Best Road. Walking in the door was as painful as I'd imagined it would be. I showered and flitted around, doing my best to avoid the anxiety that was building. Had I made a mistake? Could Titi have rallied? What was this house without any of my loves?

On the way to the meeting, the anxiety bloomed into a full-on panic attack, and I pulled off the side of the road into a parking lot, panting. I called Michele.

"I killed Titi! How could I have done it?" I was sobbing, gasping.

"It was his time to go, I promise."

"But, but he was, he'd rallied, so many times, he was so vulnerable, did he know I loved him? Did he know I didn't want him to go?"

"Yes, my friend. He knew."

I was shaking in my car in a post office parking area in the dark, not far from a church where Jon and I went to recovering couples meetings together, on a road I mostly avoided—so many roads and restaurants and movie theaters and stores it took me months to get myself anywhere near—and I was to speak in twenty minutes, to tell my story of addiction into the hope of recovery at a different meeting in a different church. All the meetings, all the churches, all the griefs becoming one grief. My guy was gone. It hit like that. Again and again. A whack to the chest. The Jon grief overtaking them all.

I rarely, if ever, struggled with stepping up to speak at a meeting, but I wasn't sure I could do it this time. I couldn't catch my breath. Michele talked me through the panic until I could get back on the road to the meeting—a better option than sleeping in my car at the post office, which I briefly considered. I sobbed through my share. A solid fifteen minutes. But I was there.

After the meeting, I realized I hadn't packed up anything to bring to Mary's house. There was zero chance I could go to Best at night, that night, without triggering another panic attack. Mary said she'd make sure I had everything I needed. She was heading there now, and I could come anytime. I told her I'd be close behind her.

Driving was easier than on the way. I bypassed Best and headed farther out in the county to her house. The farther I got from the main roads, the darker the sky became and the brighter the stars. I thought about all the help right here for me. The community that had been so instrumental in my getting through what I would never have been able to do on my own. I turned up a road I'd traveled in all my scouting about for nature preserves—a long, winding road curving up and onto the biggest set of hills in the county, really one big plateau, that led also to my friend's house. The stars spoke to me.

What if I stayed right here in the county? What if I moved up on this very hill? It was a place I'd actually tried to talk Jon into one night when we were both at Mary's house at a bonfire. He was not having it.

"Bense, you work from home. I've got to drive to work. These roads would be impossible in winter."

He was right. But there was something so alluring about hearing Mary, her husband, and other neighbors say things like "down in town" or "off the hill" to describe anywhere that wasn't home. At the time there was nothing to do but let it go. It would not have been fair to Jon.

Now, though. Those stars. And how many people did I already know who lived up here on the plateau? As I thought about it, it turned out quite a few. Close friends, too. Dawn lived out here. And my good friend Lisa, whose home was surrounded by forest. I'd been to her house many times to walk in the woods out her back door. It was something I hoped for myself one day. I thought at some point Jon would retire, or remote work would ease the burden of a daily commute, or something might pave the way for us to live this vision of mine without compromising his.

He wanted that for me. To be fulfilled. He was so, so sorry he couldn't be part of it, anymore. He was so sorry to leave.

Sleep was fitful that night, but better than being at Best alone, no doubt. The following day, Sunday, left me one more night to get through until I might hear about the two orange cats from the rescue. Dawn said I could stay with her, so that evening I made my way out to their place for the night. The next morning Dawn and I sat at her kitchen table having coffee. I told her about the stars and that maybe I would stay right here in this county after all. And then there were those two adorable kitties who might come with me. I checked my phone. Nothing yet from the rescue. But then I didn't have service out at Dawn's. I used her phone to call the pet store. They hadn't heard from the director yet. I urged them. *Please!* Let her know I was out of cell range and would be heading home straightaway.

I hustled back to Best to see if she'd called the landline. She had. She had a few more questions. I sat on a stool in the kitchen and called her back. She said the competition for these two had become really intense over the weekend. Even more applications had come in. I remained calm. I tried not to be too weird about it, but I told her I was sure that those cats belonged with me. At last, she agreed, and Murphy, who turned out to be a big boy, and little Becca who I immediately renamed Emma after Emma Goldman, a red-headed firebrand of an anarchist activist back in the early 1900s, came home with me.

Their energy changed everything in the house. Their nosing into every corner and trotting through each room charged the place with young life. They were gingers with an extra toe on each paw. Hemingway cats. Spiritually advanced, some said. No one had to tell me, though. These kitties were a godsend. They were exactly what I needed. Now all I had to do was find us a new home. Once again, I took to looking online and driving around back roads in the county. At least now I had a target area. I wanted to live on the big hill. But what I wanted and what I might be financially eligible for on my own had little overlap. In fact, the filters for price and location brought me to exactly one listing: a former community church up on the plateau.

"I can't live in a church."

I scrolled.

I scrolled back.

"That's ridiculous."

It was ridiculous. It was also ridiculously cheap, as houses go. Something I would be able to afford with the sale of Best Road, it seemed. I studied the pictures. Two floors, each a big open space. The upstairs, what would have been their room of worship, had one pew remaining in the back corner of the big, boxy room and a series of rafters high up toward the ceiling. I had an immediate vision of stringing them with white twinkle lights. Happy lights. Downstairs might have been their fellowship hall, another big open room with a small galley kitchen and two half baths at the back end. That could be the living space. It also looked like behind the church was completely wooded. I decided to investigate further.

It being December, I grabbed my showshoes and headed to one of the nature preserves I'd discovered that happened to be down the road from the church. Once I got close, I dropped my speed and drove past the place slowly, taking a long, hard look as I turned onto the road to the pond I was going to hike around in the snow, more of which had begun to come down as I drove up onto the hill. At the dead end where the parking area for the nature preserve was located, mine was the only car. It was afternoon at this point, and the storm was growing. I strapped on my snowshoes and set out on the trails.

I'd been to this preserve before but not more than once or twice. Even if I had been more familiar with the terrain, heavy snow changes everything. It is easy to feel isolated and remote. All on one's own. I pounded my way through the elements.

"I can't live in a fucking church."

Stomp stomp stomp.

"I'm going to be the weird church cat lady."

Snow battered my face to the point of forcing me to squint and turn my head from the wind as I pressed forward. I saw through the trees and the slanting snow one, then a second, round hump of sticks and small tree limbs mounded up above the frozen pond. I was pretty sure I was looking at beaver lodges. I pictured them hunkered down in their abodes as I tromped along the edge of the pond. Or who knew? Maybe they were diving down into the water on a play date.

Could I do it? Could I move—not *on*, as my hospice counselor reminded me, but forward?

I got back to my car just before dusk. I drove carefully in the accumulating snow back to the curved, hilly road toward the church, imagining what it would be like to be heading to it if it was mine. When I got to the end of the road, there it was across from me. I pulled into the parking lot that was lined with pine trees taller than the building. I stared up at the spire as the snow squalled and whirled around it. When the dark finally settled in, an industrial fluorescent outdoor light blinkered on from the corner of the lot.

"Oh, that will have to go."

Apparently, I'd found my new home.

CHAPTER 27

BLACK-CAPPED CHICKADEES

(The forest, up close and personal)

2019–2020

Chickadees have gained a reputation among songbirds for being some of the most friendly creatures in the forest. [They] are some of the most social both within their species and beyond. . . .

—Nature Mentor, "Why are chickadees friendly?"

As with Emma and Murphy, I knew the church was mine. But I would need a lot more faith, flexibility, and fortitude before landing up on the hill in this one-of-a-kind home. It took almost two full seasons of negotiating, inspecting, going before the planning board—twice—haggling back and forth on price, on who would have the cross removed from atop the spire, and on how to deal with the septic tank that was suitable for a diminishing amount of Sunday worshipers but would not be enough to accommodate residential use, even if that use was by only one person and her two cats. Even the NY State Supreme Court needed to get involved for the sale of a church to go through.

At one particularly frustrating juncture in the process, I became willing to walk away. I had no idea where else I would go. Likely this was the only "house" I could afford, and after that I'd be looking at apartment rentals that would wind up costing more on a monthly basis than the church. It was during this impasse, as I took my walks in the woods, muttering to myself, muttering to god, muttering to Jon, that it hit me. This was the big, boxy building that the one spiritual reader had mentioned. It was sacred. Surely weddings had taken place there. Jon would be with me. It would become very important to me. All of these—yes, or so I hoped on those last two in particular.

She proved to be right. It took another season to sell Best and for everything to be sorted on both ends, during which the house that Jon and I had shared started to feel more like a burden that I needed to relinquish than the home I couldn't imagine leaving. At last, all was settled, and I made the leap. I moved forward and up onto the hill. I became the church lady with her cats. The relocated widow. This building would become important. Jon would be with me. In spirit and in his things.

I brought the bookshelves from our not-dining room and all of his books and CDs up to the church. I tried to order his library the way he'd had it, but it was a definite jumble, and our music and books got mixed in together (his CD collection swallowed mine whole, but my books held their own). I lugged more than a few boxes of "keepsakes" I couldn't bear to part with, as well as the bag of his ashes. I had a quilt made of his clothes that I wasn't able to look at without sobbing, so I put it up on a shelf in the one storage room I had for the whole house.

Not all of it was so heavy. I also had framed a vintage illustration of hummingbirds, stuffing their faces into flowers, that he'd bought from a print shop, and I hung it inside the door downstairs in the living space. I transplanted some of the bee balm that he got for Best to the church property. I also brought a patch of the turtlehead flowers that he so loved watching the bumblebees crawl in and out of. Behind the church, fully visible from the window over the kitchen sink and tucked into the edge of the woods that surrounded my new home, I put up a bird feeder.

His beloved birds would be with me, too.

Some of the first to the feeder were the black-capped chickadees. It got to the point where they became so comfortable that they'd fly to me when I came out with a cup of seed to refill the feeder. My spirits lifted when they hovered all around as I poured the seed into the tube. It wasn't long before they were dipping at the seed out of the cup as I held it, and then eating it right out of the palm of my hand. With them came the nuthatches and the titmice. The titmice stayed close in the branches of the large trees that I'd placed the feeder near, but didn't take the same risks the chickadees did. Same with the nuthatches. They hitched their way down the trunks while I refilled, but would only fly to the feeder when I gave them more room.

Beyond the woods at the edge of the church property, which was about an acre and a third, was what looked like unending forest. The plateau, I learned, was one of the larger contiguous forests in all of New York State. My little parcel and what immediately surrounded it were a fraction of that, but it was all interconnected. These lots around me, who owned them? Would they stay wooded? I got my nose into the tax maps. On the one side of me was a family whose land extended behind me for about an acre or so. On the other side was a much larger parcel, about two hundred acres, that clearly had been abandoned more than a decade ago if the dilapidated house situated close to the road was any indication. These acres connected with what looked like well over a thousand acres that had few to no houses for large tracts. I thought about all the many nature preserves that I'd discovered in the county and particularly up on the plateau. Would the local land trust that stewarded these forests be interested in the two hundred acres that bordered the church? The activist in me kicked in—the first time since Jon's death—and I picked up the phone to the director of the land alliance. He was immediately friendly and accessible. He told me one thing that would be helpful to the cause was knowing the land—were there any natural features that were important to protect? Could it connect to other parcels to help create a wildlife corridor? He did ultimately say that they would be interested if the land came up for sale. I said I'd keep my eyes on it and would let him know if I saw any movement over there.

There was no one around to ask permission, so I decided I would start walking in the woods to get to know them better. My first venture was with a neighbor I'd met when I was pounding the mailbox post into the ground out front. She lived about a half mile down the hill and clearly was one of my people—a walker. Another day she came passing by while I was getting the mail. She asked if I wanted to join her to "walk old back road." I didn't know what that meant, but I immediately said yes.

We walked our road for a little under a mile before turning onto a dirt road that ran down and through the woods behind my house and that eventually petered out to an unmaintained road passable only by quads, ATVs, and feet. I'd been on this road previously, years before moving to the hill. This was where Lisa lived, tucked up into the woods, and I'd visited her multiple times, us walking out her back door and into an astonishing amount of forested land that she did have permission to be on. There were cliffs and ponds, centuries-old pines, but there were no summits as such to achieve, so the land didn't register for me the way bigger mountains did. Now I was a church lady. A widow with cats, who wanted to know where the birds who visited me lived.

Once my neighbor and I passed the last of the houses on that side of old back road, we cut into the woods at what seemed like a random spot to follow a stone wall up through forest, when lo, there through the trees was my home, the spire pointing skyward coming into view. When we got to my place, she drew a very basic map to show me how to get to a pond she'd mentioned. She said it was across the dirt road at the gate. Did I remember the gate? I did not. Never mind, she said. Follow the stone wall down, and I'll see it. Pass through, then bear right when I come to the first clearing and turn down past the baby white pines. I was fairly certain I'd never find the pond from this, but I held onto the hand-drawn map anyway.

It wasn't until that winter that I set out to find it, this time on my own and from behind the church. A storm had dumped over a foot of snow onto the hill, and the woods were beckoning. I strapped into snowshoes and headed out my back door and down along the stone wall I'd walked along with my neighbor. The snow was deep, and heavy clumps dropped onto me from above. Animal tracks were everywhere, criss-crossing the land like a backcountry Grand Central.

I got down to old back road, and there was the gate! I passed through and trudged down another slope and then up to what had to be the clearing my neighbor had mentioned. At this point in such deep snow and having done some meandering, I decided to turn back, knowing I'd definitely return. On the way up, I picked out landmarks to guide me on future walks and aimed between two blocky boulders as signposts to guide me home.

That winter I trekked out again and again. I did find the pond, a stunning gem surrounded by white pines and marshy reed grasses and what I learned were tamarack trees. A rocky slope rose above the far side of the pond. After the crunch of snowshoeing around to it, I would stop in the small clearing under the towering pines to take it all in. The hush of the woods, particularly in snow, captivated me in a way that I was sure would have attracted Jon. I stood still for lengthy periods of time, sweeping my gaze over the frozen landscape and listening to the tiny chips of birds flitting above me in the trees, until my shivering body nudged me back into motion.

Sometimes I met Lisa in the woods halfway between our houses. When the pandemic shut everything down, we coped by getting out in the forest nearly every day. We ventured all over that part of the plateau, hauling ourselves up onto ledges, ducking under sagging snow-laden branches, following animal tracks in the snow on the ground and along downed limbs, guessing who could have made them when it was anything other than the obvious split-toed deer hoof. She mentioned coyote. I'd heard them yipping and howling more than once since moving to the church, so I knew they were neighbors. There were also fox. And mink! I'd seen an elongated lustrously coated critter scampering up through the snow outside my window one day and squealed. The tracks could have been anyone, it seemed. We examined various piles, lumps, and coils of scat, poking at them with sticks. We could see the fur in some of it, indicating a meat eater. We listened for owls hooting through the tall hemlocks, a sound Jon and I had known at Best.

"Bense! Hear that?"

We'd both go still and aim our ears.

Hoot hoot hoo hoo, hoot hoot hoo hoo.

Smiles lit our faces. Did we know how lucky we were?

Lisa offered the *who cooked for you, who cooked for you* birder's phonic interpretation of the barred owl, text I confirmed in Jon's *Birds of North America* book once I trekked my now familiar path home. I reveled in the snowshoe trail I was making from my door into the woods at the back corner of the church property near two sugar maples the pastor's wife had spoken about in a way that made me think that she was going to miss them.

As winter gave way to spring, walking in the woods changed. Where snow had covered everything, now new growth was coming up through the forest floor. I brushed through the knee-high green near the sugar maples and was up onto the old stone wall I'd been snowshoeing near all winter. I walked a few feet on the rocks, then popped off over on the other side, the abandoned property. It was untrammeled forest, save paths deer had repeatedly traveled. With the snow cover gone, I was wary of crushing ferns or other understory that was filling the forest floor in swells and patches, poking up through the leafy ground cover. I stuck close to the stone wall for as long as I could to contain the impact of my footfalls to the same line of travel each time I entered.

Down below my two rocky guideposts were multiple wet areas that were filled with rocks coated with lush moss that I didn't want to tear up. There were some old lumbering roads back there that neighbors rode their quads on, so they were filled with deep, muddy ruts that were ridiculous to travel on foot. I carefully added downed limbs at the side of these furrows to create a small foot bridge so I wouldn't have to trash the moss in order to avoid the mud. I was pleased by my handiwork. I took pride in the minimal intervention my presence required (not like those intrusive petrol-burning four-wheelers, I thought). I touched with fondness the great oaks who populated my route, often stopping to stand with my hands and body pressed to them for long enough that I got self-conscious I might be witnessed by a quad-riding neighbor. There were few who shared these woods, but they were there. *Church-living tree hugger.* I looked odd to myself. And yet it was all so natural. I'd been led. This place was special. Sacred. Jon was with me still.

CHAPTER 28

CANADA GEESE

(Disruption)

2021–2022

This big "Honker" is among our best-known waterfowl. Once considered a symbol of wilderness, this goose has adapted well to civilization.

—*Audubon Bird Guide*, "Canada goose"

I became intimately familiar with these woods that had no peaks but were rich with undulating ridges and streams, rocky ledges and hemlock swamps, ponds and cliffs, and more animal dens tucked into crevices and tree trunks and tunneled under the ground than I'd ever discover despite the enormous amount of time I was now spending among them all. I became curious the way Jon had been curious. I heard the questions he would have asked, the comments he might have made. I wanted to know everything. I stayed in touch with the local land alliance, and through them I started meeting and walking with a small fleet of experts—trackers, birders, historians, botanists, ecologists, mycologists, geomorphologists, biologists, entomologists, and all sorts of crossovers and overall enthusiasts in multiple fields of study. I was awed by the stories that could be read in the land as I traveled it. I brought all of this burgeoning knowledge back to the woods behind the church, and it infiltrated my walks. I was constantly poking, prodding, dropping to my knees, looking up, looking down, sticking my head into tree cavities and rock gaps, and listening, always listening for the birds.

And looking. The red-winged blackbirds were often visible atop the marsh reeds at the edge of the pond. Dark-eyed juncos scattered themselves across the ground ahead of me, sipping in the runoff of a spring or water body, pecking at the dirt to find something to eat, or just generally hopping about at foot and eye level. Sometimes I was blessed with extraordinary sightings—a bald eagle taking flight over the water, a great blue heron, a pair of trumpeter swans floating. And then there were the geese. My god, how they yelled at me. As it was, it didn't take much to trigger in me a feeling of being an intruder in this environment even as I crawled all over it, but their raucous protesting at my presence was truly over the top. Yet even these honkers I looked for on my trips down to the pond, and I felt lonely when they weren't around. There was always somebody, though. Slopes and contours and mossy nubs and boulders and the creepy crawlers and flyers, all had personality. Tadpoles squirming around in the pond. Wood frogs clacking away in vernal pools. The scent of fox urine lingering in the air telling me a den was likely nearby. Tamaracks who shed their needles in fall. White pines whispering in the wind. The forest became the company I kept most often (unless one counts the cats, which one should).

Over time I did meet some of the other landowners as I noodled around back there and was given permission to walk the various parcels of woods they held the deed to. I always wanted to say nobody owns the land, something the original human inhabitants of the area knew so well, the Mohicans, who I also studied as I took my deep dives on the history of the regional forest and its varying manifestations before and after contact with Europeans. I could hear Jon say to me, *Hearts and minds, Bense. Hearts and minds.* Something he'd said frequently when I was amping up to launch one of my screeds into a casual conversation. Besides, I held my own deed to property, a church of all things, so who was I to say anything? Mostly I kept my mouth shut early on. I didn't tell my neighbors for quite a while the circumstances that had brought me to the hill. The way that Jon left. This childless cat woman in her fifties, alone in a church, a relative novice to real woods learning, a widow, still.

I could say anything in the woods, though, and did. The forest held space for me. Gave me room to walk and to cry (ever crying, ever grieving, about which *not enough enough is said*) and my need for this, for them—yes, *them!*—grew the more known they became to me. I was still so tender, but even when I got batted in the face by a tree limb or bumped my shin on a boulder, I was grateful for the contact. The way Jon's presence was a means of locating myself, of seeing myself in the reflection of his eyes, the forest became a way to be myself, to experience myself and to witness how I moved in the world so tangibly, even as I struggled at times with the traces I left behind. My visible path in the ground cedar next to the stone walls. Crushing trout lily leaves underfoot when there was no other option. Tearing moss no matter how carefully I walked. Was I taking more than I was giving? Did I belong? How could I contribute?

I started planting more native flowers on the church land. I was determined to seed Joe Pye weed into a wild space at the back of the property that was filled with goldenrod, St. John's wort, spirea, and wild blueberry, blackberry, and raspberry bushes, among countless other species I was still learning. Lisa and I began digging out the invasive barberry that was growing near the pond down behind us both. I got a bird bath and kept it filled with fresh water for when the progressively hot weather dried up local sources for my avian friends. We were in a season of severe heat and drought for the northeastern United States, and it was sending birds, bear, and deer on the move out of the forest looking for expanded opportunities for eating and drinking. One result was that the roads became littered with dead animal bodies due to increased car strikes.

Witnessing firsthand the stresses we humans were putting on the planet, on the more than human world, was breaking my already broken heart all over again. The climate change clock had been ticking for decades, of course, but smoky skies reaching the hill from wildfires across the continent, superstorms flooding nearby valleys and even the church basement, exploding tick populations ravaging humans and wildlife alike due to warming winters, and the list went on, all of it was hitting harder and heavier every season. Not just for me, it was in the air—climate grief—and it felt like there was nowhere to turn for solace.

And then the chainsaws came.

The firing up, revving, and wielding of a chainsaw in order to chew into tree trunks makes a noise that can cut through a forest and into a body from miles away. This chainsaw was as close as the delicate foot bridges I'd made, the oaks I'd touched, the mossy stones I'd avoided, the blocky boulders I'd followed. It was right behind me, on the hill between the church and old back road. A neighbor who'd graciously given me permission to cross his land was now logging it for timber, and I had no way to stop it, no way to stop the noise, the incessant grinding and buzzing, followed by the resounding thumps that signaled the felling of trees I'd touched and loved, which isn't to say that I didn't try.

In the early days of hearing the start-up of the machine—unmistakable sound—I tried to shrug it off. Maybe it was farther off than I thought. Maybe it was the culling of a few ailing trees. As the sawing and falling dragged on and sounded as if it was only getting closer by the day, it was impossible to ignore what I was afraid was going down back there. On a short lull in the activity one afternoon, I put on my boots and headed into the woods to investigate.

I entered at my usual spot by the sugar maples, hoofed up and over the stone wall, and worked my way down the hill through the two boulders. So far so good. But when I got to the lower areas, the place was decimated. Gone were the great oaks I'd hugged. The mud ruts in the old lumbering road were gargantuan now, rifts that were three feet deep and wide. The moss I'd worked so hard to leave intact was completely chewed off the tops of the rocks in most areas, buried by limbs and tree litter in others. It looked like a bomb had gone off and killed all my friends.

Where would the birds go? What about all the critters who'd called this home? Who didn't make it out of the way in time? That was not to mention the trees themselves. Trees I'd hugged, said hello to coming and going, looked forward to seeing around each next bend, always relieved for the company. Majestic beings. Dead. I sat on a stump and wept. This neighbor had every right to log his land, but did he have to? How many acres was he planning to cut? In fact, what were his intentions? From deep in the woods, I started making calls. I would track him down and be my most accommodatingly insistent self to encourage him toward conservation. I would save the land.

Through the dubious miracle of Internet searches, I found his number. I texted.

> Hey! It's Cara from the church. We met on old back road and you said I could walk your land. Can I ask what's going on back there?
>
> Hi. I'm logging my land.
>
> Are you gonna develop it?
>
> No
>
> I waited a moment, but nothing more followed. I texted again.
>
> What are your plans?
>
> Why, do have something in mind?
>
> If you want to sell, you could probably sell it to the local land trust. Just saying.
>
> :)

What was there to say to a smiley face? I didn't know. Plus, I didn't want to be too pushy and risk losing a future possibility for conservation. The next morning, the logger was at it with his chainsaw again. As he buzzed and ground his way up the hill, coming closer to the church every day, I found it increasingly difficult to be home when he was active. I couldn't tolerate the noise and what it represented—not only for these woods, but I felt the acceleration of deforestation all over the planet in the crashing thud of each and every tree that fell. At first I tried to stick it out, getting white noise going as I'd done at Best Road, but eventually I fled. The moment the saw started up in the morning, I dropped whatever I was doing, packed up for the day, and drove away, only coming home close to sunset when surely he'd finished his work.

I kept the feeder filled all winter believing the birds needed the seed now more than ever, but I avoided going out back otherwise and went nowhere near the woods down the hill. I would not be walking out my door and into the forest for the foreseeable future. I simply couldn't bear to face any more loss.

CHAPTER 29

RUBY-THROATED HUMMINGBIRDS

(A lyric ode, a portrait)

Time-lapse

The ruby-throated hummingbird is the only breeding hummingbird in Eastern North America. When they go around looking for nectar, they pick up pollen on their bodies and bring it to other flowers. . . .

—Antietam-Conococheague Watershed Alliance, "Meet the ruby-throated hummingbird"

The last time I saw the love of my life he was smiling. He hugged me. He had the temperament of a soul who should have inherited the earth. Instead, he abandoned it. And yet. *No one gets out of here alive.* I came to say it often. Jon would have appreciated this as a very Cara thing to say, I was sure of it. He was my perfect foil. My Viking from another lifetime. A wounded man. Weary. I don't know what it takes for others to stay here, why some do and some don't, or can't.

Jon was the one who wanted to understand how the universe worked, how the planet functioned. He dove into the particulars, even when the details seemed unbearable to fathom. The way whale song was diminishing. Bird populations plummeting. World languages declining. Glaciers retreating. He wanted the underdogs to win. The good guys to catch a break. Kindness and civility to prevail. One of his pet peeves: He truly disliked that the intentional foul in basketball had become an accepted strategy.

Yet he was a hawk lover—all raptors, really. He set the snap traps to kill the mice at Best to protect the house. *Bense, they'll chew the wires! It's dangerous.* I acquiesced. He loved watching football. He was dedicated to his beleaguered Minnesota Vikings. "They snatch defeat from the jaws of victory," he was fond of saying. His team had never won a Superbowl. There was one other team that hadn't yet either, and he was a fan of them by proxy. The Buffalo Bills. One afternoon he called me into the living room to watch the unlikely love Buffalo gave its team after a heartbreaking loss. The player who'd missed the field goal at the buzzer to lose them the most important game was called for by the crowd of thousands. Cheered as he took the podium. It was an unbelievable gesture of care. Jon called me in, tears in his eyes, nearly unable to relate what he'd just seen in the documentary he was watching. He replayed the painful game end. The team greeted by fans in their hometown. The unexpectedly upbeat chanting. We both cried. Was it the human capacity for forgiveness? For encouragement? To root one another on in a spirit of unity? That was his word. *I'm rooting for us,* he always said. Rooting for us as a species to figure it out before we take down the ship, irrevocably.

How could he not root for himself?

"We are vast, we contain multitudes," he misquoted the Walt Whitman line often.

"Large," I'd say. "And it's I. I am large, I contain multitudes," I corrected him.

He preferred his version. He treasured the line that one of the many musicians he followed had said. *Our mistakes are what make us original.* Also that the best critical response to a piece of art was to make another piece of art. He traced illustrations of species that had gone extinct onto vellum. He asked a poet friend of mine to record lines from a Dorothy Allison book he adored. He wanted to make a soundscape. *Two or three things I know for sure.* But they were never the same two or three things.

The last time I saw the love of my life he was smiling. He pet our cat, I believe, through the spindles of the railing, then walked over to me in my happy corner to give me a hug. I smiled when he approached. I was eager for him to let me in. I sat up straight. He leaned forward, then pulled back. He was subdued. Muted. Smiling. Nothing made sense. I'd talk to him about it all at dinner.

I'd wanted a partner who would step up to the plate. Who could say, *This is what I want, and that this is you, and me, that this is us.* And he had! As had I. We'd done it. We'd risked the kind of heartbreak that can take people like us out of the game for good. I'd been so close to not coming back. I'd escaped the drive so many times. As an addict who'd made recovery, so had Jon. Until he hadn't.

I didn't miss anything. It was nothing I did. I was to believe that I could not have changed his mind, even if I'd been given the chance to try. *Of course* I would have tried. Which is why he set me up on date night. That was the only way. He must have intended it for the previous day, the day Titi tanked, but our beloved feline needed us, needed him, and he gave it one more day. He gave it everything he had. The tremendous effort in his end-of-life notes. He was rooting for me even then. For us all. He'd be sitting on the couch reading, leaning over a crossword puzzle at the kitchen island, lying in bed next to me at night. I'd be wearing the destruction of the planet and her creatures *so* heavily, images of cruelty and suffering replaying in my mind, consumed with fear, with terror, with anxiety. I knew that Jon was deeply affected, too, in the DNA of his very being, and yet he could summon it up when that was what was most needed, this holding out the possibility that the good in us all could still prevail.

The hummingbirds he so wanted to see did come to Best. I was home more often, so it made sense that I'd be the recipient of these precious visitations at first. They buzzed unexpectedly close! I'd be sitting on the front steps for no particular reason, and the sudden thrumming of their wings would whir near my head. They came for the bee balm Jon had given me to plant for this purpose. I was reluctant to tell him I'd been gifted with their presence when he was the one who longed for them. I'm so glad they finally showed for him. I'm so grateful I told him as often as I did. *My life is better for you in it.* I'm with you until the end.

He didn't have it in him to face what was coming.

What was coming?

Was it the issue with the job? His health? Was it Titi's impending death? The end of life as we know it on earth? The last of the hummingbirds?

One morning, lying in bed, looking up through the skylights at the tremendous pine tree above our heads, Jon rolled over to me.

"One of the largest mass strandings of whales is happening," he said. "Something like six hundred have beached."

"What?! What's going on?" I hadn't heard.

"There are a lot of theories. Naval sonar sends them off their course. Plus, their food source is overfished, so they have to get closer to shore to feed."

We lay there in silence. He spoke after a time.

"I hope the smaller fish come back."

Our last visit to the island off the coast of Maine for summer holiday had been tainted by a bloody nose. He'd been having them more frequently, and these bleeds were becoming quite severe. Sometimes clots of blood poured out of his nose, once sending us to the emergency room. On the island, he was horrified by how public his health became when he needed help. I stood behind him in the bathroom of our room cleaning the blood splatter off the walls and handing him the phone when he was able to get one of his healthcare team on the line. He needed nose spray. A nasal coagulant. I went down to the front desk of the inn and asked if they had any. The gears of support started turning. Someone called the owner of the market on the island. Another guest of the inn was a doctor. We got ice. Supplies. Advice. We stopped the bleeding after a few harrowing hours. The last night of our holiday. We took the early ferry back to the mainland the next day. One of his happy places now a source of shame, he felt. I could see it on his face. He never got to the bottom of the cause of the bleeds that I was aware of, but he did seem to figure out how to manage them better. Or perhaps they stopped altogether. It wasn't clear. He didn't like talking about his health with me generally at this point. He stopped letting me in.

The last time I saw the love of my life was an unexpectedly sunny day of a three-day weekend. I felt a lightness of spirit after what had been such a heavy period. We needed a win. Jon would come around. He'd be glad soon enough. There is something very old about the way the world chews certain people up. The way some can't root for themselves. The way help doesn't reach everyone. He was smiling. Nothing I could have done for him. Just something he'd forgotten to take care of. I heard him in his office, the clacking of the CDs. He did not want his boss at the funeral. He said so in one of his notes that fell to me to deliver. I honored his wishes. *Of course* I did. He didn't let his therapist in on what was going on with him, either, and said so in another note. We cried together at his funeral when I told her.

Did he find out bad health news? Why hadn't he told me about his boss looking at other options? Was that the smoking gun? The straw that broke him? When did he make a plan? *It was nothing I—or anyone else—did.* It was all of it. He'd been a beautiful boy. A tender man. And yet he could also be seethingly angry. He wanted the world to stop hurting those who were the most vulnerable, of which, on paper, he didn't appear to be one. A white man. U.S. citizen. And yet. Not one of us gets out of here alive.

"There are two types of people," he liked to say. "The kind who puts people into categories, and those who don't. Which kind are you?"

"If the nonviolent become violent in response to violence," he also said, "then the violent people have won." He'd usually follow this by mentioning the success of Gandhi's commitment to nonviolence.

"Yeah, but weren't there some more radical factions pushing for independence at the same time?" I countered, ever the Hallmark writer. "Like Malcolm X and MLK. The British preferred dealing with Gandhi in the Indian fight for independence the way the U.S. government decided to meet with King."

Who wins when the cause for justice takes up the means of the unjust? He wanted to know. He was right. His version of the Whitman line was better. He was wrong to end his life the way he did. I'm not sure that's for me to say. He was my perfect foil. My Viking from another lifetime. He was rooting for us all.

He was a good guy. The love of my life. He carried the weight of, if not the world, a deep, deep wound, the way some souls are bound to repeat again and again to get their lessons, or so it seems. It's not that simple. He had the keenest eye for red-tailed hawks roadside. Some of the most joyous times in his life were with me and Titi. His kids and I were the best things to happen to him while he was here on the planet. One night at a house concert he'd found out about by following a trio of musicians now living in Armenia, Jon was reluctant to elbow in for a seat, though he truly could have been their most ardent and nuanced admirer. He let himself be relegated to a standing spot off in the kitchen. I made no bones about getting us places to sit and triumphed as the first set began. I gestured to him. He looked horrified at causing any disruption during a song, at walking in front of anyone. I held firm, my hand on the seat for him, when or if he should want it. At some point he slowly made his move through the crowd to join me. Once seated, I could see the relief on his face. And then his delight in the music.

During the break, Jon was eager to approach the musicians. He had all of their previous CDs and was excited that a new release was available. (Another line of his that became ours: *I have all your records*. Something he'd gushed when he had an unexpected encounter with one of his musical heroes, the ultimate goofy fan utterance escaping his usual reserve.) The crowd swelled around the keyboardist, the one whom Jon had most wanted to connect with, and Jon was edged out. I watched as one after the other of the attendees chatted with the musician, often stepping in front of Jon to get their moment. This was an evening in what became the last year of Jon's life. I knew on some level that living was taking its toll on him in ways that I could do nothing about. I wanted those goddamned interlopers to let Jon have his turn! I wanted Jon to nudge in there! And then it happened. The musician himself turned to Jon, put his hand on Jon's shoulder, and leaned in to hear him. I nearly cried. They had a lengthy conversation, interrupted only by the necessity of the second set. Jon returned to his seat, next to me, smiling. He told me later in the car on the way home how much the musician appreciated Jon's response to his music. He didn't say it this way, but I felt that Jon had been seen for who he was. Appreciated at a level that he—like all of us—deserved. I was so thankful he had that experience, even if it didn't keep him here.

Was MLK right? Does the moral arc of the universe bend toward justice? Jon believed in that possibility. He was what I most needed. A thoughtful man. A tender soul. He must have thrown his phone from the car so he couldn't be tracked. He hoped the little fish would come back. He was vast, he contained multitudes. He was my guy, for a time, and then he flew away.

CHAPTER 30

ROSE-BREASTED GROSBEAKS

(Commitment)

Evergreen

This bird's sweet, robin-like song has inspired many a bird watcher to pay tribute to it. A couple of early twentieth-century naturalists said it is "so entrancingly beautiful that words cannot describe it," . . . Present-day bird watchers have variously suggested it sings like a robin that has had opera training, is drunk, refined, in a hurry, or unusually happy.

—Cornell Lab of Ornithology, All About Birds, "Rose-breasted Grosbeak"

Eventually the tree cutting ceased. It took a few months, but come spring I couldn't keep myself from the woods behind the church any longer and started walking past the maples and over the stone wall again. I circumvented the logged area, cutting a new path to the north of it through young open hardwoods and down into a tremendous hemlock stand that towered over and darkened the forest floor no matter the time of day. I could see through the trees to my former route, but I never looked for long. I angled to walk along yet another stone wall that lined a meadow that looked like a previous domestic site or that had been cleared for grazing at one time. Here I connected up with my old path past the meadow and could reach the gate without too much issue. Beyond the gate remained much the same, save for the occasionally deepened ruts by neighbors on their quads, but again, who was I to say anything? We were all guests back here. And these neighbors were doing their part to keep the deer population in check by hunting during season, something I was learning was essential to support reforestation. Deer browse, due to their exploding numbers for a variety of mostly human-caused reasons, had become an increasing threat to forest regeneration. Humans had killed off their main predators in the Northeast and created suburbanized landscapes that favored the cloven-hoofed species, so these beauties were not really to be blamed. But hunting them would provide the most sustainable meat in the area, even if I would never have been able to be the one to pull the trigger.

Instead I began a practice of lobbing acorns onto the logged property from the new route I walked and even collected some to germinate in a container I kept in my kitchen. I would plant them next season. It was symbolic, perhaps, all simply token gestures, but these actions helped me to feel a part of the process of regeneration. I could be kindred with squirrels burying their food cache, with bears shitting out seeds, with the trees themselves who'd left behind the origins of their offspring. And with the birds—pollinating, dispersing, and fertilizing from below and above.

Hummingbirds came to the church to feed from the transplanted bee balm, which happily proliferated in the front near the former access ramp into the sanctuary. I also transported the two chairs Jon and I used to sit in to watch the birds and positioned them on a landing in the access ramp for a version of a front porch. I reclined in the chair, my feet up in the sun, and could hear the thrum and chirps of these tiny marvels behind my head on breaks from the work I'd finally been able to return to.

Out back, the cornucopia of species who came to the feeder continued to bring me great joy. One in particular that Jon and I had been delighted by at Best, the rose-breasted grosbeak with his shock of eponymous color covering his neck and chest, always boosted my spirits when he showed up in spring on his way north from wintering farther south. Using Jon's well-worn birding book and other guides I'd been acquiring to expand my resources, I was able to identify the less obvious female when she appeared as well.

I also learned more about the growth I walked on and among, notably the ground cedar. I found out that they, like princess pine and other species I made my path in, were called clubmosses and had towered more than a hundred feet over the swamps they reigned some 400 million years ago. These miniature Christmas trees, now typically about four to six inches in height, had been the kings and queens of the planet at one time, prime examples of survival and adaptation. I remained careful with my footfalls and kept to the same line each trip through them.

One of the forest experts I walked with talked about the need to shepherd as many species as possible—plant, insect, avian, mammal, reptilian, and so on—through this bottleneck of multiple climate stresses. I read about creating *refugios*, akin to the pockets of life that survived in the volcanic tar after the blow of Mt. St. Helens in the Pacific Northwest in the 1980s. Flora and fauna came back to the blast zone far more expeditiously than expected due to these pockets of life that somehow managed to survive in the volcanic matter.

I continued engaging with the local land trust and began helping to fundraise. I wanted them to be able to preserve as much as possible. Each time I crossed paths with the director I told him, "Buy all the land. All. Of. It." And I rarely missed an opportunity to spread the word about this and other organizations I knew that were doing the work to steward habitat, to advocate for biodiversity, to fight for climate justice and for a healthy planet. I followed as best I could the various ups and downs of legislative wins and losses, writing and calling representatives and other decision-makers, and took to the streets with others with my homemade cardboard calls for action. It didn't feel like enough, never enough, with tipping points coming ever closer, and too often I felt too overwhelmed with grief and fear to stay engaged. It was too easy to consider giving up. And then I'd hear him.

Bense, not only am I rooting for us, I'm rooting for you.

My Jon, who I could so clearly see as beautiful but who could not see it for himself, who struggled to take up space, who I did not—*for one second*—regret committing myself to no matter how he left, could he show me with his life and death how to live now? Could loving and losing him make me a better person? Could it help me to stay in the game?

I've heard it said that addiction is born of a refusal to grieve. Addicts will go to extraordinary lengths to avoid feeling loss, no matter the consequences. I don't necessarily subscribe to any one cause or condition for why someone becomes driven to engage in activity that will ultimately destroy them. What does seem to be the case, though no one asked my opinion when setting it up this way (if in fact that's even how it works—*design* intelligent, creative, divine, or otherwise and not simply *manifestation* intelligent, creative, divine, or otherwise—whatever one may believe about spirit and matter and how they meet (or not), I myself have come to believe in something beyond that's actually right here at the same time, and that something is love, is grace, is the possibility of a moral arc of the universe bending toward justice), it does seem to be true that loss is not only an unmistakable part of being alive, but it has everything to do with loving. We make that contract with ourselves when we choose to love—a partner, a parent, a cat, the planet—whether we are conscious of it or not. We will get our hearts broken. Again and again. Some of us seem to get handed more than we can take. I don't know why. I don't know why I stayed. But I did.

Winter came, and it was cold in the church basement, even with my two snuggling purring roommates. It was almost five years on from Jon's death by suicide. I took the quilt I'd had made of his clothes down from the shelf and wrapped myself in it at last. I laid on the futon that had come from his divorced dad apartment and listened to *Music for Airports* on repeat, the CD of his I listened to the day he first went hiking while I was bound indoors writing a paper for grad school. I curled into myself and let the gentle tinkle of the piano, the soft repetition of minimalist patterns coax tears out of me onto the patchwork of his T-shirts and jeans. My cats slowly made their way over and settled into the nooks of my body. All around the church, the birds who remained north for the season, after fluffing their feathers for warmth, were hunkering down for the night in the bare trees.

EPILOGUE

Now, ever after

We're standing at a confluence of gaping valleys framed by enormous, jagged peaks. Our group has been backpacking through the Chugach National Forest in Alaska for the better part of a week on an outdoor leadership course for women. The program is geared toward wilderness and environmental advocacy, so most of us here are on some kind of mission. One would almost have to be. It's cold for August, if not for Alaska, and raining. We've just climbed up and over a high mountain pass carrying sixty pounds on our backs and need to figure out which way to head next. There's a glacial lake we're aiming for to set up camp for the night.

We're exhilarated—and exhausted. The pass was serious business, and we're relieved to have successfully made it over. But some of us are starting to shiver, and there's more climbing to do, potentially quite a bit more. Our instructor pulls out the map, and we huddle around. We've crossed a stream, there's always a stream, and we're trying to locate which one on the map. Finally we get oriented and get on the move again, one heavy step at a time.

This is grizzly country. We've been pooping together in groups of four all week and hollering every few feet when bushwhacking through thick alders and willows so we don't startle one. It's both exciting and humbling, learning how to walk among them. How to give grizzlies, goats, the tundra and the mountains, the rocks, the water, the moose, and *of course* the birds the respect they deserve. (We had a willow ptarmigan sighting!)

At fifty-five, I am the oldest of the group. This has earned me a certain status for being out here "at that age." I have shared with them the circumstances of my particular loss *(no one gets out of here alive),* and yet here I am. Here we are. I may be the oldest, but I'm no stranger to exerting effort in backcountry and have been more than holding my own. When the instructor asked on the other side of the pass if anyone wanted to lead us up the steep, scree slope, I spoke up. The way the boulders of miracles in the Adirondacks my first overnight when getting sober were suddenly my friends, the sharp peaks here in Alaska let me know I could climb through them. And so I stepped up to go first.

But now we have another ridge to gain. Each step forward requires enormous energy, and my pack feels heavier in the rain. We're grunting, cold and sweaty, and beyond ready for something warm to eat and drink. The slopes in front of us seem insurmountable, even as they're lower than the pass. The sky is varying shades of gray, and the rain is biting into our faces. After fantasizing out loud about how good it will feel to get into our sleeping bags after a hot meal, the topic of having a view—or not, as the case may be—comes up.

"I've never hiked for the view," I announce.

No one says anything.

"I hike to be hiking," I continue, because that's what I do.

"Whenever I hear people talk about missing views on a hike I think about the movie *A Room with a View.* Has anybody seen it?"

No one had. I take this as cause to do a dramatic reenactment for everyone while we climb.

"It's the Victorian era," I begin, breathing heavily between sentences. "Some varyingly well-to-do English tourists are on holiday in Italy. Notably two women and two men, each duo having one elder person and one younger."

I stop talking for a minute to catch my breath. I look around at the women all hoofing up the hill. Someone encourages me to continue.

"The younger female is played by Helena Bonham Carter and her guardian by none other than the incomparable Dame Maggie Smith."

Grumbles of recognition from the group for the actresses.

"The older male is the marvelous Denholm Elliott. Julian Sands plays his son."

Less recognition.

"Of course, there's a whiff of potential romance in the air around the younger two, as movies are wont to do. But there's this whole hubbub about the women not having a view. Hence, the title of the movie."

Heavy breathing. Mindless climbing. I go on.

"So they're all down at a shared dinner table with the other English guests in the *pensione*, and Maggie Smith is complaining about not having a view and just generally making a fuss."

I break into a slightly hyperbolic English accent.

"We were specifically promised a room with a view," I say as the Maggie Smith character. "I'll talk to the mistress. The first room that comes available with a view of the Arno is to be yours."

"'Why not to you,' Helena's character says."

"'No, no, I insist,' she says. So English. 'Your mother would never forgive me if I took the view.'"

"Mother would want you to have it,' Helena's character says, getting frustrated with Maggie's, what can I call it, with her excessive protest. As in, me thinks she doth . . ."

"'On no account,' Maggie declares," I continue. "The view of the Arno is yours."

"'I don't know why we're arguing because we don't have it,' Helena's character finally says. 'We have no view.'"

Now I'm really huffing from all the effort of climbing and speaking simultaneously but still manage the voices while we carry on with our slog.

"'I have a view,' Denholm Elliot's character exclaims from across the table, butting into their conversation. 'So does my son George. You can have our rooms, and we'll have yours. We can change.' Denholm looks so pleased with the idea of it."

"Maggie, however, looks completely affronted. And, as I said, this is the Victorian era. Decorum is of the utmost importance, and swapping rooms could seem improper. Of course her character is ridiculously prudish, played to comedic perfection. But so is Denholm's performance as the affable if somewhat blundering Englishman. It's brilliant."

"Anyway, Maggie sharply declines the offer," I say trudging, then muster up the exaggerated accent. "'Thank you very much, indeed,' she says, 'but we could not impose on your kindness.'"

"'But why shouldn't they have it?' Denholm says. 'It's ridiculous, these niceties. Let them have their view if they want it. We don't mind, do we George?' he says to Julian Sands's character."

"Julian Sands agrees. 'It's obvious they should have it. And there really isn't anything more to say about it.'"

We're nearly to the ridge. I summon it up for the last push.

"Then Denholm says—and this is the best part—he says, 'I don't care what I see outside because my vision is inside. *Here* is where the birds sing!' he cries out, poking his chest with his fork," I tell the women as I mimic the action with my finger toward my own heart. "*Here* is where the sky is blue!"

I pause, panting.

"Helena is about to say something when Maggie grabs her by the elbow. They leave the table. Denholm repeats, 'They should have their view if they want it. Oh, George, go after them.'"

Here we reach the ridge. We stop to catch our breath and to take in the vista. It's a short hike down to the lake, where we'll set up camp for the night. The water is glowing a stunning ice blue and surrounded by magnificent mountains as backdrop. It's still cold and gray, but the rain has stopped. We'll have something hot to eat and climb into our tents before long. I can't say that we wouldn't have made it to the top without my storytelling, but I'd like to think it played a part.

A FEW NOTES . . .

If you need help, get it. Then let it in when it comes. Whether it's mental health, alcoholism, addiction, domestic abuse, suicidal thoughts, or some overlap of these, please know THERE ARE RESOURCES AVAILABLE. Reach out. Talk to a safe person. Call a counselor. Find a meeting. Contact the 988 Suicide and Crisis Lifeline by dialing 988, text "988" to the Crisis Text Line at 741741, or go to 988lifeline.org if you have any thought of ending it.

The planet needs us! There are so many ways to make a difference. Land conservation, climate justice, biological diversity, clean energy, reducing waste, protecting wildlife, and more—for each of these issues, there are people and organizations already doing amazing work. Land trusts. Earth lawyers. Food co-ops. Black and Indigenous farmers. Climate shareholder activists. The list goes on. A quick search will get you to who's working on the cause(s) you care about. Then—join in! Root for us to win!

A quick thought on logging. It is healthy, I've learned, to partake in responsible forestry. Engaging with my local land trust, attending talks via the Yale School of the Environment, and conversing with Robin Wall Kimmerer have disabused me of the notion that all land and her creatures need are for us to leave them alone. As animals, we humans do have an ecological role to play. May we as a species be better cohabitants going forward.

A word on cats and birds. Though cats do occasionally get snatched up by owls and other raptors, the percentages are dismal for domestic cats killing our avian friends. Please consider keeping your cats inside. No, I didn't know this when I got Ed. Yes, Murphy and Emma are lucky they have a huge church to rumble around in. No matter your circumstances, keep in mind the fact that the domestic feline species is doing just fine while we've already lost over two-thirds of the world's bird population.

More to do for birds: If you have bird feeders, please clean them regularly. Put reflective decals on your windows to prevent birds from flying into them. (I have ones that shoot rainbows throughout my house when the light shines through—they're awesome.) During migration seasons, keep outside lights dark. In winter in cold climates, make sure feeders are full before first light; these little ones lose lots of heat overnight, and it's crucial that their first try for food is successful. And take part in the backyard bird count! It's a fun way to connect with the global birding community.

Lastly, but importantly, I do not speak for any recovery program. What you have read is just one person's experience, strength, and (hopefully) hope. There are as many stories as there are people in recovery. If you have one to tell, please do! We need you.

ACKNOWLEDGMENTS

I'll start with my agent Jennifer Thompson and editor Darcie Abbene. The whole team at HCI and Smith Publicity. Sumanth Prabhaker of *Orion*. Amy Brady, who is an amazing literary citizen and overall good person. Rob Bower of *The Sun*, whose generous and insightful feedback on an early essay version of this story changed the course of the work, and Tracy Frisch for connecting us. Thank you to everyone mentioned and to so many others in the literary community. Storytelling matters.

Hudson Taconic Lands for doing the good work of conserving land through community. Jim, thanks for picking up the phone when I called.

To my NOLS Alaska crew: You are all amazing women who make the world a better place. And a special thank-you to Lauren for helping me confirm the ptarmigan sighting.

Catherine and Julie—my writing sisters! I love you both. Lisa, thank you for adopting your lil buddy. And for all the walks and encouragement. Michele. I'm not sure I'd have made it without you. Period.

Dad and Donna! My Benson blood. Mom. Mariann Elizabeth Corby Benson Shepard (Shapiro). I have your smile. Your laugh. Your love of telling stories. I hope I'm making you proud.

Nick, Matt, and Lauren. You are beautiful souls. Jon's life was better for the three of you (he said so often). I'm so grateful for your blessings.

Thank you to recovery communities everywhere. I would not be alive without this help. And to hospice counseling. Psychiatry. Mental health professionals. Domestic Violence Services. To every addict or alcoholic who picks up the phone in the middle of the night. You all are my heroes.

Most of all, I'm grateful to Jon. Forever my beloved. You are who I most needed. I am a better person for having had you in my life. As you can see, I included your letter. It felt like the best way to speak to the moment was to let you have your say. I hope I did us right.

ABOUT THE AUTHOR

Cara Benson's writing has been published in *The New York Times, Boston Review, Orion, Sierra Magazine, The Brooklyn Rail, Terrain,* and selected for *Best American Poetry.* Her first book, an idiosyncratic collection of prose poems called *(made),* was well reviewed in *The Huffington Post* and *The Brooklyn Rail.* She has received a New York Foundation for the Arts Fellowship and the bpNichol Award. Benson wrote a series on walking in the woods for the *Best American Poetry* website and taught poetry in a New York State Correctional Facility for eight years. She lives in a former church on the ancestral homelands of the Stockbridge-Munsee Band of Mohicans in upstate New York. www.carabensonwriter.com.